GCSE OCR Gateway Physics Higher Revision Guide

This book is for anyone doing **GCSE OCR Gateway Physics** at higher level.
It covers everything you'll need for your year 10 and 11 exams.

GCSE Science is all about **understanding how science works**.
And not only that — understanding it well enough to be able to **question** what you hear on TV and read in the papers.

But you can't do that without a fair chunk of **background knowledge**. Hmm, tricky.

Happily this CGP book includes all the **science facts** you need to learn, and shows you how they work in the **real world**. And in true CGP style, we've explained it all as **clearly and concisely** as possible.

It's also got some daft bits in to try and make the whole experience at least vaguely entertaining for you.

What CGP is all about

Our sole aim here at CGP is to produce the
quality books — carefully written, immaculatel
and dangerously close to being funn

Then we work our socks off to get them out to you — at the cheapest possible prices.

Contents

Module P4 — Radiation for Life

Module P5 — Space for Reflection

Module P6 — Electricity for Gadgets

Published by CGP

From original material by Richard Parsons.

Editors:
Helen Ronan, Lyn Setchell, Jane Towle, Julie Wakeling, Dawn Wright.

Contributors:
Barbara Mascetti, John Myers.

ISBN: 978 1 84762 633 2

With thanks to Ian Francis, Helena Hayes,
Glenn Rogers and Sarah Williams for the proofreading.

With thanks to Jan Greenway for the copyright research.

With thanks to Science Photo Library for permission to reproduce the image used on page 14.

Graph to show trend in atmospheric CO_2 concentration and global temperature on page 39 based on data by EPICA Community Members 2004 and Siegenthaler et al 2005.

Data used to construct stopping distance diagram on page 60 From the Highway Code.

Groovy website: www.cgpbooks.co.uk

Printed by Elanders Ltd, Newcastle upon Tyne.
Jolly bits of clipart from CorelDRAW®

The Scientific Process

You need to know a few things about how the world of science works — both for your exams and your controlled assessment. Investigate these next few pages and you'll be laughing all day long on results day.

Scientists Come Up with Hypotheses — Then Test Them

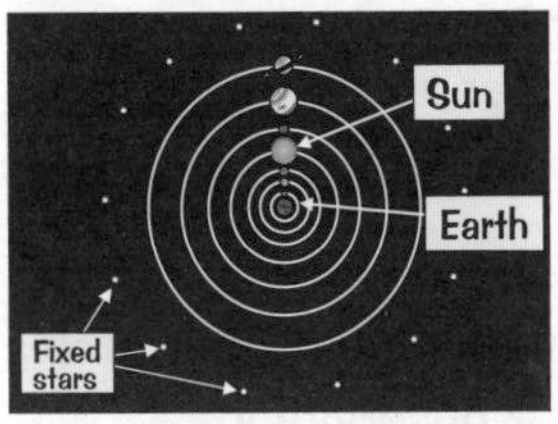

About 500 years ago, we still thought the Solar System looked like this.

1) Scientists try to explain things. Everything.
2) They start by observing or thinking about something they don't understand — it could be anything, e.g. planets in the sky, a person suffering from an illness, what matter is made of... anything.
3) Then, using what they already know (plus a bit of insight), they come up with a hypothesis — a possible explanation for what they've observed.
4) The next step is to test whether the hypothesis might be right or not — this involves gathering evidence (i.e. data from investigations).
5) To gather evidence the scientist uses the hypothesis to make a prediction — a statement based on the hypothesis that can be tested by carrying out experiments.
6) If the results from the experiments match the prediction, then the scientist can be more confident that the hypothesis is correct. This doesn't mean the hypothesis is true though — other predictions based on the hypothesis might turn out to be wrong.

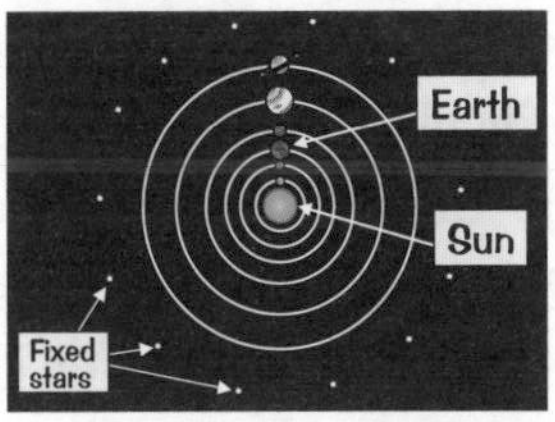

Then we thought it looked like this.

Scientists Work Together to Test Hypotheses

1) Different scientists can look at the same evidence and interpret it in different ways. That's why scientists usually work in teams — they can share their different ideas on how to interpret the data they find.
2) Once a team has come up with (and tested) a hypothesis they all agree with, they'll present their work to the scientific community through journals and scientific conferences so it can be judged — this is called the peer review process.
3) Other scientists then check the team's results (by trying to replicate them) and carry out their own experiments to collect more evidence.
4) If all the experiments in the world back up the hypothesis, scientists start to have a lot of confidence in it.
5) However, if another scientist does an experiment and the results don't fit with the hypothesis (and other scientists can replicate these results), then the hypothesis is in trouble. When this happens, scientists have to come up with a new hypothesis (maybe a modification of the old explanation, or maybe a completely new one).

Scientific Ideas Change as New Evidence is Found

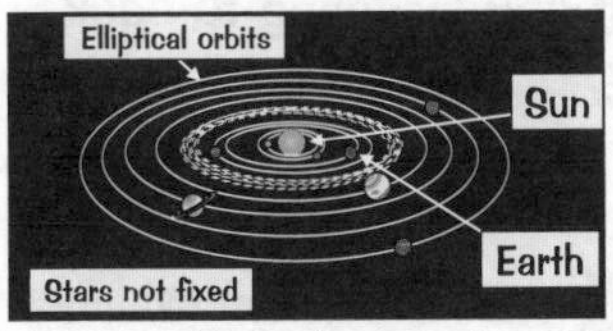

Now we think it's more like this.

1) Scientific explanations are provisional because they only explain the evidence that's currently available — new evidence may come up that can't be explained.
2) This means that scientific explanations never become hard and fast, totally indisputable fact. As new evidence is found (or new ways of interpreting existing evidence are found), hypotheses can change or be replaced.
3) Sometimes, an unexpected observation or result will suddenly throw a hypothesis into doubt and further experiments will need to be carried out. This can lead to new developments that increase our understanding of science.

You expect me to believe that — then show me the evidence...

If scientists think something is true, they need to produce evidence to convince others — it's all part of testing a hypothesis. One hypothesis might survive these tests, while others won't — it's how things progress. And along the way some hypotheses will be disproved — i.e. shown not to be true.

Evaluating Hypotheses and Scientific Information

In everyday life (and in your exams unfortunately) you'll encounter lots of scientific information. It's important that you know a few things about how to evaluate any evidence you're given.

Some Hypotheses are More Convincing Than Others

1) You might have to evaluate hypotheses that give different explanations for the same thing. Basically, this just means you need to say which one you think is better, and then explain why.
2) The most convincing hypotheses are based on reliable evidence (e.g. data that can be reproduced by others in independent experiments, see p. 5) — not opinions or old wives' tales.
3) Reliable evidence comes from controlled experiments in laboratories (where you can control variables to make it a fair test — see p. 4), studies (e.g. into the effects of radiation), or observations (e.g. of the solar system).
4) Evidence that's based on samples that are too small doesn't have much more credibility than opinions. A sample should be representative of the whole population (i.e. it should share as many of the various characteristics in the population as possible) — a small sample just can't do that.

Scientific Information Isn't Always Very Good Quality

When you're given some scientific information, don't just believe it straight away — you need to think critically about what it's saying to work out how good the information really is.

1) Scientific information can be presented by a person who is biased.
2) When a person is biased, it means that they favour a particular interpretation of the evidence for a reason that's incorrect or unrelated to the scientific information.
3) This can be unintentional — the scientist might not realise they're being affected by something which makes them biased.
4) It can also be intentional — a scientist might give a particular interpretation on purpose because they have a personal reason for doing so.
5) A person who is intentionally biased might misrepresent the evidence — give the true facts, but present them in a way that makes them misleading. This might be to persuade you to agree with them...

EXAMPLE

Scientists say 1 in 2 people are of above average weight

Sounds like we're a nation of fatties. It's a scientific analysis of the facts, and almost certainly true.

But an average is a kind of 'middle value' of all your data. Some readings are higher than average (about half of them, usually). Others will be lower than average (the other half).

So the above headline (which made it sound like we should all lose weight) could just as accurately say:

Scientists say 1 in 2 people are of below average weight

6) A person who is intentionally biased might also give scientific information without any evidence to back it up. This might be because there's no evidence to support what they're saying, or it could be that the person is just ignoring the evidence that exists (e.g. because it contradicts what they're saying).
7) Information that isn't backed up with any evidence could just be an opinion — you've got no way of telling whether it's true or not.

EXAMPLE

"Global warming is just something that ice cream sellers have made up."

There's no evidence to back up this claim so it could just be completely made up.

It's a scientific fact that the Moon's made of cheese...

Whenever you're given any kind of scientific information just stop for a second and ask yourself how convincing it really is — think about the evidence that's been used (if any) and the way that the information's been presented.

Scientific Development, Ethics and Risk

Scientific developments have a bit of a bumpy ride and yep, you guessed it, you need to know why this is.

Society Influences the Development of Science

1) You might think that scientific and technological developments are always a good thing. But society doesn't always agree about new developments.
2) Take space exploration. Different people have different opinions on it. For example:

Some people say it's a good idea... it increases our knowledge about the Universe, we develop new technologies that can be useful on Earth too, it inspires young people to take an interest in science, etc.

Other people say it's a bad idea... the vast sums of money it costs should be spent on more urgent problems, like providing clean drinking water and curing diseases in poor countries. Others say that we should concentrate research efforts on understanding our own planet better first.

3) The question of whether something is morally or ethically right or wrong can't be answered by more experiments — there is no "right" or "wrong" answer.
4) In an ideal world, the best decision about any moral or ethical dilemma would have the best outcome for the majority of people involved.

Other Factors Can Affect Scientific Development Too

There are other factors that can influence the development of science and the way it's used:

Economic factors:
- Companies very often won't pay for research unless there's likely to be a profit in it.
- Society can't always afford to do things scientists recommend (e.g. investing heavily in alternative energy sources) without cutting back elsewhere.

Social factors: Decisions based on scientific evidence affect people — e.g. should fossil fuels be taxed more highly (to invest in alternative energy)? Should alcohol be banned (to prevent health problems)? Would the effect on people's lifestyles be acceptable...?

Cultural factors: Cultural feelings can sometimes affect whether research is carried out or given funding, e.g. some people are against research involving animal testing.

Scientific Development Has Benefits and Risks

1) Like most things, developments in scientific technology have both benefits and risks.

2) There often needs to be a balance between personal risk and the overall benefit to society. For example, building a nuclear power station poses a risk to the people who work there and those living nearby (because they may be exposed to radiation), but it will also supply a large section of society with a reliable source of electricity.
3) Scientists try to find ways of reducing the risks involved, e.g. introducing strict safety measures at the power station.

Scientific development — a nice quiet estate of labs on the edge of town...

As you can see, science isn't just about knowing your facts — you need to think about the factors that affect the development of science, the ethical issues raised and the benefits and risks that come with scientific development.

Planning Investigations

That's all the dull stuff about the world of science over — now onto the hands-on part. The next few pages show how practical investigations should be carried out — by both professional scientists and you.

To Make an Investigation a Fair Test You Have to Control the Variables

An important part of planning an investigation is making sure it's a fair test.

1) In a lab experiment you usually change one variable and measure how it affects the other variable.

> EXAMPLE: you might change only the angle of a slope and measure how it affects the time taken for a toy car to travel down it.

2) To make it a fair test everything else that could affect the results should stay the same (otherwise you can't tell if the thing that's being changed is affecting the results or not — the data won't be reliable).

> EXAMPLE continued: you need to keep the slope length the same, otherwise you won't know if any change in the time taken is caused by the change in angle, or the change in length.

3) The variable that you change is called the independent variable.
4) The variable that's measured is called the dependent variable.
5) The variables that you keep the same are called control variables.
6) Because you can't always control all the variables, you often need to use a control experiment — an experiment that's kept under the same conditions as the rest of the investigation, but doesn't have anything done to it. This is so that you can see what happens when you don't change anything at all.

> EXAMPLE continued:
> Independent = angle of slope
> Dependent = time taken
> Control = length of slope

The Equipment Used has to be Right for the Job

1) The measuring equipment you use has to be sensitive enough to accurately measure the chemicals you're using, e.g. if you need to measure out 11 ml of a liquid, you'll need to use a measuring cylinder that can measure to 1 ml, not 5 or 10 ml.
2) The smallest change a measuring instrument can detect is called its **RESOLUTION**. E.g. some mass balances have a resolution of 1 g and some have a resolution of 0.1 g.
3) You should also be able to explain why you've chosen each bit of kit.

Experiments Must be Safe

1) Part of planning an investigation is making sure that it's safe.
2) There are lots of hazards you could be faced with during an investigation, e.g. radiation, electricity, gas, chemicals and fire.
3) You should always make sure that you identify all the hazards that you might encounter.
4) You should also come up with ways of reducing the risks from the hazards you've identified.
5) One way of doing this is to carry out a risk assessment:

> For an experiment involving a Bunsen burner, the risk assessment might be something like this:

Hazard: Bunsen burner is a fire risk.
Precautions:
- Keep flammable chemicals away from the Bunsen.
- Never leave the Bunsen unattended when lit.
- Always turn on the yellow safety flame when not in use.

Hazard: revision boredom. Precaution: use CGP books

Wow, all this even before you've started the investigation — it really does make them run more smoothly though.

Getting the Data Right

There are a few things that can be done to make sure that you get the best results you possibly can.

Trial Runs Help Figure out the Range and Interval of Variable Values

1) Before you carry out an experiment, it's a good idea to do a trial run first — a quick version of your experiment.
2) Trial runs help you work out whether your plan is right or not — you might decide to make some changes after trying out your method.
3) Trial runs are used to figure out the range of variable values used (the upper and lower limit).
4) And they're used to figure out the interval (gaps) between the values too.

Slope example from previous page continued:

- You might do trial runs at 20, 40, 60 and 80°. If the time taken is too short to accurately measure at 80°, you might narrow the range to 20-60°.
- If using 20° intervals gives you a big change in time taken you might decide to use 10° intervals, e.g. 20, 30, 40, 50...

Data Should be as Reliable and Accurate as Possible

1) Reliable results are ones that can be consistently reproduced each time you do an experiment. If your results are reliable they're more likely to be true, so you can make valid conclusions from them.
2) When carrying out your own investigation, you can improve the reliability of your results by repeating the readings and calculating the mean (average, see next page). You should repeat readings at least twice (so that you have at least three readings to calculate an average result).
3) To make sure your results are reliable you can also take a second set of readings with another instrument, or get a different observer to cross check.
4) Checking your results match with secondary sources, e.g. studies that other people have done, also increases the reliability of your data.
5) You should also always make sure that your results are accurate. Really accurate results are those that are really close to the true answer.

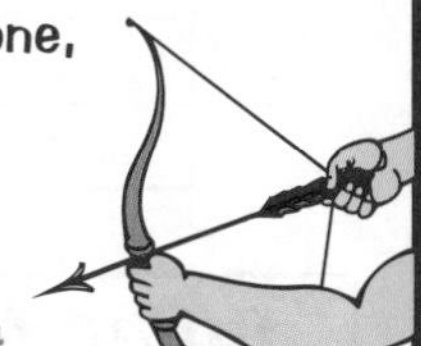

6) You can get accurate results by doing things like making sure the equipment you're using is sensitive enough (see previous page), and by recording your data to a suitable level of accuracy. For example, if you're taking digital readings of something, the results will be more accurate if you include at least a couple of decimal places instead of rounding to whole numbers.

You Can Check For Mistakes Made When Collecting Data

1) When you've collected all the results for an experiment, you should have a look to see if there are any results that don't seem to fit in with the rest.
2) Most results vary a bit, but any that are totally different are called anomalous results.
3) They're caused by human errors, e.g. by a whoopsie when measuring.
4) The only way to stop them happening is by taking all your measurements as carefully as possible.
5) If you ever get any anomalous results, you should investigate them to try to work out what happened. If you can work out what happened (e.g. you measured something wrong) you can ignore them when processing your results.

Reliable data — it won't ever forget your birthday...

All this stuff is really important — without good quality data an investigation will be totally meaningless. So give this page a read through a couple of times and your data will be the envy of the whole scientific community.

Processing, Presenting and Interpreting Data

The fun doesn't stop once you've collected your data — it then needs to be processed and presented...

Data Needs to be Organised

1) Data that's been collected needs to be organised so it can be processed later on.
2) Tables are dead useful for organising data.
3) When drawing tables you should always make sure that each column has a heading and that you've included the units.
4) Annoyingly, tables are about as useful as a chocolate teapot for showing patterns or relationships in data. You need to use some kind of graph or mathematical technique for that...

Test tube	Result (ml)	Repeat 1 (ml)	Repeat 2 (ml)
A	28	37	32
B	47	51	60
C	68	72	70

Data Can be Processed Using a Bit of Maths

1) Raw data generally just ain't that useful. You usually have to process it in some way.
2) A couple of the most simple calculations you can perform are the mean (average) and the range (how spread out the data is):

- To calculate the mean ADD TOGETHER all the data values and DIVIDE by the total number of values. You usually do this to get a single value from several repeats of your experiment.
- To calculate the range find the LARGEST number and SUBTRACT the SMALLEST number. You usually do this to check the accuracy and reliability of the results — the greater the spread of the data, the lower the accuracy and reliability.

Test tube	Result (ml)	Repeat 1 (ml)	Repeat 2 (ml)	Mean (ml)	Range
A	28	37	32	(28 + 37 + 32) ÷ 3 = 32.3	37 – 28 = 9
B	47	51	60	(47 + 51 + 60) ÷ 3 = 52.7	60 – 47 = 13
C	68	72	70	(68 + 72 + 70) ÷ 3 = 70.0	72 – 68 = 4

Different Types of Data Should be Presented in Different Ways

1) Once you've carried out an investigation, you'll need to present your data so that it's easier to see patterns and relationships in the data.
2) Different types of investigations give you different types of data, so you'll always have to choose what the best way to present your data is.

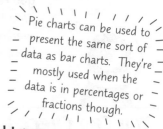

Pie charts can be used to present the same sort of data as bar charts. They're mostly used when the data is in percentages or fractions though.

Bar Charts

If the independent variable is categoric (comes in distinct categories, e.g. blood types, metals) you should use a bar chart to display the data. You also use them if the independent variable is discrete (the data can be counted in chunks, where there's no in-between value, e.g. number of people is discrete because you can't have half a person).

There are some golden rules you need to follow for drawing bar charts:

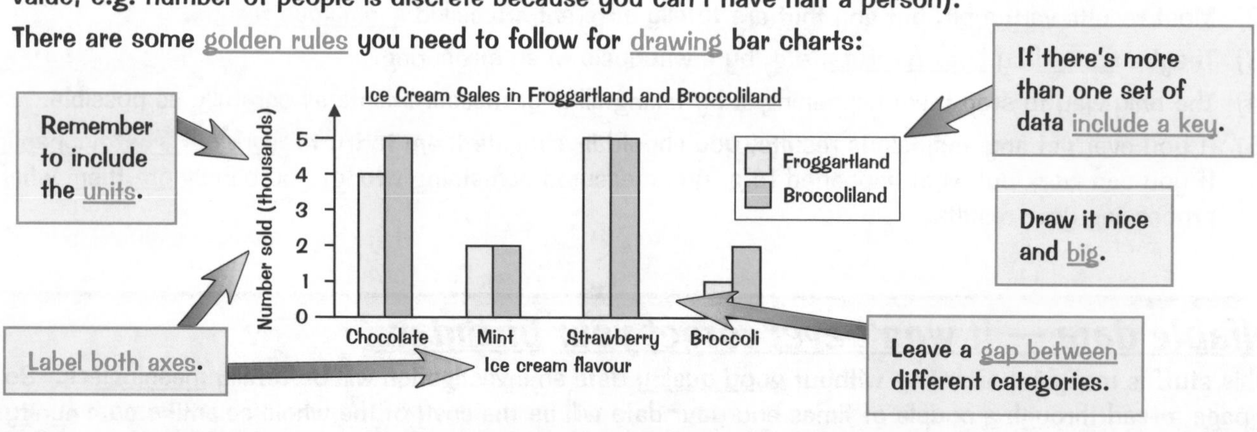

Processing, Presenting and Interpreting Data

Line Graphs

If the independent variable is continuous (numerical data that can have any value within a range, e.g. length, volume, time) you should use a line graph to display the data.

Remember to include the units.

The dependent variable (the thing you measure) goes on the y-axis (the vertical one).

The independent variable (the thing you change) goes on the x-axis (the horizontal one).

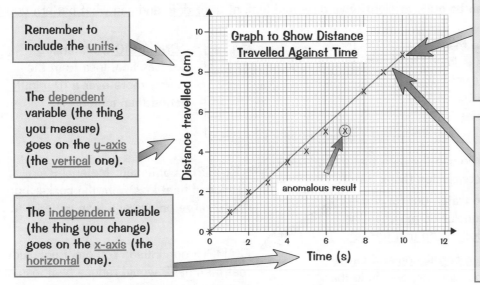

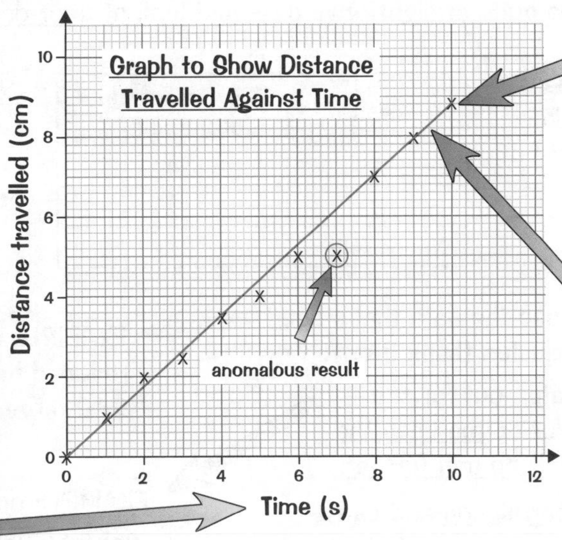

When plotting points, use a sharp pencil and make a neat little cross (don't do blobs).

Don't join the dots up. You should draw a line of best fit (or a curve of best fit if your points make a curve). When drawing a line (or curve), try to draw the line through or as near to as many points as possible, ignoring anomalous results.

You can also use line graphs to process data a bit more. For example, if 'time' is on the x-axis, you can calculate the gradient (slope) of a line graph to find things like the rate of travel (speed):

1) Gradient = y ÷ x
2) You can calculate the gradient of the whole line or a section of it.
3) The rate would be in cm/s.

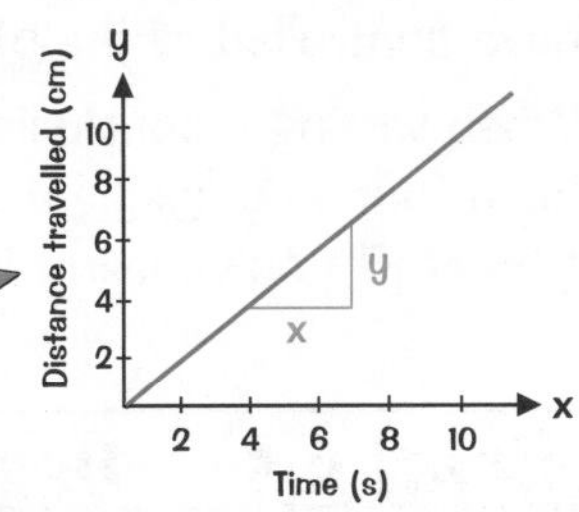

Line Graphs Can Show Relationships in Data

1) Unfortunately, when you're carrying out an investigation it's not enough to just present your data — you've got to analyse it to identify any patterns or relationships there might be.
2) Line graphs are great for showing relationships between two variables.
3) Here are the three different types of correlation (relationship) shown on line graphs:

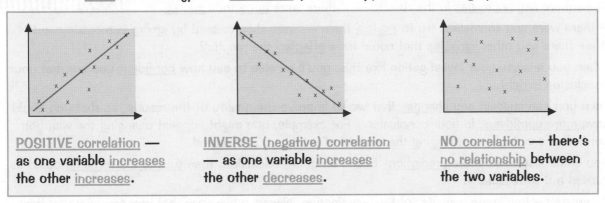

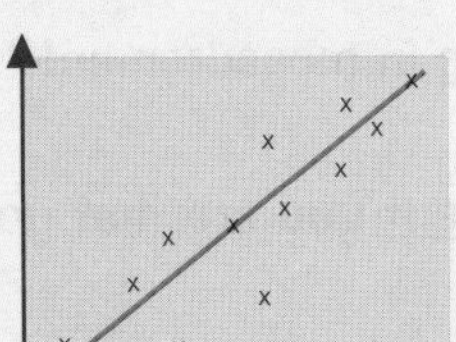

POSITIVE correlation — as one variable increases the other increases.

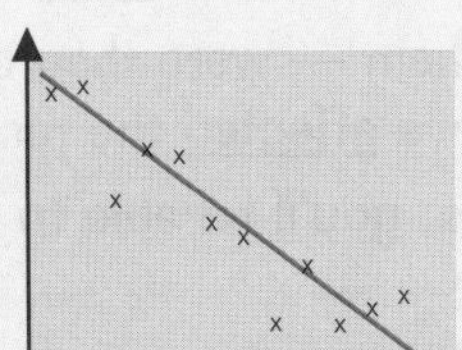

INVERSE (negative) correlation — as one variable increases the other decreases.

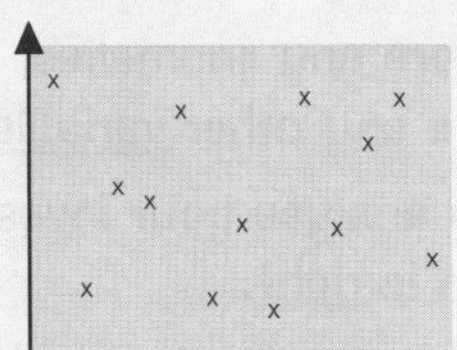

NO correlation — there's no relationship between the two variables.

4) You've got to be careful not to confuse correlation with cause though. A correlation just means that there's a relationship between two variables. It doesn't mean that the change in one variable is causing the change in the other (there might be other factors involved).

There's a positive correlation between age of man and length of nose hair...

Process, present, interpret... data's like a difficult child — it needs a lot of attention. Go on, make it happy.

Concluding and Evaluating

At the end of an investigation, the conclusion and evaluation are waiting. Don't worry, they won't bite.

A Conclusion is a Summary of What You've Learnt

1) Once all the data's been collected, presented and analysed, an investigation will always involve coming to a conclusion.
2) Drawing a conclusion can be quite straightforward — just look at your data and say what pattern you see.

EXAMPLE: The table on the right shows the decrease in temperature of a beaker of hot water insulated with different materials over 10 minutes.

Material	Mean temperature decrease (°C)
A	4
B	2
No insulation	20

CONCLUSION: Material B reduces heat loss from the beaker more over a 10 minute period than material A.

3) However, you also need to use the data that's been collected to justify the conclusion (back it up).

EXAMPLE continued: Material B reduced heat loss from the beaker by 2 °C more on average than material A.

4) There are some things to watch out for too — it's important that the conclusion matches the data it's based on and doesn't go any further.

EXAMPLE continued: You can't conclude that material B would reduce heat loss by the same amount for any other type of container — the results could be totally different. Also, you can't make any conclusions beyond the 10 minutes — the material could fall to pieces.

5) Remember not to confuse correlation and cause (see previous page). You can only conclude that one variable is causing a change in another if you have controlled all the other variables (made it a fair test).
6) When writing a conclusion you should also explain what's been found by linking it to your own scientific knowledge (the stuff you've learnt in class).

Evaluations — Describe How it Could be Improved

I'd value this E somewhere in the region of 250-300k
E

An evaluation is a critical analysis of the whole investigation.

1) You should comment on the method — was the equipment suitable? Was it a fair test?
2) Comment on the quality of the results — was there enough evidence to reach a valid conclusion? Were the results reliable, accurate and precise?
3) Were there any anomalies in the results — if there were none then say so.
4) If there were any anomalies, try to explain them — were they caused by errors in measurement? Were there any other variables that could have affected the results?
5) When you analyse your investigation like this, you'll be able to say how confident you are that your conclusion is right.
6) Then you can suggest any changes that would improve the quality of the results, so that you could have more confidence in your conclusion. For example, you might suggest changing the way you controlled a variable, or changing the interval of values you measured.
7) You could also make more predictions based on your conclusion, then further experiments could be carried out to test them.
8) When suggesting improvements to the investigation, always make sure that you say why you think this would make the results better.

Evaluation — in my next study I will make sure I don't burn the lab down...

I know it doesn't seem very nice, but writing about where you went wrong is an important skill — it shows you've got a really good understanding of what the investigation was about. It's difficult for me — I'm always right.

Controlled Assessment

At some point you'll have to do the controlled assessment. Here's a bit about it, but make sure you can recite all the stuff we've covered in this section first — it'll really help you out.

There are Three Parts to the Controlled Assessment

1) Research and Collecting Secondary Data

For Part 1 you'll be given some material to introduce the task and a research question.
You'll need to read this through and then:

1) Carry out research and collect secondary data (data that other people have collected, rather than data you collect yourself).
2) Show that you considered all the different sources you could have used (e.g. books, the Internet) and chose the ones that were most suitable. You also need to explain why you chose those sources.
3) Write a full list (bibliography) of all the sources you used.
4) Present all the data you collected in an appropriate way, e.g. using tables.

2) Planning and Collecting Primary Data

For Part 2 you'll be given some more information to get your head around. Read this through and then:

1) Come up with a hypothesis based on the information you've been given.
2) Plan an experiment to test your hypothesis. You'll need to think about:
    - What equipment you're going to use (and why that equipment is right for the job).
    - What measurements you're going to take of the dependent variable.
    - How you're going to minimise errors so that your results are accurate and reliable.
    - What range of values you will use for the independent variable.
    - What interval you will use for the independent variable.
    - What variables you're going to control (and how you're going to do it).
    - How many times you're going to repeat the experiment.

There's lots of help on all of these things on pages 4-5.

3) Explain all the choices you made when planning the experiment.
4) Write a risk assessment for the experiment.
5) Carry out the experiment to collect primary data, taking any precautions from the risk assessment.
6) Present all the data you collected in an appropriate way, e.g. using tables.

3) Analysis and Evaluation

For Part 3 you'll have to complete a question paper which will ask you to do things like:

1) Process (e.g. using a bit of maths) and present (e.g. using graphs) both the primary and secondary data you collected in Part 1 and Part 2 in the most appropriate way.
2) Analyse and interpret the data to identify any patterns or relationships.
3) Compare your primary and secondary data to look for similarities and differences.
4) Write a conclusion based on all the data you collected and back it up with your own scientific knowledge. Say whether the secondary data you collected supports the conclusion.
5) Look back to your hypothesis and say whether the data supports the hypothesis or not.
6) Evaluate the methods you used to collect the data and the quality of the data that was collected.
7) Say how confident you are in your conclusion and make suggestions for how the investigation could be improved. You'll also need to say why your suggestions would be an improvement.

Read this through and your assessment will be well under control...

You could use this page like a tick list for the controlled assessment — to make sure you don't forget anything.

Moving and Storing Heat

When it starts to get a bit nippy, on goes the heating to warm things up a bit.
Heating is all about the transfer of energy. Here are a few useful definitions to begin with.

Heat is a Measure of Energy

1) When a substance is heated, its particles gain kinetic energy (KE). This energy makes the particles in a gas or a liquid move around faster. In a solid, the particles vibrate more rapidly. This is what eventually causes solids to melt and liquids to boil.
2) This energy is measured on an absolute scale. (This means it can't go lower than zero, because there's a limit to how slow particles can move.) The unit of heat energy is the joule (J).

Temperature is a Measure of Hotness

1) Temperature is a measure of the average kinetic energy of the particles in a substance. The hotter something is, the higher its temperature, and the higher the average KE of its particles.
2) Temperature is usually measured in °C (degrees Celsius), but there are other temperature scales, like °F (degrees Fahrenheit). These are not absolute scales as they can go below zero.

Energy tends to flow from hot objects to cooler ones. E.g. warm radiators heat the cold air in your room — they'd be no use if heat didn't flow.

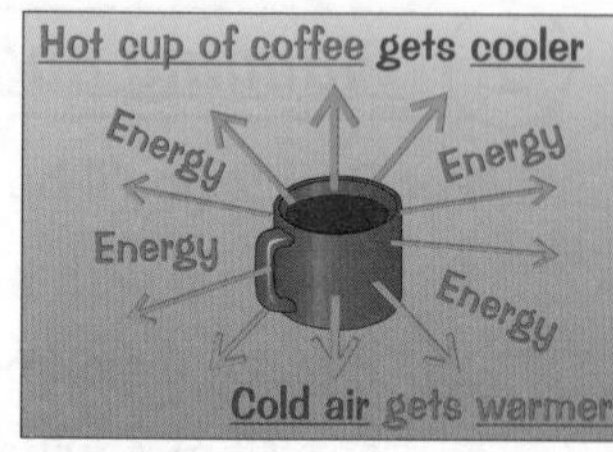

If there's a DIFFERENCE IN TEMPERATURE between two places, then ENERGY WILL FLOW between them.

The greater the difference in temperature, the faster the rate of cooling will be.
E.g. a hot cup of coffee will cool down quicker in a cold room than in a warm room.

Specific Heat Capacity Tells You How Much Energy Stuff Can Store

1) It takes more heat energy to increase the temperature of some materials than others. E.g. you need 4200 J to warm 1 kg of water by 1 °C, but only 139 J to warm 1 kg of mercury by 1 °C.
2) Materials which need to gain lots of energy to warm up also release loads of energy when they cool down again. They can 'store' a lot of heat.
3) The measure of how much energy a substance can store is called its specific heat capacity.
4) Specific heat capacity is the amount of energy needed to raise the temperature of 1 kg of a substance by 1 °C. Water has a specific heat capacity of 4200 J/kg/°C.
5) The specific heat capacity of water is high. Once water's heated, it stores a lot of energy, which makes it good for central heating systems. Also, water's a liquid so it can easily be pumped around a building.
6) You'll have to do calculations involving specific heat capacity. This is the equation to learn:

$$\text{Energy} = \text{Mass} \times \text{Specific Heat Capacity} \times \text{Temperature Change}$$

EXAMPLE: How much energy is needed to heat 2 kg of water from 10 °C to 100 °C?
ANSWER: Energy needed = $2 \times 4200 \times 90 =$ 756 000 J

Flick to the inside front cover for more on formula triangles.

If you're not working out the energy, you'll have to rearrange the equation, so this formula triangle will come in dead handy. You cover up the thing you're trying to find. The parts of the formula you can still see are what it's equal to.

Energy
Mass × SHC × Temp Ch

EXAMPLE: An empty 200 g aluminium kettle cools down from 115 °C to 10 °C, losing 19 068 J of heat energy. What is the specific heat capacity of aluminium?

Remember — you need to convert the mass to kilograms first.

ANSWER: $\text{SHC} = \dfrac{\text{Energy}}{\text{Mass} \times \text{Temp Change}} = \dfrac{19\,068}{0.2 \times 105} =$ 908 J/kg/°C

I wish I had a high specific fact capacity...

There are two reasons why water's used in central heating systems — it's a liquid and it has a high specific heat capacity. This makes water good for cooling systems too. Water can absorb a lot of energy and carry it away.

Melting and Boiling

If you heat up a pan of water on the stove, the water never gets any hotter than 100 °C. You can carry on heating it up, but the temperature won't rise. How come, you say? It's all to do with latent heat...

You Need to Put In Energy to Break Intermolecular Bonds

1) When you heat a liquid, the heat energy makes the particles move faster. Eventually, when enough of the particles have enough energy to overcome their attraction to each other, big bubbles of gas form in the liquid — this is boiling.
2) It's similar when you heat a solid. Heat energy makes the particles vibrate faster until eventually the forces between them are overcome and the particles start to move around — this is melting.
3) When a substance is melting or boiling, you're still putting in energy, but the energy's used for breaking intermolecular bonds rather than raising the temperature — there are flat spots on the heating graph.

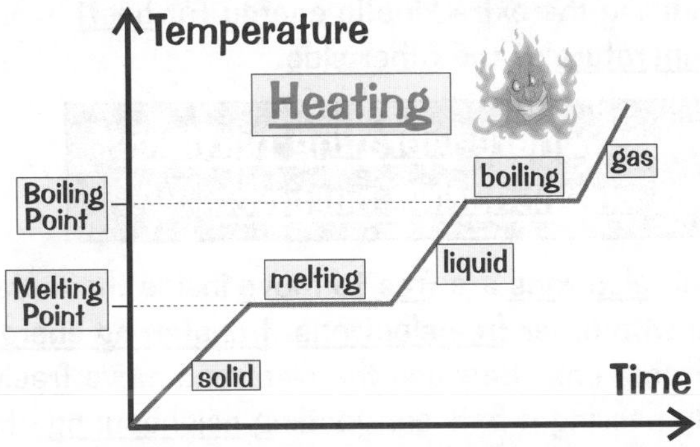

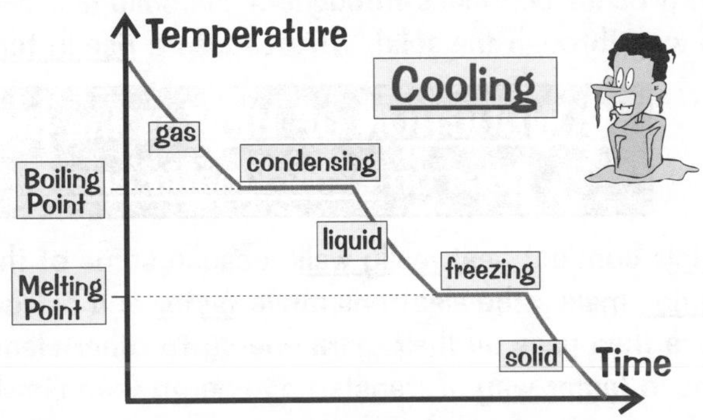

4) When a substance is condensing or freezing, bonds are forming between particles, which releases energy. This means the temperature doesn't go down until all the substance has turned into a liquid (condensing) or a solid (freezing).

Specific Latent Heat is the Energy Needed to Change State

1) The specific latent heat of melting is the amount of energy needed to melt 1 kg of material without changing its temperature (i.e. the material's got to be at its melting temperature already).
2) The specific latent heat of boiling is the energy needed to boil 1 kg of material without changing its temperature (i.e. the material's got to be at its boiling temperature already).
3) Specific latent heat is different for different materials, and it's different for boiling and melting. You don't have to remember what all the numbers are, though. Phew.
4) There's a formula to help you with all the calculations. And here it is:

Energy = Mass × Specific Latent Heat

EXAMPLE: The specific latent heat of water (for melting) is 334 000 J/kg. How much energy is needed to melt an ice cube of mass 7 g at 0 °C?

ANSWER: Energy = 0.007 × 334 000 J = 2338 J

If you're finding the mass or the specific latent heat you'll need to divide, not multiply — just to make your life a bit easier here's the formula triangle.

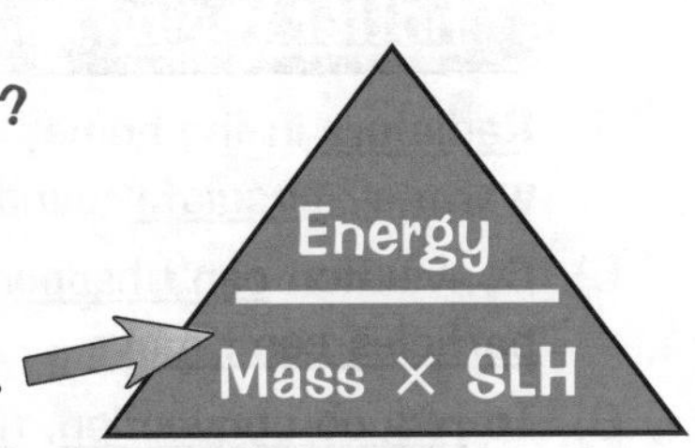

EXAMPLE: The specific latent heat of water (for boiling) is 2 260 000 J/kg. 2 825 000 J of energy is used to boil dry a pan of water at 100 °C. What was the mass of water in the pan?

ANSWER: Mass = Energy ÷ SLH = 2 825 000 ÷ 2 260 000 J = 1.25 kg

Breaking Bonds — Blofeld never quite manages it...

Melting a solid or boiling a liquid means you've got to break bonds between particles. That takes energy. Specific latent heat is just the amount of energy you need per kilogram of stuff. Incidentally, this is how sweating cools you down — your body heat's used to change liquid sweat into gas. Nice.

Conduction and Convection in the Home

If you build a house, there are regulations about doing it properly, mainly so that it doesn't fall down, but also so that it keeps the heat in. Easier said than done — there are several ways that heat is 'lost'.

Conduction Occurs Mainly in Solids

Houses lose a lot of heat through their windows even when they're shut. Heat flows from the warm inside face of the window to the cold outside face mostly by conduction.

1) In a solid, the particles are held tightly together. So when one particle vibrates, it bumps into other particles nearby and quickly passes the vibrations on.
2) Particles which vibrate faster than others pass on their extra kinetic energy to neighbouring particles. These particles then vibrate faster themselves.

3) This process continues throughout the solid and gradually the extra kinetic energy (or heat) is spread all the way through the solid. This causes a rise in temperature at the other side.

CONDUCTION OF HEAT is the process where vibrating particles pass on extra kinetic energy to neighbouring particles.

4) Metals conduct heat really well because some of their electrons are free to move inside the metal. Heating makes the electrons move faster and collide with other free electrons, transferring energy. These then pass on their extra energy to other electrons, etc. Because the electrons move freely, this is a much faster way of transferring energy than slowly passing it between jostling neighbouring atoms.
5) Most non-metals don't have free electrons, so warm up more slowly, making them good for insulating things — that's why metals are used for saucepans, but non-metals are used for saucepan handles.
6) Liquids and gases conduct heat more slowly than solids — the particles aren't held so tightly together, which prevents them bumping into each other so often. So air is a good insulator.

Convection Occurs in Liquids and Gases

1) When you heat up a liquid or gas, the particles move faster, and the fluid (liquid or gas) expands, becoming less dense.
2) The warmer, less dense fluid rises above its colder, denser surroundings, like a hot air balloon does.
3) As the warm fluid rises, cooler fluid takes its place. As this process continues, you actually end up with a circulation of fluid (convection currents). This is how immersion heaters work.

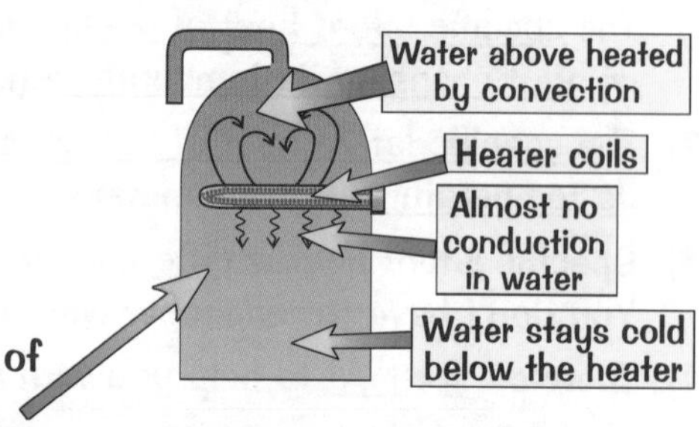

CONVECTION occurs when the more energetic particles move from the hotter region to the cooler region — and take their heat energy with them.

4) Radiators in the home rely on convection to make the warm air circulate round the room.
5) Convection can't happen in solids because the particles can't move — they just vibrate on the spot.
6) To reduce convection, you need to stop the fluid moving. Clothes, blankets and cavity wall foam insulation all work by trapping pockets of air. The air can't move so the heat has to conduct very slowly through the pockets of air, as well as the material in between.

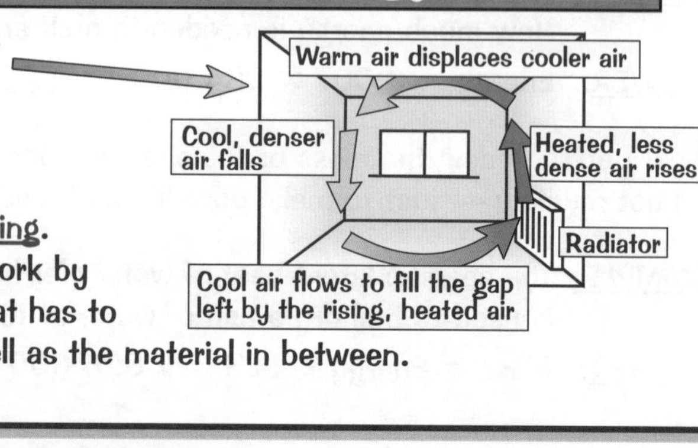

And the good old garden spade is a great example...

If a garden spade is left outside in cold weather, the metal bit will always feel colder than the wooden handle. But it isn't colder — it just conducts heat away from your hand quicker. The opposite is true if the spade is left out in the sunshine — it'll feel hotter because it conducts heat into your hand quicker.

Heat Radiation

Houses in Mediterranean countries are often painted white, to reflect heat from the Sun. In cold, cloudy Britain, we tend to leave our houses slate grey or brick red to absorb the heat. (Saves on paint, too.)

Radiation is How We Get Heat from the Sun

As well as by conduction and convection, heat can be transferred by radiation. Heat is radiated as infrared waves — these are electromagnetic waves that travel in straight lines at the speed of light (see p. 20).

Radiation is different from conduction and convection in several ways:

1) It doesn't need a medium (material) to travel through, so it can occur in a vacuum, like space. This is the only way that heat reaches us from the Sun.
2) It can only occur through transparent substances, like air, glass and water.
3) The amount of radiation emitted or absorbed by an object depends to a large extent on its surface colour and texture. This definitely isn't true for conduction and convection.

All Objects Emit and Absorb Heat Radiation

1) All objects are continually emitting and absorbing heat radiation.
2) The hotter an object gets, the more heat radiation it emits.
3) Cooler objects will absorb the heat radiation emitted by hotter things, so their temperature increases. You can feel heat radiation, for example if you're indoors and the Sun shines on you through a window.
4) Matt black surfaces are very good absorbers and emitters of radiation. You should really paint your radiators black to help emit heat radiation, but leave your fridge a nice shiny white to help reflect it.
5) Light-coloured, smooth and shiny objects are very poor absorbers and emitters of radiation. They effectively reflect heat radiation — e.g. some people put shiny foil behind their radiators to reflect radiation back into the room rather than heat up the walls.

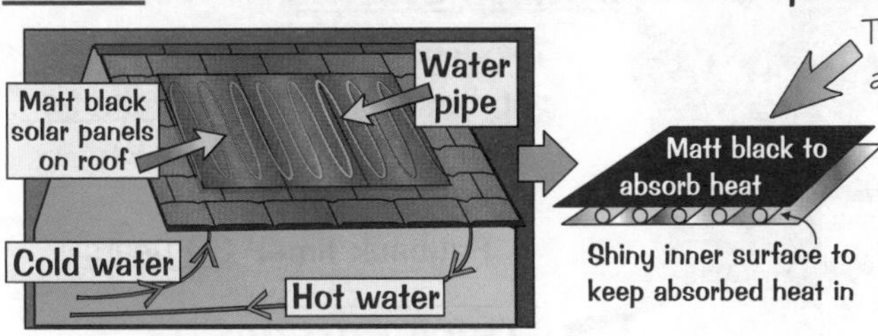

The panels for solar water heating are painted matt black to absorb as much heat as possible.

The shiny surface on a patio heater reflects heat downwards — onto the patio.

Heat Radiation is Important in Cooking

1) Grills and toasters heat food by infrared (heat) radiation. The heat radiated by a grill is absorbed by the surface particles of the food, increasing their kinetic energy. The heat energy is then conducted or convected to more central parts.
2) People often line their grill pan with shiny foil. This reflects the heat radiation back onto the bottom of the food being grilled, so the food is cooked more evenly. (It also stops the grill pan getting dirty, of course.)
3) Microwave ovens also use radiation to cook food — microwaves are electromagnetic waves that have a different wavelength to infrared (see p. 20).
4) Microwaves penetrate about 1 cm into the outer layer of food where they're absorbed by water or fat molecules, increasing their kinetic energy. The energy is then conducted or convected to other parts.
5) You don't cover food with foil in a microwave oven though — the microwaves will be reflected away so they won't cook the food, AND it can cause dangerous sparks inside the oven. It's okay to cover the food with glass or plastic though as microwaves can pass right through.

Radiate happiness — stand by the fire and smile...

The most confusing thing about radiation is that those white things on your walls called 'radiators' actually transfer most of their heat by convection, as rising warm air. They do radiate some heat too, of course, but whoever chose the name 'radiator' obviously hadn't swotted up their physics first.

Saving Energy

It's daft to keep paying for energy to heat your house only to let the heat escape straight out again.

Insulating Your House Saves Energy and Money

'Sources' can also waste energy if they're not very efficient.

1) Energy in the home is emitted and transferred (or wasted) in different areas.
2) Things that emit energy are called sources, e.g. radiators.
   Things that transfer and waste or lose energy are called sinks, e.g. windows and computers.
3) To save energy, you can insulate your house so the sinks 'drain' less energy, e.g. use curtains to reduce energy loss. You can also make sources and sinks more efficient, so they waste less energy, e.g. use energy-saving light bulbs instead of normal ones.
4) It costs money to buy and install insulation, or buy more efficient appliances, but it also saves you money, because your energy bills are lower.
5) Eventually, the money you've saved on energy bills will equal the initial cost — the time this takes is called the payback time.
6) If you subtract the annual saving from the initial cost repeatedly then eventually the one with the biggest annual saving must always come out as the winner, if you think about it.
7) But you might sell the house (or die) before that happens. If you look at it over, say, a five-year period then a cheap and cheerful hot water tank jacket wins over expensive double glazing.

$$\text{payback time} = \frac{\text{initial cost}}{\text{annual saving}}$$

Loft Insulation

Fibreglass 'wool' laid across the loft floor reduces conduction through the ceiling into the roof space.
Initial Cost: £200
Annual Saving: £100
Payback time: 2 years

Hot Water Tank Jacket

Reduces conduction.
Initial Cost: £60
Annual Saving: £15
Payback time: 4 years

These figures are rough. It'll vary from house to house.

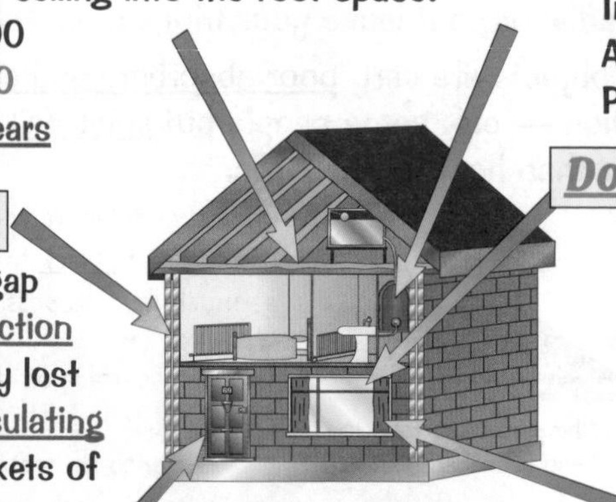

Cavity Walls & Insulation

Two layers of bricks with a gap between them reduce conduction but you still get some energy lost by convection. Squirting insulating foam into the gap traps pockets of air to minimise this convection.
Initial Cost: £150
Annual Saving: £100
Payback time: 18 months
(Heat is still lost through the walls by radiation though. Also, if there are any spaces where air is not trapped there'll still be some convection too.)

Double Glazing

Two layers of glass with an air gap between reduce conduction.
Initial Cost: £2400
Annual Saving: £80
Payback time: 30 years

Draught-proofing

Strips of foam and plastic around doors and windows stop hot air going out — reducing convection.
Initial Cost: £100
Annual Saving: £15
Payback time: 7 years

Thick Curtains

Reduce conduction and radiation through the windows.
Initial Cost: £180
Annual Saving: £20
Payback time: 9 years

Thermograms Show Where Your House is Leaking Heat

1) A thermogram is a picture taken with a thermal imaging camera.
2) Objects at different temperatures emit infrared rays of different wavelengths. The thermogram displays these temperatures as different colours. The hotter parts show up as white, yellow and red, whilst the colder parts are black, dark blue and purple. If a house looks 'hot', it's losing heat to the outside.
3) In this thermogram, the houses on the left and right are losing bucket-loads of heat out of their roofs (shown as red/yellow), but the one in the middle must have loft insulation as it's not losing half as much.

It looks like this house doesn't have any double glazing either... tut, tut.

TONY MCCONNELL/ SCIENCE PHOTO LIBRARY

I went to a physicist's stag night — the best man had booked a thermogram...

Insulating your house well is a really good way to save energy. Drawing the curtains is like putting on a jumper.

Efficiency

An open fire looks cosy, but a lot of its heat energy goes straight up the chimney, by convection, instead of heating up your living room. All this energy is 'wasted', so open fires aren't very efficient.

Machines Always Waste Some Energy

1) Useful machines are only useful because they convert energy from one form to another. Take cars for instance — you put in chemical energy (petrol or diesel) and the engine converts it into kinetic (movement) energy.

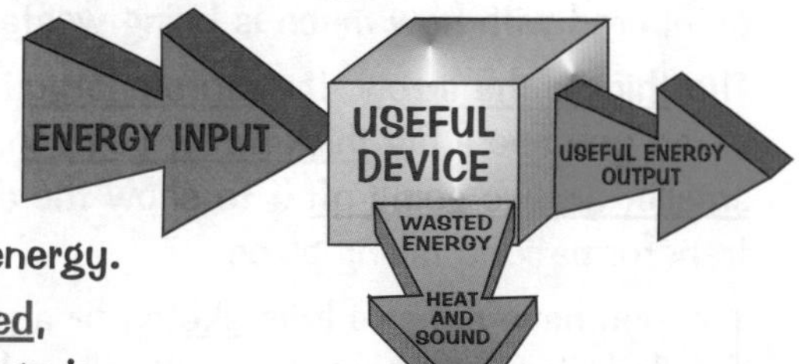

2) The total energy output is always the same as the energy input, but only some of the output energy is useful. So for every joule of chemical energy you put into your car you'll only get a fraction of it converted into useful kinetic energy.
3) This is because some of the input energy is always lost or wasted, often as heat. In the car example, the rest of the chemical energy is converted (mostly) into heat and sound energy. This is wasted energy — although you could always stick your dinner under the bonnet and warm it up on the drive home.
4) The less energy that is wasted, the more efficient the device is said to be.

More Efficient Machines Waste Less Energy

The efficiency of a machine is defined as:

$$\text{Efficiency} = \frac{\text{USEFUL Energy OUTPUT}}{\text{TOTAL Energy INPUT}} \quad (\times 100\%)$$

1) To work out the efficiency of a machine, first find out the Total Energy INPUT. This is the energy supplied to the machine.
2) Then find how much useful energy the machine delivers — the Useful Energy OUTPUT. The question might tell you this directly, or it might tell you how much energy is wasted as heat/sound.
3) Then just divide the smaller number by the bigger one to get a value for efficiency somewhere between 0 and 1. Easy. If your number is bigger than 1, you've done the division upside down.

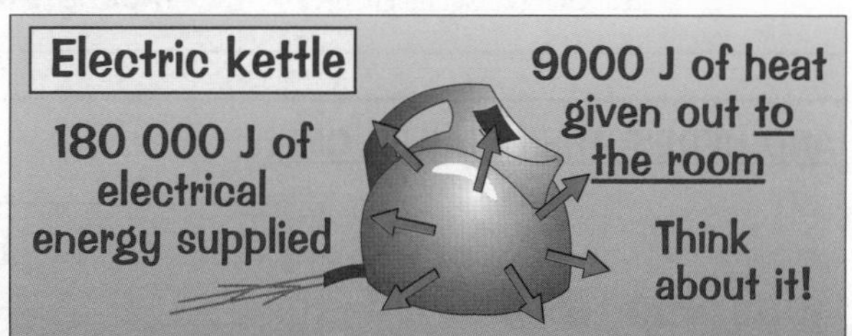

$$\text{Efficiency} = \frac{\text{Useful En. Out}}{\text{Total En. In}} = \frac{171\,000}{180\,000} = 0.95$$

4) You can convert the efficiency to a percentage, by multiplying it by 100. E.g. 0.6 = 60%.
5) In the exam you might be told the efficiency and asked to work out the total energy input, the useful energy output or the energy wasted. So you need to be able to rearrange the formula.

EXAMPLE: An ordinary light bulb is 5% efficient. If 1000 J of light energy is given out, how much energy is wasted?

ANSWER: $\text{Total Input} = \frac{\text{Useful Output}}{\text{Efficiency}} = \frac{1000\text{ J}}{0.05} = 20\,000\text{ J},$

so Energy Wasted = 20 000 – 1000 = 19 000 J

Shockingly inefficient, those ordinary light bulbs. Low-energy light bulbs are roughly 4 times more efficient, and last about 8 times as long. They're more expensive though.

6) You can use information like this to draw a Sankey diagram, or use the equation to work out the efficiency of something from a Sankey diagram — coming up on the next page.

Efficiency = pages learned ÷ cups of tea made...

Some new appliances (like washing machines and fridges) come with a sticker with a letter from A to H on, to show how energy-efficient they are. A really well-insulated fridge might have an 'A' rating. But if you put it right next to the oven, or never defrost it, it will run much less efficiently than it should.

Sankey Diagrams

This is another opportunity for a MATHS question. Fantastic.
So best prepare yourself — here's what those Sankey diagrams are all about...

The Thickness of the Arrow Represents the Amount of Energy

Sankey diagrams are just energy transformation diagrams — they make it easy to see at a glance how much of the input energy is being usefully employed compared with how much is being wasted.

The thicker the arrow, the more energy it represents — so you see a big thick arrow going in, then several smaller arrows going off it to show the different energy transformations taking place.

You can have either a little sketch or a properly detailed diagram where the width of each arrow is proportional to the number of joules it represents.

Example —TV:

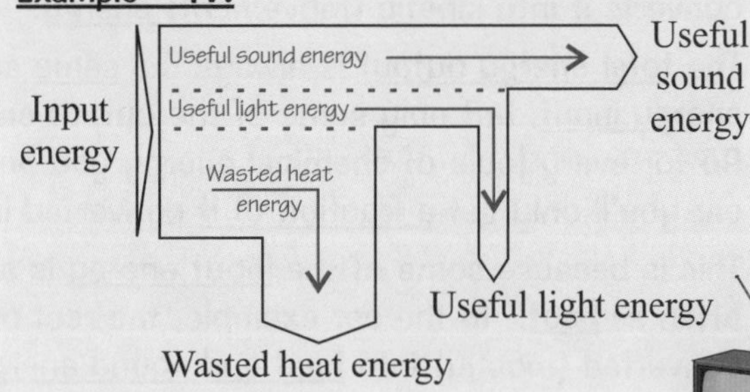

EXAMPLE — SANKEY DIAGRAM FOR A SIMPLE MOTOR:

HERE'S THE SKETCH VERSION:

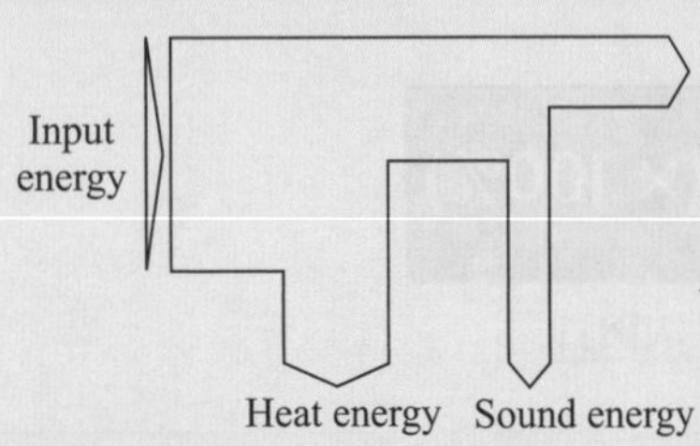

You don't know the actual amounts, but you can see that most of the energy is being wasted, and that it's mostly wasted as heat.

EXAM QUESTIONS:

With sketches, they're likely to ask you to compare two different devices and say which is more efficient. You generally want to be looking for the one with the thickest useful energy arrow(s).

AND HERE'S THE DETAILED ONE:

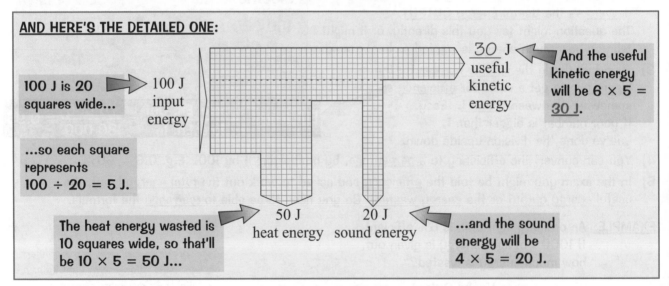

100 J is 20 squares wide...

...so each square represents 100 ÷ 20 = 5 J.

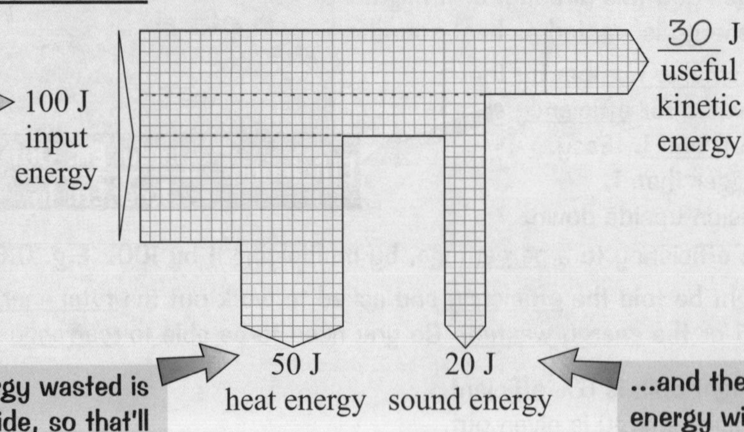

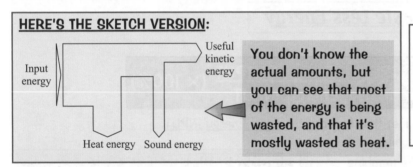

And the useful kinetic energy will be 6 × 5 = 30 J.

The heat energy wasted is 10 squares wide, so that'll be 10 × 5 = 50 J...

...and the sound energy will be 4 × 5 = 20 J.

EXAM QUESTIONS:

In an exam, the most likely question you'll get about detailed Sankey diagrams is filling in one of the numbers or calculating the efficiency. The efficiency is straightforward enough if you can work out the numbers (see p. 15).

Skankey diagrams — to represent the smelliness of your socks...

If they ask you to draw your own Sankey diagram in the exam, and don't give you the figures, a sketch is all they'll expect. Just give a rough idea of where the energy goes. E.g. a filament lamp turns most of the input energy into heat, and only a tiny proportion goes to useful light energy.

Wave Basics

Think about a toaster that glows when it heats up. It emits infrared radiation (heat) and a reddish light. You could conclude that heat and light must be similar forms of radiation — you'd be right. They're both electromagnetic waves, but before we move on to them, let's start with some wave basics.

Waves Have Amplitude, Wavelength and Frequency

Waves have certain features:

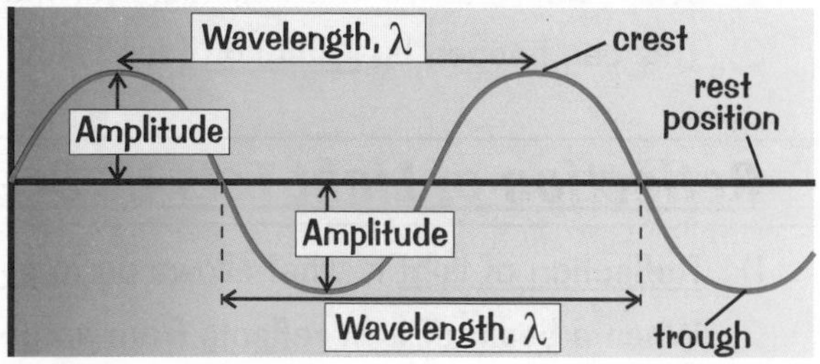

1) The amplitude is the displacement from the rest position to the crest. (NOT from a trough to a crest)
2) The wavelength is the length of a full cycle of the wave, e.g. from crest to crest.
3) Frequency is the number of complete cycles or oscillations passing a certain point per second. Frequency is measured in hertz (Hz). 1 Hz is 1 wave per second.

Wave Speed = Frequency × Wavelength

You need to learn how to use this equation:

Speed (m/s) = Frequency (Hz) × Wavelength (m) OR $v = f\lambda$

Speed (v is for velocity)
Wavelength (that's the Greek letter 'lambda')
Frequency

EXAMPLE Eva is building a sandcastle. She estimates that 1 wave passes her sandcastle every 2 seconds, and that the crests of the waves are 90 cm apart. Calculate the speed, in metres per second, of the waves passing Eva's sandcastle.

In one second, half a wave passes, so the frequency is 0.5 Hz (hertz).

ANSWER: Speed = 0.5 × 0.90 = 0.45 m/s (Remember to change the 90 cm into metres first.)

You might be asked to calculate the frequency or wavelength instead of the speed though, so you need the good old triangle too...

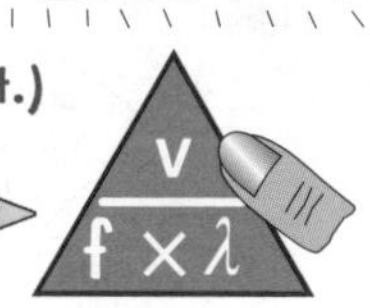

You Need to Convert Your Units First

1) The standard (SI) units involved in wave equations are: metres, seconds, m/s and hertz (Hz). Always CONVERT INTO SI UNITS (m, s, m/s, Hz) before you work anything out.
2) The trouble is waves often have high frequencies given in kHz or MHz, so make sure you learn this too:

1 kHz (kilohertz) = 1000 Hz   1 MHz (1 megahertz) = 1 000 000 Hz

3) Wavelengths can also be given in other units, e.g. km for long-wave radio.
4) There's worse still: The speed of light is 3×10^8 m/s = 300 000 000 m/s. This, along with numbers like 900 MHz = 900 000 000 Hz won't fit into some calculators. That leaves you three choices:
   1) Enter the numbers as standard form. For example, to enter 3×10^8, press [3] [EXP] [8].
   (Your calculator might have a different button for standard form — if you don't know what it is, find out...)
   2) Cancel three or six noughts off both numbers (so long as you're dividing them!) or...
   3) Do it entirely without a calculator (no really, I've seen it done).

EXAMPLE: A radio wave has a frequency of 92.2 MHz. Find its wavelength. (The speed of all EM waves is 3×10^8 m/s.)

ANSWER: You're trying to find λ using f and v, so you've got to rearrange the equation.
You need to convert the frequency into the SI unit, Hz: 92.2 MHz = 92 200 000 Hz
So $\lambda = v \div f = 3 \times 10^8 \div 92\,200\,000 = 3 \times 10^8 \div 9.22 \times 10^7 = 3.25$ m

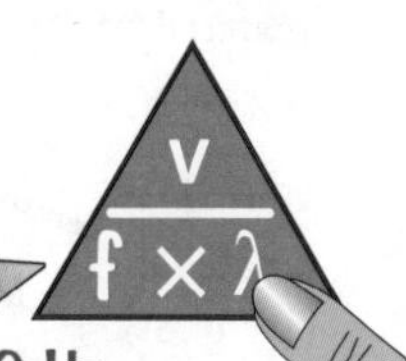

It's probably easiest to use standard form here.

This stuff on formulas is really painful — I mean it MHz...

Yep, there's a helluva lot of maths on this page. Make sure you get your head around all the definitions too.

Wave Properties

Now you know the basics, let's have a look at some wave properties...

All Waves Can be Reflected, Refracted and Diffracted

1) Waves travel in a straight line through whatever substance they're travelling in.
2) When waves arrive at an obstacle (or meet a new material), their direction of travel can be changed.
3) This can happen by reflection (see below) or by refraction or diffraction (see next page).

Reflection of Light Lets Us See Things

1) Reflection of light is what allows us to see objects. Light bounces off them into our eyes.
2) When a beam of light reflects from an uneven surface such as a piece of paper, the light reflects off at different angles.
3) When it reflects from an even surface (smooth and shiny like a plane mirror) then it's all reflected at the same angle and you get a clear reflection.
4) The LAW OF REFLECTION applies to every reflected ray:

Angle of INCIDENCE = Angle of REFLECTION

The normal is an imaginary line that's perpendicular (at right angles) to the surface at the point of incidence (where the light hits the surface).

Note that these two angles are ALWAYS defined between the ray itself and the NORMAL, dotted below. Don't ever label them as the angle between the ray and the surface. Definitely uncool.

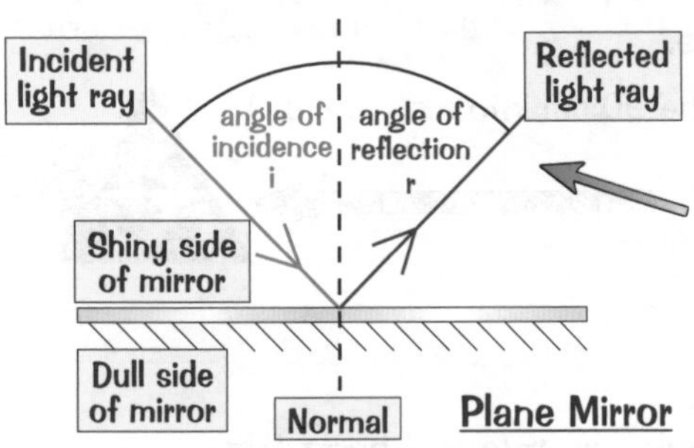

Plane Mirror

You have to know how to use ray diagrams like these two to show reflection. Just remember to draw in the normal first, then the incident and reflected rays at the same angle either side of this. Use a ruler.

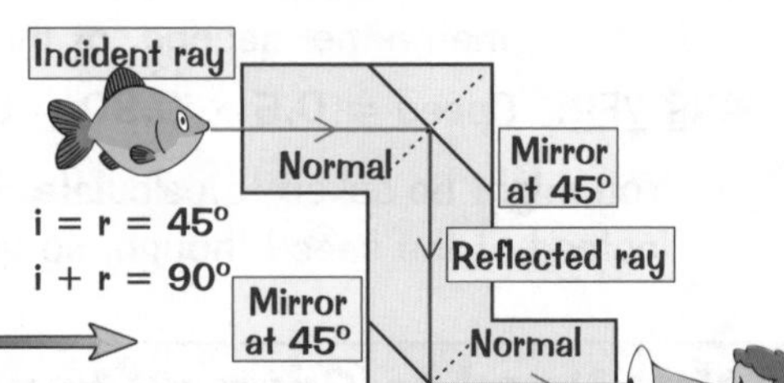

Simple Periscope

Total Internal Reflection Depends on the Critical Angle

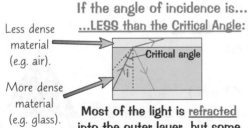

1) A wave hitting a surface can experience total internal reflection. This can only happen when the light ray travels through a dense material like glass, water or Perspex® towards a less dense substance like air.
2) If the angle of incidence is big enough, the ray doesn't come out at all, but reflects back into the material.
3) Big enough means bigger than the critical angle for that particular material — every material has its own, different critical angle.

If the angle of incidence is...

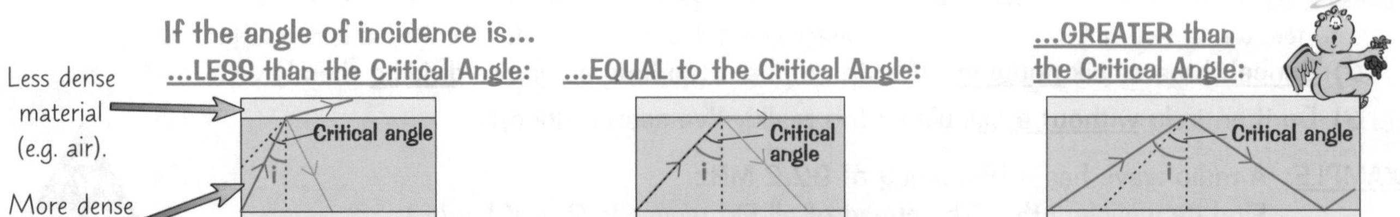

Most of the light is refracted into the outer layer, but some of it is internally reflected.

The ray would go along the surface (with quite a bit of internal reflection as well).

No light comes out. It's all internally reflected, i.e. total internal reflection.

Plane mirrors — what pilots use to look behind them...

This stuff on reflection ain't too complicated — and it's easy marks in the exam. Make sure you can scribble down some nice, clear ray diagrams and you should be well on your way to a great mark. Don't forget your ruler

Diffraction and Refraction

If you thought reflection was good, you'll just love diffraction and refraction — it's awesome. If you didn't find reflection interesting then I'm afraid it's tough luck — you need to know about all three of them. Sorry.

Diffraction — Waves Spreading Out

1) All waves spread out ('diffract') at the edges when they pass through a gap or pass an object.
2) The amount of diffraction depends on the size of the gap relative to the wavelength of the wave. The narrower the gap, or the longer the wavelength, the more the wave spreads out.
3) A narrow gap is one about the same size as the wavelength of the wave. So whether a gap counts as narrow or not depends on the wave.
4) Light has a very small wavelength (about 0.0005 mm), so it can be diffracted but it needs a really small gap.
5) This means you can hear someone through an open door even if you can't see them, because the size of the gap and the wavelength of sound are roughly equal, causing the sound wave to diffract and fill the room...
6) ...But you can't see them unless you're directly facing the door because the gap is about a million times bigger than the wavelength of light, so it won't diffract enough.

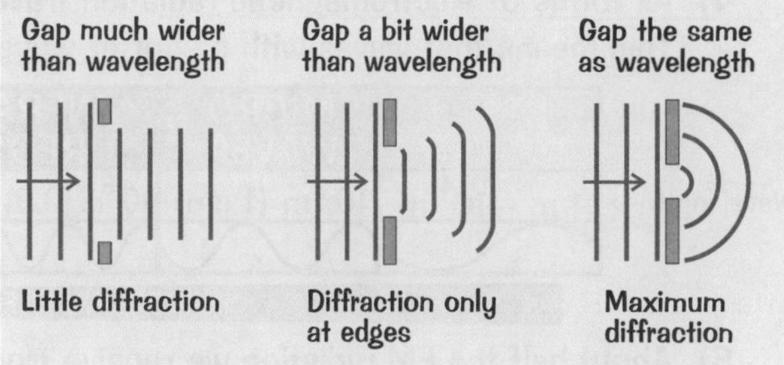

7) If a gap is about the same size as the wavelength of a light, you can get a diffraction pattern of light and dark fringes, as shown here.

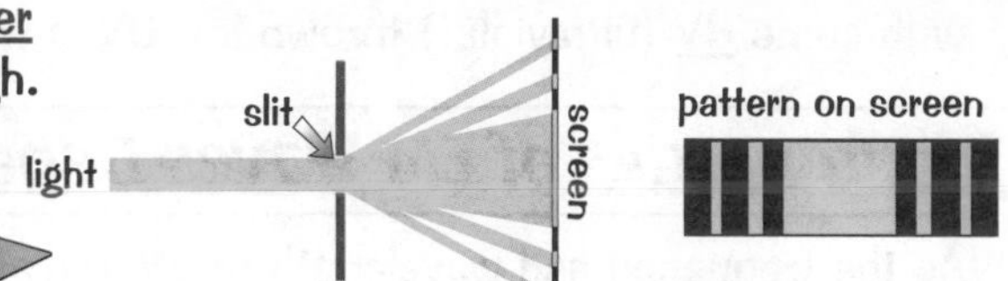

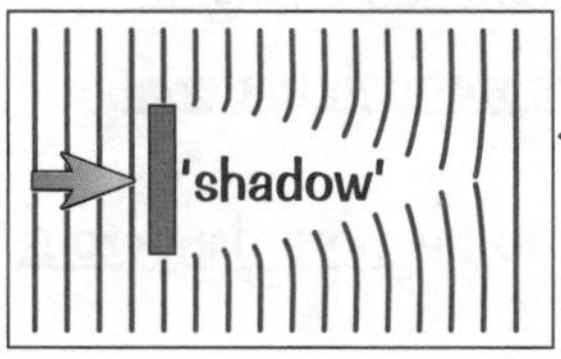

8) You get diffraction around the edges of obstacles too. The shadow is where the wave is blocked. The wider the obstacle compared to the wavelength, the less diffraction it causes, so the longer the shadow.

Refraction — Changing the Speed of a Wave Can Change its Direction

1) Waves travel at different speeds in substances which have different densities. So when a wave crosses a boundary between two substances (from glass to air, say) it changes speed:

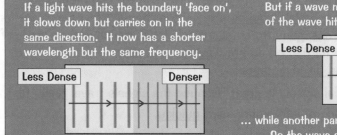

If a light wave hits the boundary 'face on', it slows down but carries on in the same direction. It now has a shorter wavelength but the same frequency.

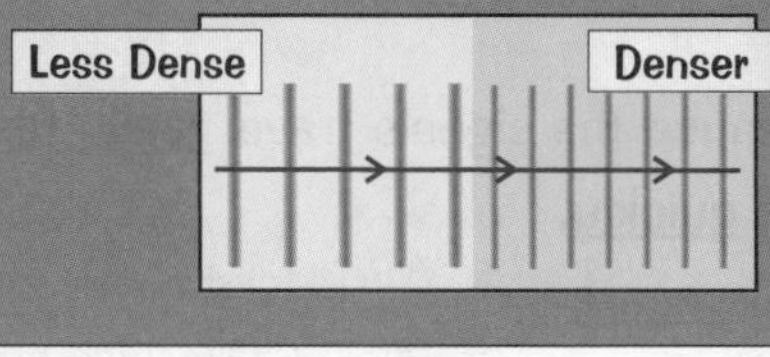

But if a wave meets a different medium at an angle, part of the wave hits the denser layer first and slows down...

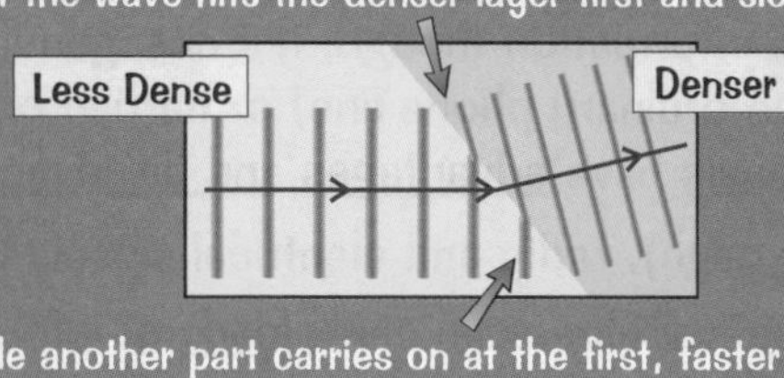

... while another part carries on at the first, faster speed for a while. So the wave changes direction — it's been REFRACTED.

2) E.g. when light passes from air into the glass of a window pane (a denser medium), it slows down — causing the light to refract towards the normal. When the light reaches the 'glass to air' boundary on the other side of the window, it speeds up and refracts away from the normal.
3) Waves are only refracted if they meet a new medium at an angle. If they're travelling along the normal (i.e. the angle of incidence is zero) they will change speed, but are NOT refracted — they don't change direction.

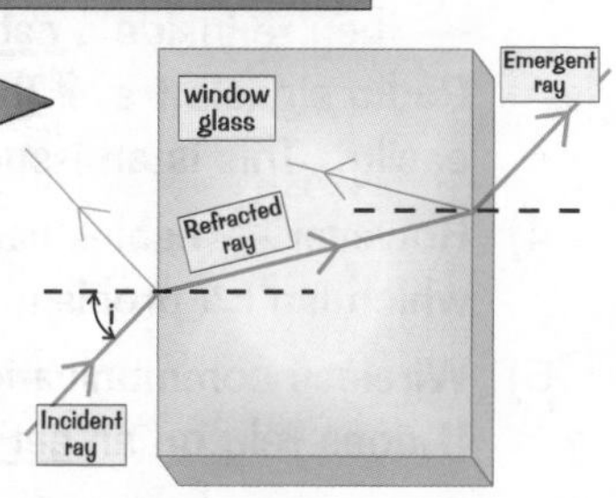

Lights, camera, refraction...

Remember that all waves can be diffracted. It doesn't matter what type of wave it is — sound, light, water... The key point to remember about refraction is that the wave has to meet a boundary at an angle.

EM Waves and Communication

Waves are brilliant. There is no end to the things you can do with a wave.
So let's have a closer look at those electromagnetic waves and marvel at their awesomeness...

There are Seven Types of Electromagnetic (EM) Waves

1) Electromagnetic radiation can occur at many different wavelengths.
2) In fact, there is a continuous spectrum of different wavelengths, but waves with similar wavelengths tend to have similar properties.
3) Electromagnetic radiation is conventionally split into seven types of waves — see below.
4) All forms of electromagnetic radiation travel at the same speed through a vacuum. This means that waves with a shorter wavelength have a higher frequency.

	RADIO WAVES	MICRO WAVES	INFRA RED	VISIBLE LIGHT	ULTRA VIOLET	X-RAYS	GAMMA RAYS
Wavelength →	1 m – 10^4 m	10^{-2} m (1 cm)	10^{-5} m (0.01 mm)	10^{-7} m	10^{-8} m	10^{-10} m	10^{-12} m

INCREASING FREQUENCY AND DECREASING WAVELENGTH →

5) About half the EM radiation we receive from the Sun is visible light. Most of the rest is infrared (heat), with some UV (ultraviolet) thrown in. UV is what gives us a suntan (see page 29).

The Properties of EM Waves Depend on Frequency and Wavelength

1) As the frequency and wavelength of EM radiation changes, its interaction with matter changes — i.e. the way a wave is absorbed, reflected or transmitted by any given substance changes.
2) As a rule, the EM waves at each end of the spectrum tend to be able to pass through material, whilst those nearer the middle are absorbed.
3) Also, the ones with higher frequency (shorter wavelength), like X-rays, tend to be more dangerous to living cells. That's because they have more energy.
4) When any EM radiation is absorbed it can cause heating and ionisation (if the frequency is high enough). Ionisation is where an atom or molecule either loses or gains electrons and it can be dangerous.

Different Sorts of Signals have Different Advantages

As well as cooking our food and keeping us warm (see p. 13), EM waves are used for communication. E.g. radio waves are used for radio, microwaves for mobile phones etc. — see the next few pages for more. Before you communicate information though, it's changed into an electrical signal, which is then sent off on its own (like you get in an ordinary phone line) or carried on an EM wave (see p. 28).
The different types of signals have advantages and disadvantages:

1) Using light (see next page), radio and electrical signals is great because the signals travel really fast.
2) Electrical wires and optical fibres can carry loads of information very quickly.
3) Information sent through optical fibres and electrical wires is pretty secure — they're inside a cable and so can't easily be tapped in to. Radio signals travel through the air, so they can be intercepted more easily. This is an issue for people using wireless internet networks.
4) However — cables can be difficult to repair if they get broken, which isn't a problem for wireless methods.
5) Wireless communication also has the advantage that it is portable (e.g. mobile phones, laptop wi-fi etc.). It does rely on an aerial to pick up a signal though, and signal strength often depends on location.

Wireless just means without wires — usually using radio and microwaves but infrared and light can be used too. TV, radio, mobile phones and computers all use wireless technology.

Where would Chris Moyles be without EM waves — I ask you...

In 1588, beacons were used on the south coast of England to relay the information that the Spanish Armada was approaching. As we know, light travels as electromagnetic waves, so this is an early example of transferring information using electromagnetic radiation — or wireless communication.

Communicating with Light

Light's a very useful wave for communicating — you can only read this book because it's reflecting light rays. But this page is really about using light to communicate over longer distances or in awkward places.

Communicating with Light Can Require a Code

1) Historically, light was used to speed up communication over long distances.
2) By creating a code of 'on-off' signals, a message could be relayed between stations far away, by flashing a light on and off in a way that could be decoded.
3) This is the principle behind the Morse code.
4) Each letter of the alphabet (and each number 0-9) is represented by a sequence of 'dots' and 'dashes' — which are pulses of light (or sound) that last for a certain length of time.
5) E.g. in the International Morse Code, the distress signal 'SOS' would be transmitted as · · · — — — · · · which is three short pulses of light, followed by three long pulses and then another three short.
6) The Morse code is a type of digital signal (see p. 28) because the light pulse is only either 'on' or 'off'.

Some letters from the International Morse Code are shown here:

A · — M — —
E · S · · ·
O — — — W · — —

E.g. the word 'awesome' is:
· — · — — · · · · — — — — — ·

Light Signals Can Travel Through Optical Fibres

Optical fibres can also be called fibre optics.

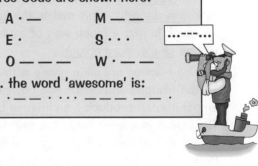

1) A more modern use of light for communication is the use of optical fibres, which can carry data over long distances as pulses of light or infrared radiation (see p. 23).
2) They work by bouncing waves off the sides of a very narrow core which is protected by outer layers.

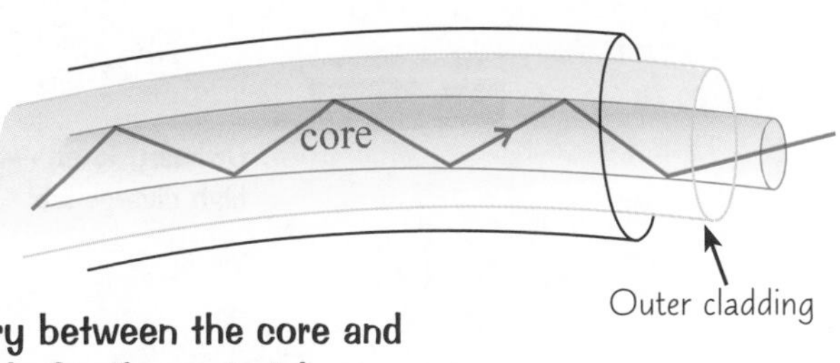

3) The ray of light enters the fibre so that it hits the boundary between the core and the outer cladding at an angle greater than the critical angle for the material. This causes total internal reflection of the ray within the core (see page 18).
4) The pulse of light enters at one end and is reflected again and again until it emerges at the other end.
5) Optical fibres are increasingly being used for telephone and broadband internet cables, replacing the old electrical ones. They're also used for medical purposes — to 'see inside' the body without having to operate. You'll probably know them best though as the things that give us twinkly lights at the ends of the branches of artificial Christmas trees... yey, Christmas.

Using Light has lots of Advantages

1) Using light is a very quick way to communicate. In a vacuum, light travels at 300 000 000 m/s — it can't travel that fast through optical fibres (it's slowed down by about 30%) but it's still pretty quick.
2) Multiplexing means that lots of different signals can be transmitted down a single optical fibre at the same time, so you don't need as many cables.
3) As it's a 'digital' signal, there's little interference.

See page 28 for more on interference and multiplexing.

If you're not sure what life's about, try total internal reflection...

Here's something to make you go 'wow' (or '· — — — — — · — —') in amazement — an optical fibre, which is thinner than a human hair, can have over one million telephone calls going down it at the same time.

Lasers

Lasers are useful in lots of areas — manufacturing, surgery, dentistry, weaponry...
They're even used in CD players.

Lasers Produce Narrow, Intense Beams of Monochromatic Light

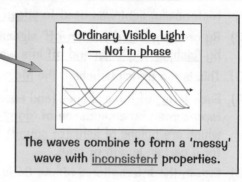

Ordinary visible light (e.g. daylight) is a combination of waves of different frequency and wavelength (and so colour) that are 'out of phase' with each other (i.e. the crests and troughs don't match).

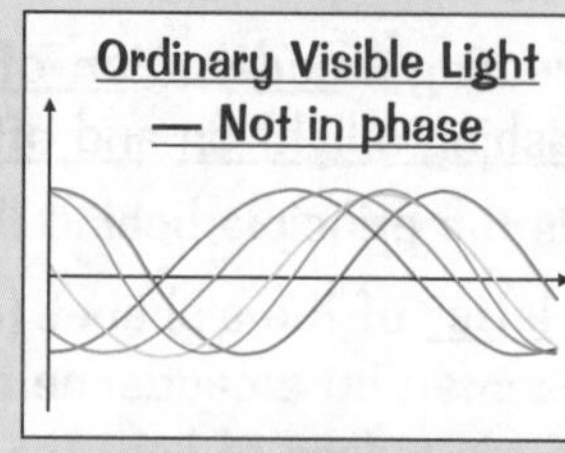

The waves combine to form a 'messy' wave with inconsistent properties.

A laser beam is just a special ray of visible light that has a few extra properties which make it special:

1) All the waves in a laser beam are at the same frequency (and wavelength). This makes the light monochromatic — which is just a fancy way of saying that it's all one single, pure colour.
2) The light waves are all in phase with each other — the troughs and crests line up, increasing the amplitude, so producing an intense beam. The waves in a laser beam are said to be coherent because they have a fixed phase difference (in this case a difference of zero, i.e. the waves are 'in phase').
3) Lasers have low divergence — the beam is narrow, and it stays narrow, even at a long distance from the light source (it doesn't diverge):

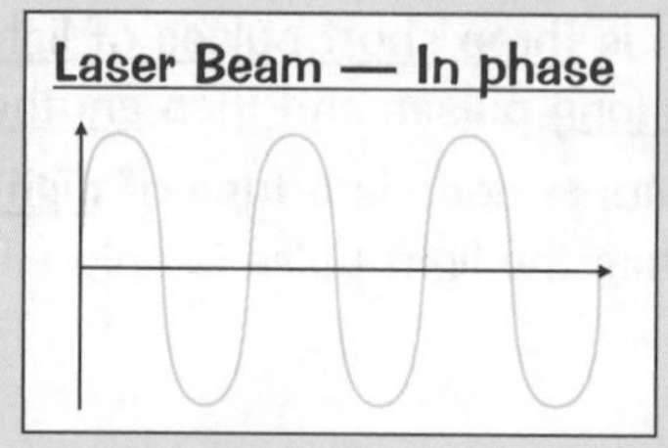

The combined wave has the same wavelength as the individual waves but an increased amplitude.

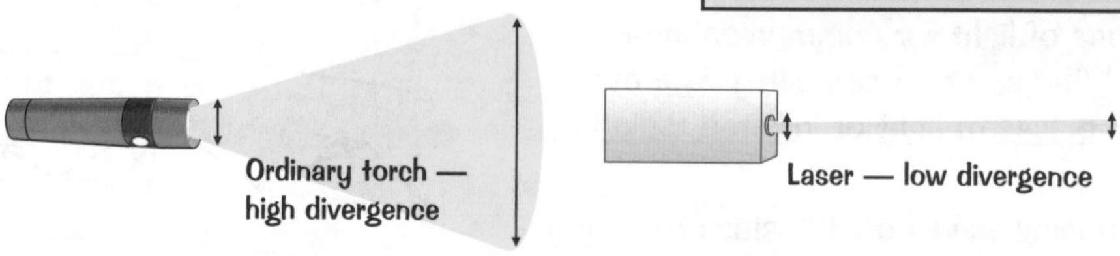

CD Players Use Lasers to Read Digital Information

1) The surface of a CD has a pattern of billions of shallow pits cut into it. The areas between the pits are called lands.
2) A laser shone onto the CD is reflected from the shiny bottom surface as it spins around in the player.
3) The beam is reflected from a land and a pit slightly differently — and this difference can be picked up by a light sensor. These differences in reflected signals can then be changed into an electrical signal.
4) The pits and lands themselves don't represent the digital ons and offs. It's actually a change in the reflected beam which represents on, while no change represents off.
5) An amplifier and a loudspeaker then convert the electrical signal into sound of the right pitch (frequency) and loudness.

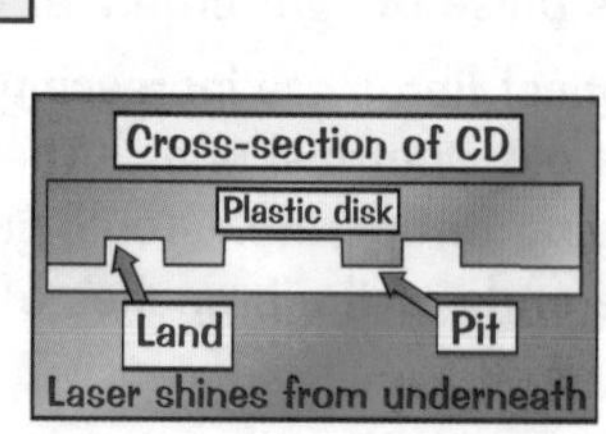

They seem like pits when you look from the top, anyway. But the laser shines from underneath, so it sees the pits as slightly raised areas.

Dynamite with a laser beam — guaranteed to blow your mind...

If you ever wondered where the name 'laser' came from, wonder no more — it stands for 'Light Amplification by Stimulated Emission of Radiation'. That won't be on the exam, but it may come up in a quiz sometime and your mates will (possibly) be impressed that you know it. The rest of the stuff IS on the exam, so go and learn it.

Infrared

Infrared radiation (or IR) may sound space-age but it's actually as common as beans on toast. You've probably used it several times today already without even knowing it.

Infrared Has Many Uses Around the Home...

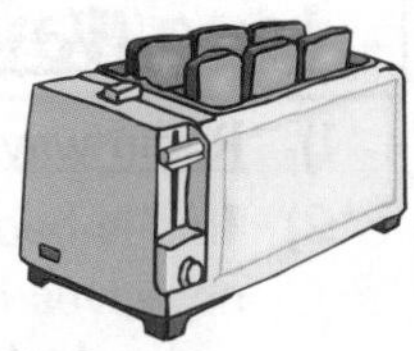

1) Infrared radiation can be used in cooking, e.g. in grills and toasters (see p. 13).
2) Remote controls transfer information to TVs and DVD players using IR.
3) It can be used to transmit information between mobile phones or computers — but only over short distances.
4) Infrared sensors are used in security systems, e.g. burglar alarms and security lights. These sensors detect heat from an intruder's body.
5) Infrared can also be used instead of visible light to carry information through optical fibres (see page 21).

IR Can be Used to Monitor Temperature

1) Infrared radiation is also known as heat radiation. It's given out by hot objects — and the hotter the object, the more IR radiation it gives out.
2) This means infrared can be used to monitor temperatures. For example, heat loss through a house's uninsulated roof can be detected using infrared sensors (see page 14).

3) Infrared is also detected by night-vision equipment. The equipment turns it into an electrical signal, which is displayed on a screen as a picture. The hotter an object is, the brighter it appears. Police and the military use this to spot baddies running away, like you've seen on TV.

IR Signals Can Control Electrical Equipment

1) Remote controls emit pulses of IR to control electrical devices such as TVs or DVD players. If it was visible, you'd see it flickering when you pressed a button on the control.
2) The pulses act as a digital ('on/off') code (see p. 28) — similar to how Morse Code works.
3) The device will detect and decode the pattern of pulses coming from the remote control and follow the coded instruction.
4) E.g. a CD player might be programmed to know that a certain sequence of pulses at a particular speed means 'play', so when it receives this signal it will play the CD. A different sequence will tell it to 'pause', etc.
5) IR signals are used in the same way to transfer information between mobile phones and computers over short distances (so they're another form of wireless communication).
6) The main drawback is that you need to be close to the device you're operating, because the IR beam from a small, low-powered remote control is fairly weak.
7) You also need to point the beam straight at the detector on the device, because the IR waves only travel in a straight line.

Some remote controls, such as the ones on electronic car keys, use radio waves rather than IR. The radio waves can bend (diffract, see p. 19) — that's why you can open the car without pointing it at it.

Don't lose control of your sensors — this page isn't remotely hard...

Compared with all that stuff on lasers, infrared seems relatively low-tech. It's still amazingly useful though, and because infrared technology is relatively cheap and cheerful we can afford to use it to make our lives a bit easier (and safer) around the home. Bad news for criminals. Remember — crime doesn't pay, revision does.

Wireless Communication — Radio Waves

Wireless communication uses all sorts of EM waves, but for the next few pages we're just focusing on radio and microwaves — and how they're used for TV, radio, mobile phones etc.

Long Wavelengths Travel Well Through Earth's Atmosphere

1) Radio waves and microwaves (see p. 26) are good at transferring information over long distances.
2) This is because they don't get absorbed by the Earth's atmosphere as much as waves in the middle of the EM spectrum (like heat, for example), or those at the high-frequency end of the spectrum (e.g. gamma rays or X-rays).

You couldn't use high-frequency waves anyway — they'd be far too dangerous.

Radio Waves are Used Mainly for Communications

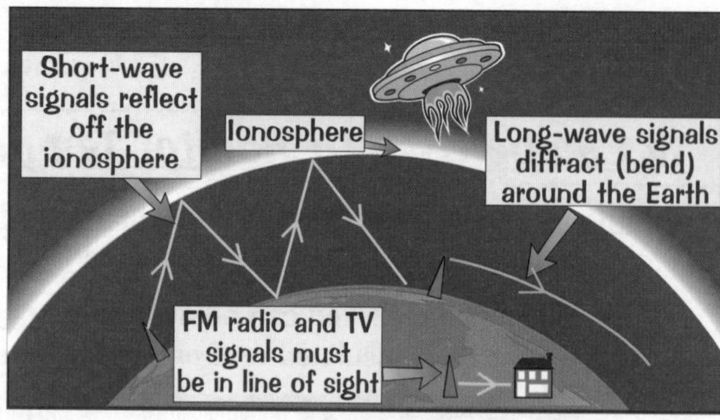

1) Radio waves are EM radiation with wavelengths longer than about 10 cm.
2) Different wavelengths of radio wave refract and diffract in different ways.
3) Long-wave radio (wavelengths of 1 – 10 km) can be transmitted from one place and received halfway round the world because they diffract (bend) around the curved surface of the Earth. This is explained in more detail below.
4) Radio waves used for TV and FM radio transmissions have very short wavelengths (10 cm – 10 m). To get reception, you must be in direct sight of the transmitter — the signal doesn't bend around hills or travel far through buildings.
5) Short-wave radio signals with wavelengths of about 10 m – 100 m can be received at long distances from the transmitter because of reflection in the ionosphere (see next page). Medium-wave signals (well, the shorter ones) can also reflect from the ionosphere, depending on atmospheric conditions and time of day.

Diffraction Makes a Difference to Signal Strength

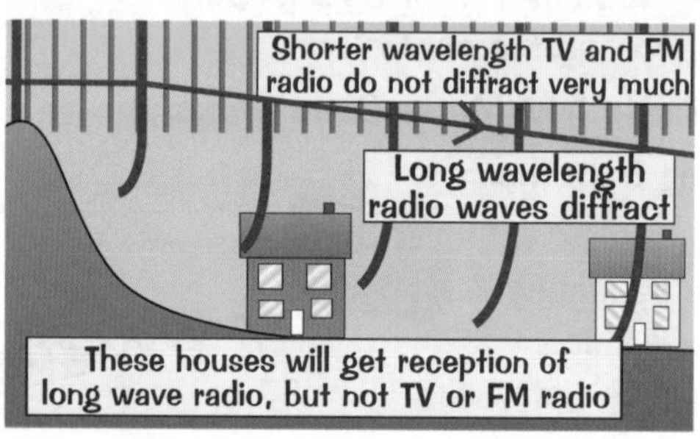

Shorter wavelength TV and FM radio do not diffract very much
Long wavelength radio waves diffract
These houses will get reception of long wave radio, but not TV or FM radio

1) Diffraction is when waves spread out at the edges when they pass through a gap or past an object (see p. 19).
2) The amount of diffraction depends on the wavelength of the wave, relative to the size of the gap or obstacle.
3) Longer wavelengths can encounter a lot of diffraction because they are large compared with the gap or obstacle.
4) This means that they are able to bend around corners and any obstacles — such as hills, tall buildings etc.
5) So longer wavelength radio waves can travel long distances between the transmitter and receiver without them having to be in the line of sight of each other. Shorter wavelength radio waves and microwaves (see p. 26) don't diffract very much, so the transmitters need to be located high up to avoid obstacles (and even then they can only cover short distances).
6) Some areas have trouble receiving shorter wavelength radio (and microwave) signals — e.g. if you live at the foot of a mountain you will probably have poor signal strength.
7) Diffraction can also occur at the edges of the dishes used to transmit signals. This results in signal loss — the wave is more spread out so the signal is weaker.

Concentrate — don't get diffracted...

So the key point on this page is that the longer the wavelength, the more it diffracts. This means that long waves bend round the Earth, while shorter waves need to be transmitted in the line of sight.

Wireless Communication — Radio Waves

It's not just diffraction that's affected by wavelength — refraction is too. And that's another property of waves which can either help or hinder communication signals.

Refraction Can Help Radio Waves Travel Further

When a wave comes up against something that has a different density, it changes speed.
If the wave hits the new substance at an angle, it changes direction. This is refraction (see p. 19).
When it happens high up in the atmosphere, it can help waves travel further for long distance communication.

1) UV radiation from the Sun creates layers of ionised atoms (atoms that have either gained or lost electrons) in the Earth's atmosphere. These electrically charged layers are called the ionosphere.
2) Radio waves travel faster through ionised parts of the atmosphere than non-ionised parts. This causes refraction.

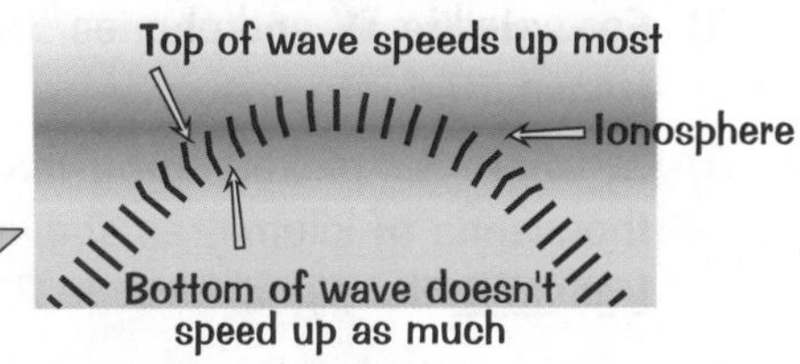
Top of wave speeds up most
Ionosphere
Bottom of wave doesn't speed up as much

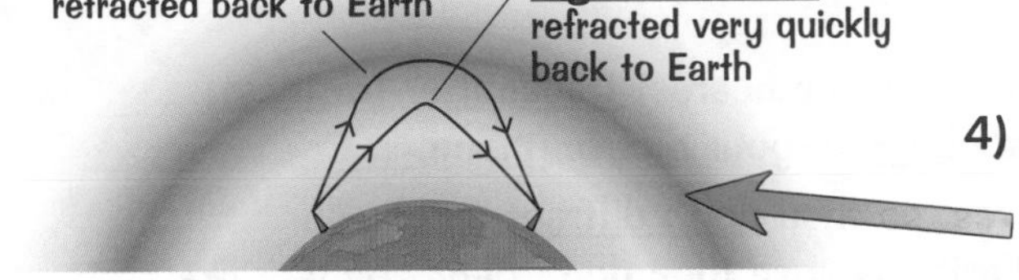
Waves with a higher frequency or transmitted at a higher angle of elevation are gradually refracted back to Earth
Waves with a lower frequency or transmitted at a lower angle of elevation are refracted very quickly back to Earth

3) Short-wave (with wavelengths of about 10 m – 100 m) and medium-wave (about 300 m) radio signals are refracted most in the ionosphere — they are effectively bounced back or reflected back to Earth. This means that short- and medium-wave radio signals can be received a long way from the transmitter.
4) The amount a wave is refracted in the ionosphere depends on its frequency and angle of elevation. High frequency / short wavelength signals such as short-wave radio don't refract as much as medium-wave.
5) Radio waves 'bounce' off the ionosphere in a similar way to how light waves totally internally reflect inside optical fibres (p. 21).
6) Refraction's not always good though. It can disrupt a signal by bending it away from the receiver dish.

Digital Radio Helps Reduce Interference

1) There's a limited number of radio wave frequencies that can be used to transmit a good analogue signal — so radio stations often broadcast using waves of very similar frequencies.
2) These analogue signals often suffer from interference because of this — similar waves covering a similar area can combine, which causes 'noise'. This is why radio stations near to each other use different frequencies — so they don't interfere as much.

Interference, noise and multiplexing are all covered on page 28.

3) Digital Audio Broadcasting (DAB) works in a different way to traditional radio broadcasts — it's digital to start with.
4) With DAB, many different signals are compressed, then transmitted as a single wave — this is known as multiplexing.
5) They are transmitted across a relatively small frequency bandwidth and separated out by the receivers at the other end. You need a DAB radio set to pick up and decode the signals.
6) DAB suffers less interference than traditional radio broadcasts, and since the signals from many stations can be broadcast at the same frequency (multiplexing), it means an increase in the potential number of radio stations available.
7) At the moment there are a limited number of DAB transmitters in the UK (and the world) so some areas can't receive digital radio signals at all.
8) Even if you can receive DAB, the sound quality is often not as good as a traditional FM radio broadcast, due to the compression of the signal.

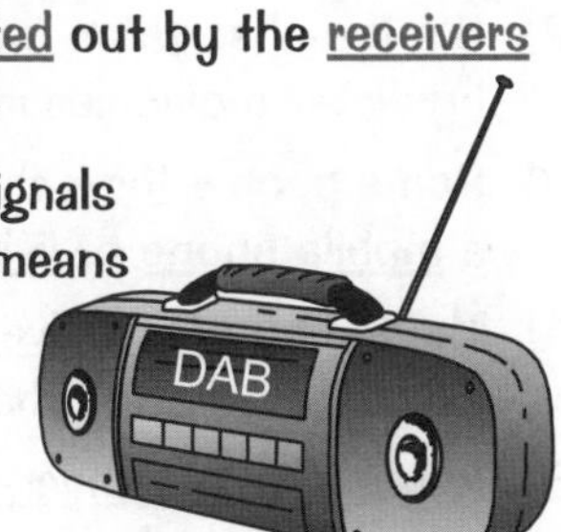
DAB

Size matters — and my wave's longer than yours...

The various types of EM radiation have different uses because they have different wavelengths and frequencies, which gives them different properties. Make sure you understand why. And make sure you understand why DAB radio is better than traditional radio in some ways, but not in other ways. Hard cheese, isn't it.

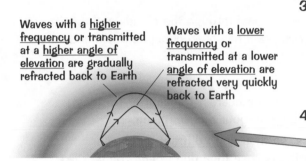

Wireless Communication — Microwaves

Microwave communication involves microwaves — but of different wavelengths from those used in ovens.

Microwaves are Used for Satellite Communication...

1) Communication to and from satellites (including satellite TV signals and satellite phones) uses microwaves. But you need to use wavelengths which can pass easily through the Earth's watery atmosphere without too much absorption.
2) For satellite TV and phones, the signal from a transmitter is transmitted into space...
3) ... where it's picked up by the satellite's receiver dish orbiting thousands of kilometres above the Earth. The satellite transmits the signal back to Earth in a different direction...

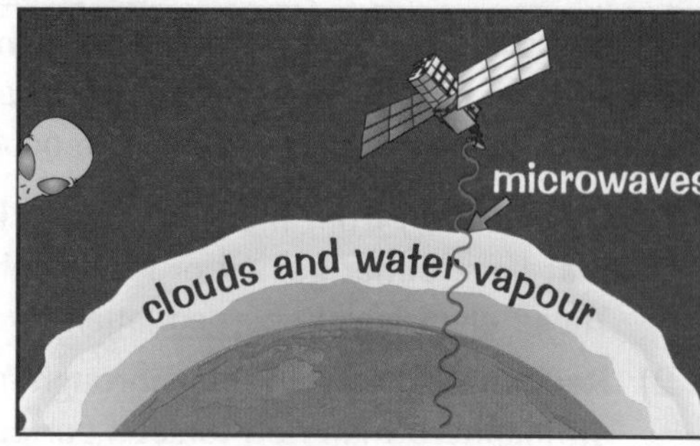

4) ... where it's received by a satellite dish on the ground.
5) Microwaves are also used by remote-sensing satellites — to 'see' through the clouds and monitor oil spills, track the movement of icebergs, see how much rainforest has been chopped down and so on.

...as well as Mobile Phones

1) Mobile phone calls travel as microwaves from your phone to the nearest transmitter (or mast). The transmitters pass signals between each other, then back to your mobile phone.
2) Microwaves have a shorter wavelength than radio waves, so they don't diffract much. This means they're affected by the curvature of the Earth because they don't bend round it like long-wave radio waves. It also means they're blocked more by large obstacles like hills because they can't bend round them.
3) This means that microwave transmitters need to be positioned in line of sight — they're usually high up on hilltops so they can 'see each other', and they're positioned fairly close together. If there's a hill or a man-made obstacle between your phone and the transmitter, you'll probably get a poor signal, or no signal at all.
4) The microwave frequencies used are partially absorbed by water, even though they can pass through the atmosphere. So in adverse weather (or if there's a lake nearby) there can be some signal loss through absorption or scattering. This is why you can lose satellite TV signal in a storm.
5) Sometimes there's interference between signals (see p. 28), which can also affect signal strength.

Mobile Masts May be Dangerous — but there's Conflicting Evidence

1) Microwaves used for communications need to pass through the Earth's watery atmosphere, but the microwaves used in microwave ovens have a different wavelength — they're actually absorbed by the water molecules in the food (see page 13).
2) It's the absorption that's harmful — if microwaves are absorbed by water molecules in living tissue, cells may be burned or killed.

3) Some people think that the microwaves emitted into your body from using a mobile phone or living near a mobile phone mast could damage your health.
4) There's no conclusive proof either way yet though. Lots of studies have been published, which has allowed the results to be checked, but so far they have given conflicting evidence.
5) Any potential dangers would be increased by prolonged exposure though — e.g. living close to a mast or using your phone all the time.
6) This means we have to carefully balance the potential risks and the benefits of this technology until we know more — in terms of where we locate masts and how much we choose to use our mobile phones.

Microwaves — used for TV AND for TV dinners...

Scientists publish the details of studies in scientific journals — this lets other scientists read and repeat the work to see if they agree. It's a good way to get results and conclusions repeated and checked.

EM Receivers

The air is chock-a-block full of EM waves, bounding around all over the shop. But most of them we can neither see nor hear. That's why we need receivers — to collect the information.

The Size of Receiver Depends on the Size of Wave

1) We use different receivers (sensors) to pick up the different types of EM waves used for communication — e.g. telescopes, satellite dishes, microscopes etc.
2) The minimum size of receiver needed is linked to the size of the wavelength of the wave — the longer the wavelength, the larger the receiver should be.
3) So radio waves need the biggest receivers, then microwaves, then infrared, then light waves...

4) This is because of diffraction (see p. 19) — when a wave enters a receiver it passes through a gap. If the wave is diffracted, it spreads out and you lose detail.
5) As you've already seen, the amount of diffraction is affected by the size of the gap compared to the wavelength — gaps about the same size as the wavelength cause lots of diffraction, but as the gap size increases there is less diffraction.
6) So the bigger the receiver compared with the wavelength of wave being received, the less diffraction it causes, so the clearer the information received is.

Telescopes Detect Different Types of EM Wave

1) Telescopes help you to see distant objects clearer — e.g. astronomers look for very distant stars and galaxies using them.
2) Different telescopes are used to collect different EM waves — e.g. optical telescopes receive visible light, radio telescopes collect radio waves etc.
3) Bigger telescopes give us better resolution (i.e. lots of detail) because they cause less diffraction, so the information is clearer (see above).
4) Telescopes with small gaps compared to the wavelength they're looking for have limited resolving power — they are said to be diffraction-limited.
5) Light waves have a relatively small wavelength compared to radio waves.
6) Since radio waves can be more than 10 000 000 000 times bigger than light waves, this would mean having a ridiculously big receiver (about the size of the UK for a decent one). So we just make do with a lower resolution (although the dishes are still pretty huge).
7) To get round this, radio telescopes are often linked together and their signals combined to get more detailed information — acting like a single giant receiver.
8) A bigger receiver can also collect more EM waves, giving a more intense image — so a bigger telescope can observe fainter objects.

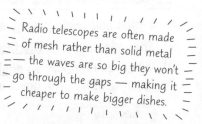

Radio telescopes are often made of mesh rather than solid metal — the waves are so big they won't go through the gaps — making it cheaper to make bigger dishes.

Optical Microscopes are Diffraction Limited

1) Optical microscopes have to be small, because you usually use them to look at small samples of tiny things in the lab — you want to collect light coming from a very small area only.
2) Their small size makes it hard to get a good resolution — the gap needs to be really small, so you still get some diffraction even though light has a small wavelength.

Mind the gap...

There's a lot more to telescopes than meets the eye (ho ho). Luckily, you don't have to know all the ins and outs of how they work for the exam, as long as you understand how diffraction limits them. Remember that telescopes can pick up invisible waves too, like microwaves and radio waves — but they have to be much much bigger. Microscopes are important too — make sure you know why their resolution is limited by size.

Analogue and Digital Signals

Sound and images can be sent as analogue signals, but digital technology is gradually taking over.

Information is Converted into Signals

1) To communicate any kind of information (e.g. sounds, pictures), it needs to be converted into electrical signals before it's transmitted.
2) These signals can then be sent long distances down telephone wires or carried on EM waves.
3) The signals can either be analogue or digital.

Analogue Signals Vary but Digital's Just On or Off

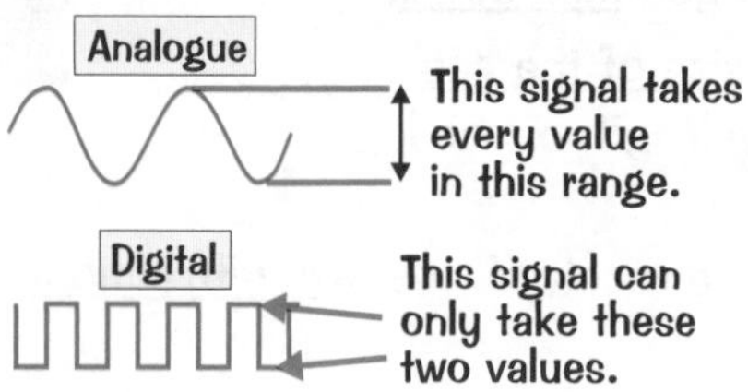

Analogue
This signal takes every value in this range.
Digital
This signal can only take these two values.

1) An analogue signal can take any value within a certain range. (Remember: analogue — any.) The amplitude and frequency of an analogue wave vary continuously.
2) A digital signal can only take two values. These values tend to be called on/off, or 1/0. For example, you can send data along optical fibres as short pulses of light.

Digital Signals Have Advantages Over Analogue

1) Digital and analogue signals weaken as they travel, so they might need to be amplified along their route.
2) They also pick up interference or noise from electrical disturbances or other signals (see box below).
3) When you amplify an analogue signal, the noise is amplified too — so every time it's amplified, the signal loses quality. The noise is easier to remove or ignore with digital, so the signal remains high quality.

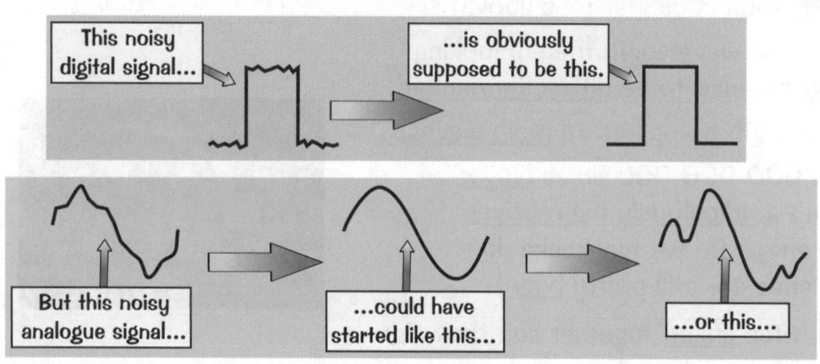

This noisy digital signal...
...is obviously supposed to be this.
But this noisy analogue signal...
...could have started like this...
...or this...

Interference

When two or more waves of a similar frequency meet, they can create one combined signal with a new amplitude.

This is called interference. You get it when two radio stations transmit on similar frequencies.

4) Another advantage of digital technology is that you can transmit several signals at the same time using just one cable or EM wave — this is called multiplexing.
5) Multiplexing happens in phone wires. When you're on the phone, your voice is converted into a digital signal and transmitted regularly at very small time intervals. In between your voice signals being transmitted, thousands of other people's voice signals can be slotted in or 'multiplexed'. The samples are separated out again at the other end so the person you called can hear you — and only you. This happens so quickly that you don't notice it.
6) The advantages of digital signals over analogue have played a big part in the 'switching over' from analogue to digital TV and radio broadcasts.

I've got loads of digital stuff — watch, radio, fingers...

Eeehh, I don't know about all this digital nonsense — ah reckon there were nowt wrong wi' carrier pigeons meself. Seriously though, digital signals are great — unless you live somewhere with poor reception of digital broadcasts, in which case you get no benefit at all. This is because if you don't get spot-on reception of digital signals in your area, you won't get a grainy signal (like with analogue TV and radio signals) — you'll get nothing at all.

Humans and the Environment

You've seen how useful EM waves can be for communication — but they can be pretty bad for us...

Ultraviolet Radiation Causes Skin Cancer

1) If you spend a lot of time in the sun, you can expect to get a tan and maybe sunburn.
2) But the more time you spend in the sun, the more chance you also have of getting skin cancer. This is because the Sun's rays include ultraviolet radiation (UV) which damages the DNA in your cells.
3) UV radiation can also cause you eye problems, such as cataracts, as well as premature skin aging (eek!).
4) Darker skin gives some protection against UV rays — it absorbs more UV radiation. This prevents some of the damaging radiation from reaching the more vulnerable tissues deeper in the body.
5) Everyone should protect themselves from the Sun, but if you're pale skinned, you need to take extra care, and use a sunscreen with a higher Sun Protection Factor (SPF).
6) An SPF of 15 means you can spend 15 times as long as you otherwise could in the sun without burning (as long as you keep reapplying the sunscreen).

EXAMPLE: Ruvani normally burns after 40 minutes in the sun. Before going to the beach, she applies sunscreen with SPF 8. For how long can she sunbathe before she will start to burn?

ANSWER: Time = 40 mins × 8 = 320 minutes = 5 hours and 20 minutes.

7) We're kept informed of the risks of exposure to UV — research into its damaging effects is made public through the media and advertising campaigns, and the government tells people how to keep safe to improve public health.
8) It's not just exposure to the Sun that's a problem — we are now being warned of the risks of prolonged use of sunbeds too. Tanning salons have time limits to make sure people are not over-exposed.

The Ozone Layer Protects Us from UV Radiation

1) Ozone is a molecule made of three oxygen atoms, O_3. There's a layer of ozone high up in the Earth's atmosphere.
2) The ozone layer absorbs some of the UV rays from the Sun — so it reduces the amount of UV radiation reaching the Earth's surface.
3) Recently, the ozone layer has got thinner because of pollution from CFCs — these are gases which react with ozone molecules and break them up. This depletion of the ozone layer allows more UV rays to reach us at the surface of the Earth (which, as you know, can be a danger to our health).

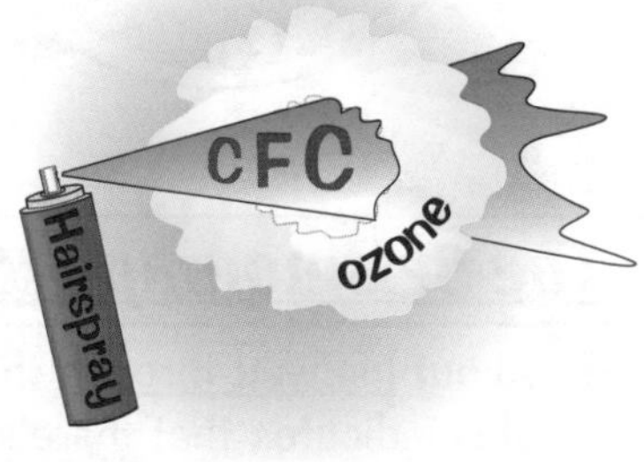

There's a Hole in the Ozone Layer over Antarctica

1) In winter, special weather effects cause the concentration of ozone over Antarctica to drop dramatically. It increases again in spring, but the winter concentration has been dropping. The low concentration looks like a 'hole' on satellite images.
2) Scientists now monitor the ozone concentration very closely to get a better understanding of why it's decreasing, and how to prevent further depletion.
3) Many different studies have been carried out internationally, using different equipment, to get accurate results — this helps scientists to be confident that their hypotheses and predictions are correct.
4) Studies led scientists to confirm that CFCs were causing the depletion of the ozone layer, so the international community banned them. We used to use CFCs all the time — e.g. in hairsprays and in the coolant for fridges — but now international bans and restrictions on CFC use have been put in place because of their environmental impact.

In 1987 lots of countries signed the Montreal Protocol, agreeing to reduce their use of CFCs.

Use protection — wear a hat...

Okay... time for a bit of risk balancing. Too much time in the sun can help cause skin cancer, but a bit of sun can be a good thing (it helps with your body's production of vitamin D). So don't avoid it altogether.

Seismic Waves

Waves don't just fly through the air — seismic waves travel inside the Earth. Scientists use seismic waves to investigate the Earth's inner structure (well it's a bit tricky to dig all the way down to have a look...).

Earthquakes Cause Different Types of Seismic Waves

1) When there's an earthquake somewhere, it produces shock waves which travel out through the Earth. We record these seismic waves all over the surface of the planet using seismographs.
2) Seismologists measure the time it takes for the shock waves to reach each seismograph.
3) They also note which parts of the Earth don't receive the shock waves at all.
4) There are two different types of seismic waves that travel through the Earth — P-waves and S-waves.

P-Waves are Longitudinal

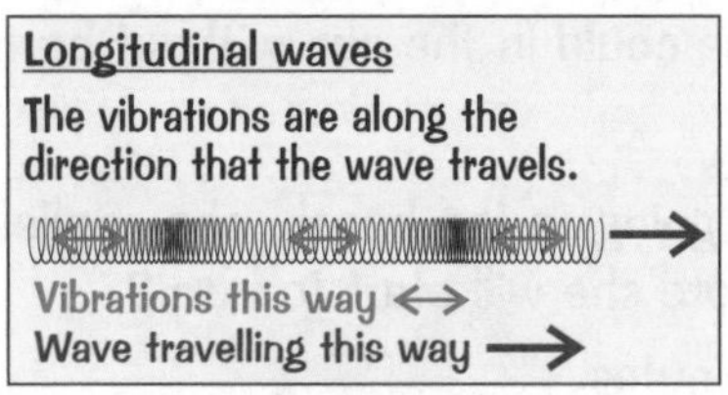

Longitudinal waves
The vibrations are along the direction that the wave travels.
Vibrations this way
Wave travelling this way

There's also a third type of wave — surface waves. But you don't need to know about those.

S-Waves are TranSverSe

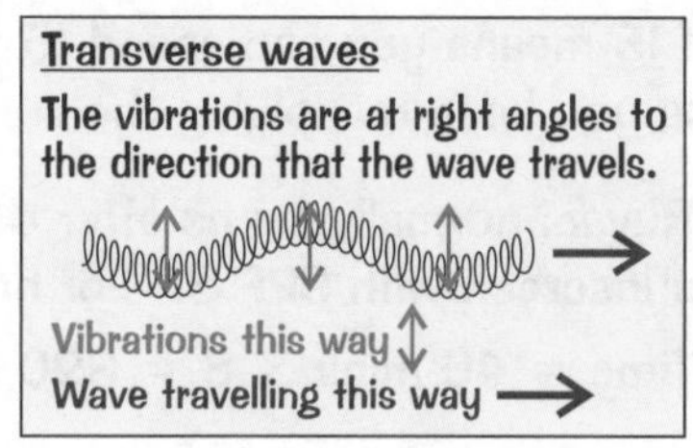

Transverse waves
The vibrations are at right angles to the direction that the wave travels.
Vibrations this way
Wave travelling this way

P-waves travel through solids and liquids. They travel faster than S-waves.

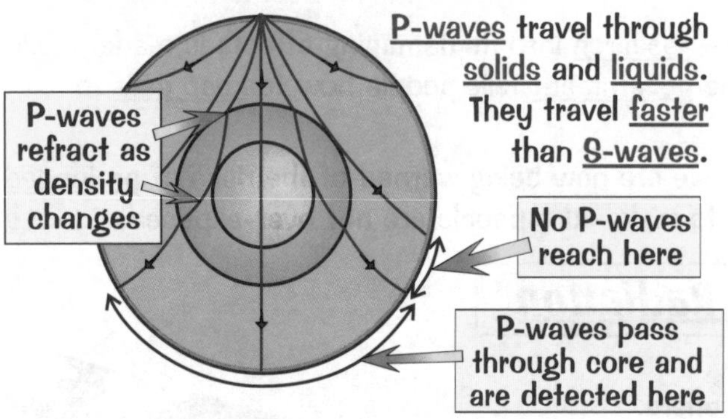

S-waves only travel through Solids. They are Slower than P-waves.

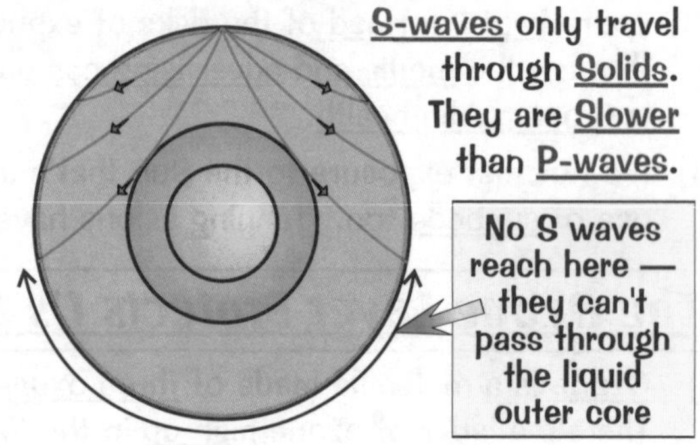

The Seismograph Results Tell Us What's Down There

1) About halfway through the Earth, P-waves change direction abruptly. This indicates that there's a sudden change in properties — as you go from the mantle to the core.
2) The fact that S-waves are not detected in the core's shadow tells us that the outer core is liquid — S-waves only pass through Solids.
3) P-waves seem to travel slightly faster through the middle of the core, which strongly suggests that there's a solid inner core.
4) Note that S-waves do travel through the mantle, which shows that it's solid. It only melts to form magma in small 'hot spots'.

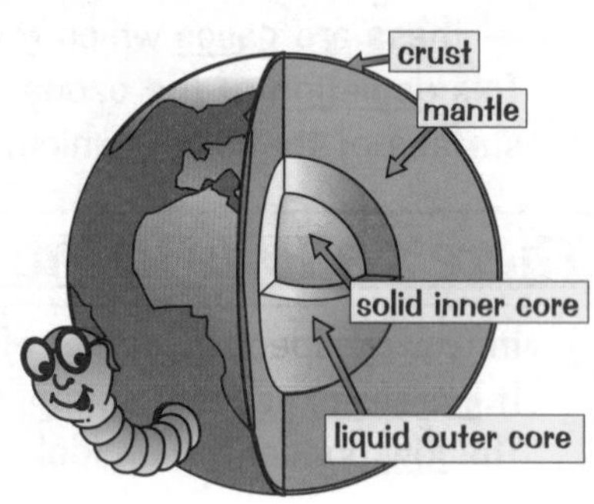

The Waves Curve with Increasing Depth

1) The waves change speed as the properties of the mantle and core change.
2) This change in speed causes the waves to change direction — which is refraction of course (see p. 19).
3) Most of the time the waves change speed gradually, resulting in a curved path.
4) But when the properties change suddenly, the wave speed changes abruptly, and the path has a kink.

Seismic waves — they reveal the terrible trembling truth...

Yet another way in which understanding about waves helps us know more about the world around us — or in this case, the world underneath us. Learning all this stuff about waves will definitely help you in your exam too, so that's a very big reason indeed to knuckle down and learn everything in this module.

Revision Summary for Module P1

Now a reward for ploughing through loads of pages of pretty intense science — a page of lovely questions. Okay, I know it seems a little daunting, but it's absolutely vital to check that you've learnt all the right stuff.

1) What is specific heat capacity?
2)* It takes 5000 J to heat 50 g of a substance by 40 °C. Calculate its specific heat capacity.
3) Explain why heating a pan of boiling water doesn't increase its temperature.
4)* How much energy is needed to boil dry a pan of 500 g of water at 100 °C? (Specific latent heat of water for boiling = 2 260 000 J/kg.)
5) Briefly describe how heat is transferred through a) conduction, b) convection, and c) radiation.
6) Describe how heat radiation is used to cook food a) under a grill, and b) in a microwave oven.
7) Describe three ways of saving energy in the home and explain how each one works.
8)* How much energy is wasted if a hairdrier that's 20% efficient has a total energy input of 200 000 J?
9) Sketch a Sankey diagram to show the energy transformations in the hairdrier mentioned above.
10) Sketch a typical transverse wave and explain all its main features.
11) Sketch and label a diagram explaining reflection in a plane mirror.
12) Briefly describe what happens to a wave when it is a) diffracted, and b) refracted.
13) List the seven types of electromagnetic wave in order of wavelength (smallest to largest).
14) Explain why Morse code is a digital signal.
15) Describe how light signals can travel through optical fibres.
16) Explain the properties of laser beams which make them a) monochromatic, and b) coherent.
17) Describe how lasers are used in CD players.
18) Briefly explain how infrared radiation is used to control electrical equipment.
19) Explain why long-wave radio waves can bend around obstacles.
20) Briefly describe what happens to radio waves in the ionosphere.
21) Give two advantages and two disadvantages of using DAB.
22) Describe how satellites are used for communication.
23) Why are microwave transmitters located in high places and close together?
24) Explain why scientists are concerned about the dangers of: a) mobile phone use, and b) the thinning of the ozone layer.
25) Explain how diffraction affects the size of receiver needed to pick up different wave signals.
26) Explain the difference between analogue and digital signals.
27) Why are CFCs so bad?
28) Name and describe two types of wave produced by an earthquake.
29) Name your top five cool bits of physics in this module.

* Answers on p. 123.

Using the Sun's Energy

The Sun is very hot and very bright — which means it's kicking out a lot of energy.

The Sun is the Ultimate Source of Loads of Our Energy

1) Every second for the last few billion years or so, the Sun has been giving out loads of energy — mostly in the form of heat and light.
2) Some of that energy is stored here on Earth as fossil fuels (coal, oil and natural gas). And when we use wind power, we're using energy that can be traced back to the Sun (the Sun heats the air, the hot air rises, cold air whooshes in to take its place (wind), and so on).
3) But we can also use the Sun's energy in a more direct way — with photocells and solar heating.

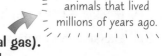

Fossil fuels are the remains of plants and animals that lived millions of years ago.

You Can Capture the Sun's Energy Using Photocells

1) Photocells (solar cells) generate electricity directly from sunlight.
2) They generate direct current (DC) — the same as a battery. Direct current just means the current flows the same way round the circuit all the time — not like mains electricity in your home (AC), which keeps switching direction (see page 35).

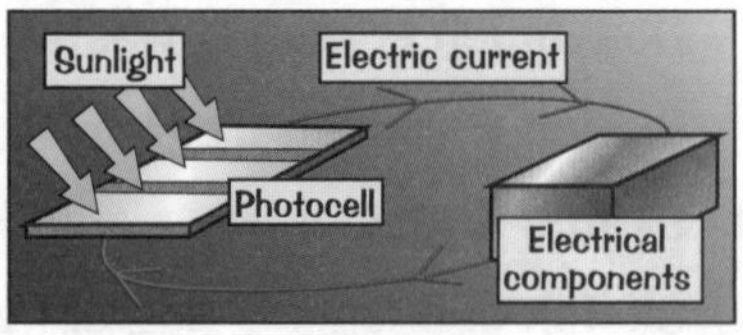

3) Photocells are usually made of silicon — a semiconductor. When sunlight falls on the cell:
   i) the silicon atoms absorb some of the energy, knocking loose some electrons,
   ii) these electrons then flow round a circuit — which is electricity.
4) The current and power output of a photocell depends on:
   - its surface area (the bigger the cell, the more electricity it produces),
   - the intensity of the light (brighter light = more electricity),
   - the distance from the light source (the closer the cell, the more intense the light hitting it will be).

Photocells have lots of advantages:

There are no moving parts — so they're sturdy, low maintenance and last a long time.
You don't need power cables or fuel (your digital calculator doesn't need to be plugged in/fuelled up).
Solar power won't run out (it's a renewable energy resource), and it doesn't pollute the environment.

But there's one major disadvantage — no sunlight, no power.
So they're rubbish at night, and not so good when the weather's bad.

Curved Mirrors can Concentrate Energy from the Sun

1) Curved mirrors focus the Sun's light and heat.
2) A single curved mirror can be used as a solar oven.
3) Large curved mirrors (or a combination of lots of smaller mirrors) can be used to generate steam to produce electricity.

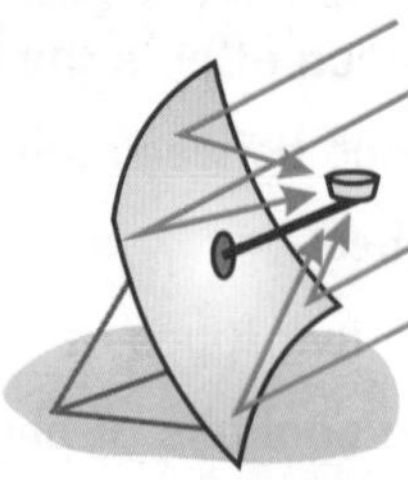

All the radiation that lands on the curved mirror is focused right on your pan.

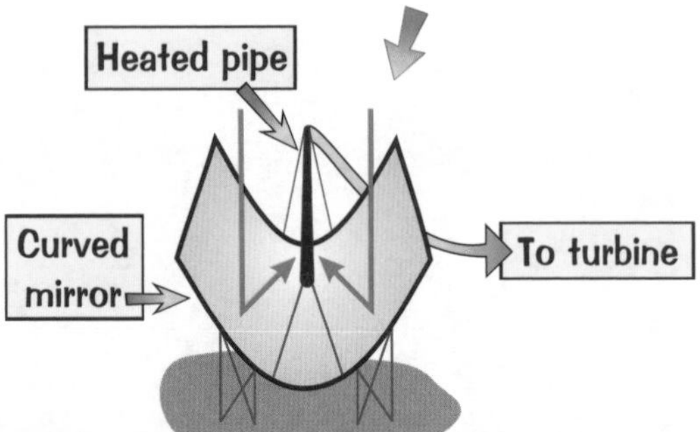

4) All devices that collect energy from the Sun (mirrors, solar cells and solar panels) are most efficient if they track the Sun's movement across the sky.
5) If collectors are pointed directly at the Sun then they can capture the maximum amount of light and heat.

Don't let the Sun go down on me — I hate cold dinners...

Although initial costs can be high with solar power, once you're up and running the energy is free and running costs are almost nil. It's even better if you live somewhere that's sunny most of the time. Not Britain then.

Solar and Wind Power

The Sun's going to be around for a long, long time and as long as there's the Sun there'll also be wind. Time to figure out how to make the most of all that free energy...

Passive Solar Heating — No Complex Mechanical Stuff

1) Passive solar heating is when energy from the Sun is used to heat something directly.
2) You can reduce the energy needed to heat a building if you build it sensibly and think about passive solar heating — e.g. it can make a big difference which way the windows face.
3) Glass lets in heat and light from the Sun, which is absorbed by things in a room, heating them up.
4) The light from the Sun has a short wavelength, so it can pass through the glass into a room.
5) But the heated things in a room emit infrared radiation of a longer wavelength, which can't escape through the glass — it's reflected back instead, just like in a greenhouse.
6) So this 'greenhouse effect' works to heat, and keep heat, inside a building.
7) Solar water heaters use passive solar heating too — the glass lets heat and light from the Sun in which is then absorbed by the black pipes and heats up the water (which can be used for washing or pumped to radiators to heat the building).

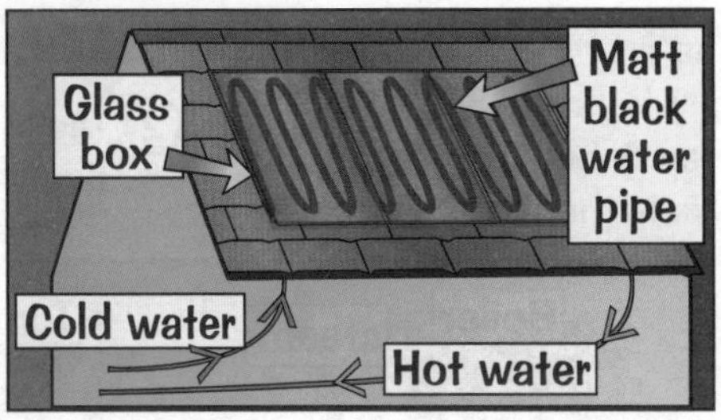

Wind Farms — Lots of Little Wind Turbines

The Sun is the reason we have wind — it's also the reason we have wind farms.

1) Wind power involves putting lots of wind turbines up in exposed places — like on moors, the coast or out at sea.
2) Energy from the Sun heats the atmosphere which causes convection currents (see p. 12), which produce wind.
3) Wind turbines convert the kinetic energy of moving air into electricity. The wind turns the blades, which turn a generator.

Wind is a Renewable Resource

Wind turbines, like any energy source, have advantages and disadvantages which you need to learn:

ADVANTAGES

1) Wind turbines are quite cheap to run — they're very tough and reliable, and the wind is free.
2) Even better, wind power doesn't produce any polluting waste.
3) Wind power is also renewable — the wind's never going to run out.

DISADVANTAGES

1) You need about 1500 wind turbines to replace one coal-fired power station.
2) Some people think that wind farms spoil the view (visual pollution) and the spinning blades cause noise pollution.
3) Another problem is that sometimes the wind isn't fast enough to generate any power.
4) It's also impossible to increase supply when there's extra demand (e.g. when Coronation Street starts).
5) It can be difficult to find a suitable place to build wind turbines — they need to be spaced out and built in places that are windy enough.
6) And although the wind is free, it's expensive to set up a wind farm, especially out at sea.

I love the feeling of wind in my hair...

Perhaps I should build a miniature wind farm into a hat, then I wouldn't need batteries to listen to music anymore. I'm sure there's a market for PowerHats™. I'll be rich, I tell you, rich! Anyway, before I go off and make my millions you need to make sure you know all about the advantages and disadvantages of wind power.

Producing and Distributing Electricity

In the UK, most electricity is generated in power stations and then distributed via the National Grid.

The National Grid Connects Power Stations to Consumers

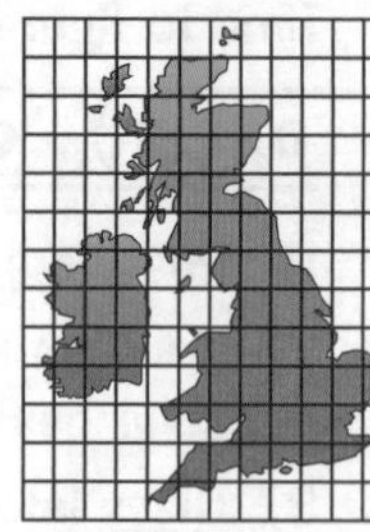

The National Grid.

1) The National Grid is the network of pylons and cables which covers the whole country.
2) It takes electricity from power stations to just where it's needed in homes and industry.
3) It enables power to be generated anywhere on the grid, and then supplied anywhere else on the grid. (See also page 36.)

All Power Stations are Pretty Much the Same

1) The aim of a power station is to convert one kind of energy (e.g. the energy stored in fossil fuels, or nuclear energy contained in the centre of atoms) into electricity. Usually this is done in three stages...

① The first stage is to use the fuel to produce heat which then generates steam — this is the job of the boiler.

② The moving steam drives the blades of a turbine...

③ ...and this rotating movement from the turbine is converted to electricity by the generator (using electromagnetic induction — see the next page).

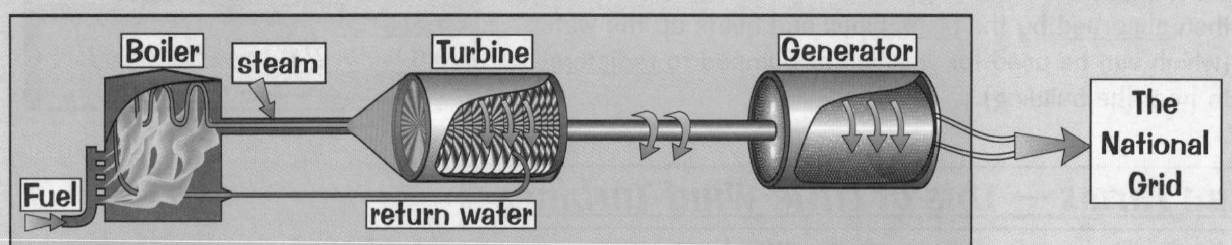

2) Most power stations are terribly inefficient — usually more than half the energy produced is wasted as heat and noise (though the efficiency of the power station depends a lot on the power source).

Different Power Sources Have Advantages and Disadvantages

You need to learn the advantages and disadvantages of different types of power source:

FOSSIL FUELS Fossil fuels are burnt to release their heat energy. At the moment, these fuels are readily available, and they're a concentrated source of energy (a little bit of coal gives a lot of heat). But burning fossil fuels causes acid rain and produces carbon dioxide (a greenhouse gas — see p. 38). Also, we buy most of our fossil fuels from other countries — which means we don't have control of the price or supply. (Plus they're running out, of course.)

BIOMASS Biomass is stuff from plants (like wood and straw) or animals (their manure) that can be burnt directly, or fermented to produce methane that's also burnt. Biomass is renewable — we can quickly make more by growing more plants and rearing more animals. Burning methane does produce carbon dioxide, but this is CO_2 that the plants took out of the atmosphere when they were growing — the process is 'carbon neutral' overall. Recently, we've started to use more biomass in the UK. You do need a lot of biomass to replace one lump of coal, and it takes a lot of room to grow it. But we don't need to import straw and poo from other countries.

NUCLEAR POWER Nuclear power stations use the heat released by uranium (or plutonium) atoms as they split during a nuclear reaction. There's more on the pros and cons of nuclear power on page 42.

PHOTO CELLS Photocells absorb energy from the Sun and convert it into electricity. There's more about the positives and negatives of photocells on page 32.

WIND POWER Wind turbines convert energy from the movement of the wind into electricity. The pros and cons of wind power are on page 33.

You could be asked to compare things like availability and environmental issues.

Power stations — nothing to get steamed up about...

Steam engines were invented as long ago as the 17th century, and yet we're still using the idea to produce most of our electricity today, over 300 years later. I doubt any of my ideas will last as long as that...

The Dynamo Effect

Generators use a pretty cool piece of physics to make electricity from the movement of a turbine. It's called electromagnetic (EM) induction — which basically means making electricity using a magnet.

ELECTROMAGNETIC INDUCTION: The creation of a VOLTAGE (and maybe current) in a wire which is experiencing a CHANGE IN MAGNETIC FIELD.

The Dynamo Effect — Move the Wire or the Magnet

1) Using electromagnetic induction to transform kinetic energy (energy of moving things) into electrical energy is called the dynamo effect. (In a power station, this kinetic energy is provided by the turbine.)
2) There are two different situations where you get EM induction:
   a) An electrical conductor (a coil of wire is often used) moves through a magnetic field.
   b) The magnetic field through an electrical conductor changes (gets bigger or smaller or reverses).

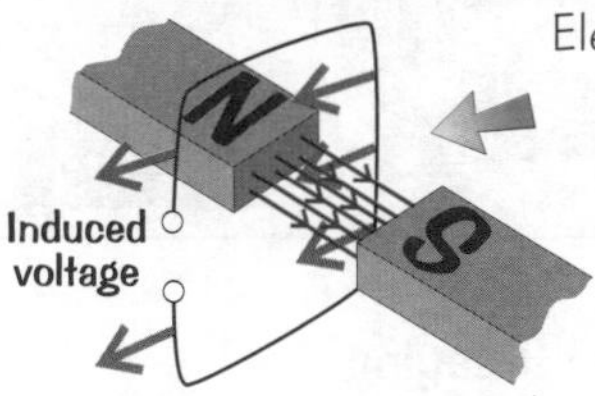

Electrical conductor moving in a magnetic field.

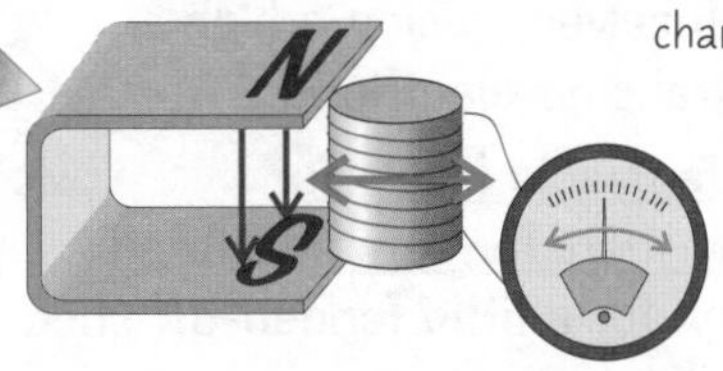

Magnetic field through a conductor changing (as the magnet moves).

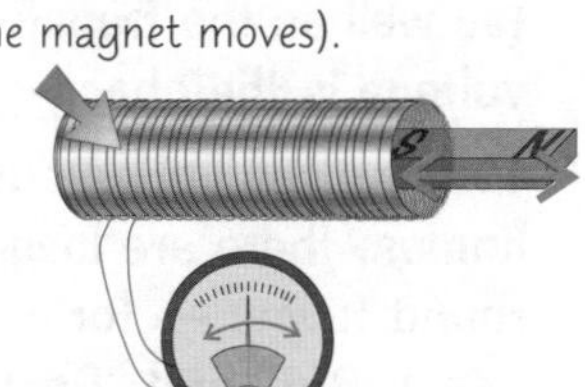

3) If the direction of movement is reversed, then the voltage/current will be reversed too.

To get a bigger voltage and current, you can increase...
1. The STRENGTH of the MAGNET
2. The number of TURNS on the COIL
3. The SPEED of movement

Generators Move a Coil in a Magnetic Field

Generators can work by rotating a magnet in a coil instead — the same principles still apply.

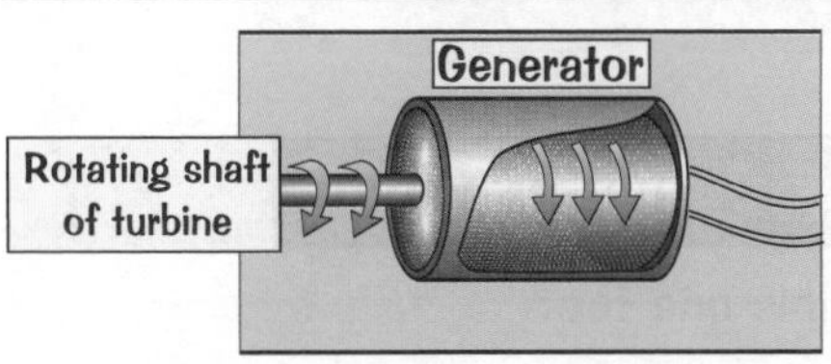

1) Generators rotate a coil in a magnetic field.
2) Every half a turn, the current in the coil swaps direction. (Think about one part of the coil... sometimes it's heading for the magnet's north pole, sometimes for the south — it changes every half a turn. This is what makes the current change direction.)
3) This means that generators produce an alternating (AC) current. If you looked at the current (or voltage) on a display, you'd see something like this...
   Turning the coil faster produces not only more peaks, but a higher voltage and current too.

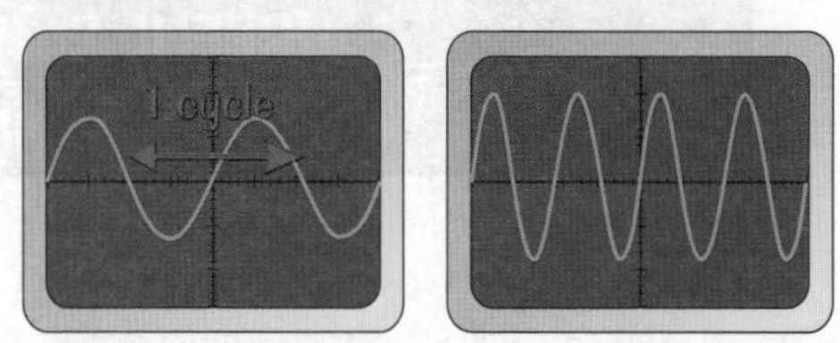

4) The frequency of AC electrical supplies is the number of cycles per second, and is measured in hertz (Hz). In the UK, electricity is supplied at 50 Hz (which means the coil in the generator at the power station is rotating 50 times every second).
5) Remember, this is completely different from the DC electricity supplied by batteries and photocells. If you plotted that on a graph, you'd see something more like this...

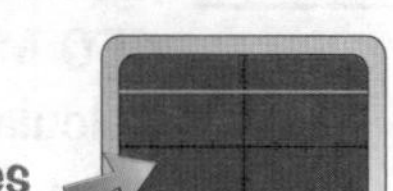

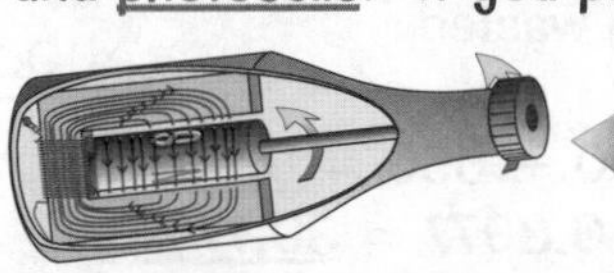

6) Dynamos on bikes work slightly differently — they usually rotate the magnet near the coil. But the principle is exactly the same — they're still using EM induction.

A conductor moving in a field — must be an open-air concert...

EM induction sounds pretty hard, but it boils down to this — if a magnetic field changes (moves, grows, shrinks... whatever) somewhere near a conductor, you get electricity. It's a weird old thing, but important — this is how all our mains electricity is generated. Not with hamsters then — I was wrong about that.

Supplying Electricity Efficiently

Sending electricity round the country is best done at high voltage.
This is why you probably weren't encouraged to climb electricity pylons as a child.

Electricity is Transformed to High Voltage Before Distribution

1) To transmit a lot of electrical power, you either need a high voltage or a high current. But... a higher current means your cables get hot, which is inefficient (all that heat just goes to waste).

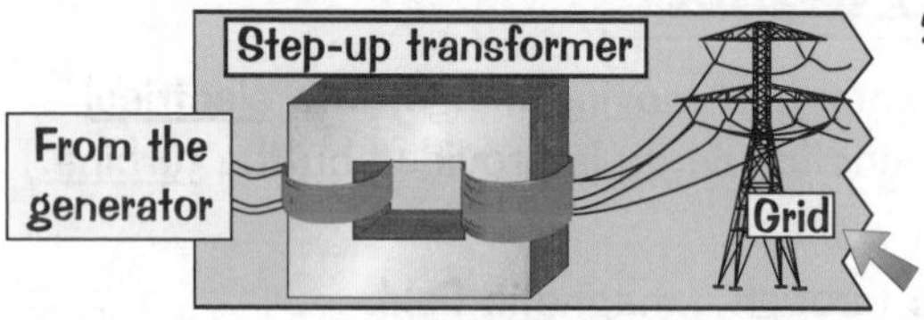

2) It's much cheaper to increase the voltage. So before the electricity is sent round the country, the voltage is transformed to 400 000 V. (This keeps the current very low, meaning less wasted energy because heating of the cables is reduced.)
3) To increase the voltage, you need a step-up transformer.

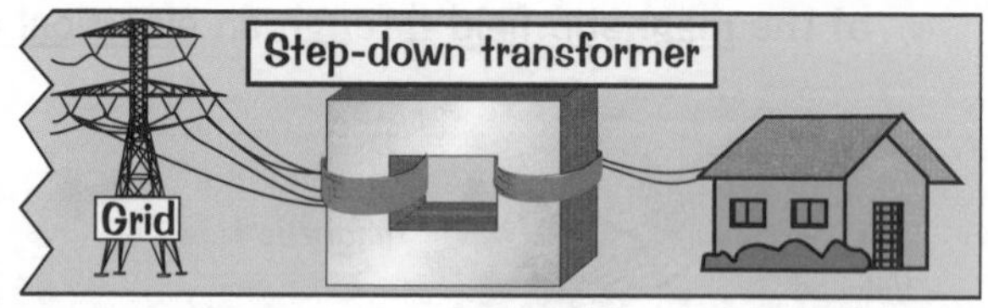

4) Even though you need big pylons with huge insulators (as well as the transformers themselves), using a high voltage is the cheapest way to transmit electricity.
5) To bring the voltage down to safe usable levels for homes, there are local step-down transformers scattered round towns — for example, look for a little fenced-off shed with signs all over it saying "Keep Out" and "Danger of Death".
6) This is the main reason why mains electricity is AC — so that the transformers work. Transformers only work on AC.

Power Stations aren't Very Efficient

1) The process of generating and supplying electricity isn't massively efficient.
2) Unfortunately most power stations produce a lot of waste energy (e.g. heat lost to the environment) as well as energy we can make use of. Basically the energy in each bit of fuel is broken down into two parts — the 'useful bit' and the 'wasted bit'. Learn this equation...

TOTAL Energy Input = USEFUL energy output + WASTE energy output

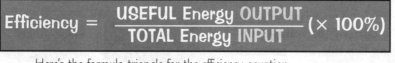

3) There's an equation for working out efficiency as well... yep, learn this one too:

$$\text{Efficiency} = \frac{\text{USEFUL Energy OUTPUT}}{\text{TOTAL Energy INPUT}} (\times 100\%)$$

Here's the formula triangle for the efficiency equation. As always, cover up the thing you want to find out — what you can still see is the formula that'll tell you how to get it.

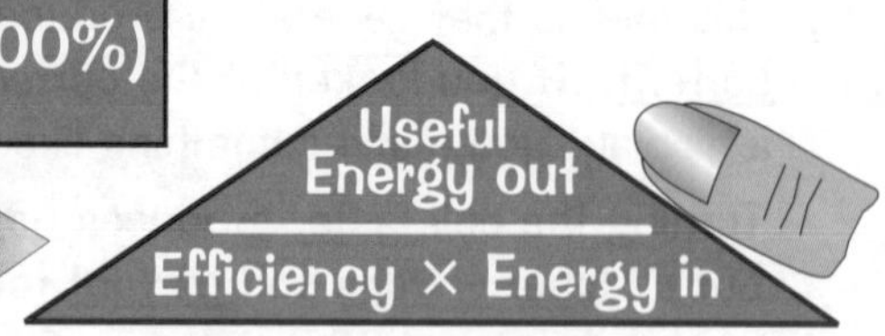

EXAMPLE: A coal-fired power station generates 200 MJ (200 000 000 J) of electrical energy per second. 450 MJ of energy is wasted per second as heat and noise.
Calculate: a) the energy used by the power station in a second,
b) the efficiency of the power station.

You can also calculate the efficiency as a decimal instead of a percentage — just don't do the '× 100%' bit.

ANSWER: a) Energy used (energy input) = useful energy output + energy wasted = 200 MJ + 450 MJ = 650 MJ
b) Efficiency = useful energy output ÷ total energy input = 200 ÷ 650 = 0.3077
Convert efficiency to a percentage by multiplying by 100, so 0.3077 = 30.77%

All that energy — straight down the grid...

Once you've generated all that electricity, you don't want to waste it by heating up miles and miles of power cables when you're distributing it. So keep the current in the power cables low, and make the voltage high. Then the good folk of John o' Groats can still afford to boil the kettle. Problem solved.

Electrical Power

Electrical power is the amount of energy converted per second. It's a hoot.

Running Costs Depend on an Appliance's Power Rating

1) Power's measured in watts (W) or kilowatts (kW) — where 1 watt means 1 joule per second.
   For example, a light bulb with a power rating of 100 W uses 100 J of electrical energy every second. And a 2 kW kettle converts electrical energy at the rate of 2000 J per second. Easy.

2) If they're both on for the same amount of time, the kettle is much more expensive to run than the bulb, because it consumes more energy (and it's energy you pay for — see below).
3) The power rating of an appliance depends on the voltage and the current it uses.
   Equation time...

Power (in W) = Voltage (in V) × Current (in A)

So to transmit a lot of power, you need either a high voltage or a high current — see p. 36.

You know the drill — learn: (i) the equation, and (ii) how to rearrange it.

EXAMPLE: Find the current flowing through a 100 W light bulb if the voltage is 230 V.
ANSWER: Current = Power ÷ Voltage = 100 ÷ 230 = 0.43 amps

Kilowatt-hours (kWh) are "UNITS" of Energy

Your electricity meter records how much energy you use in units of kilowatt-hours, or kWh.

> A KILOWATT-HOUR is the amount of electrical energy converted by a 1 kW appliance left on for 1 HOUR.

The higher the power rating of an appliance, and the longer you leave it on, the more energy it consumes, and the more it costs. Learn (and practise rearranging) this equation too...

ENERGY SUPPLIED (in kWh) = POWER (in kW) × TIME (in hours)

And this one (but this one's easy): **COST = NUMBER OF UNITS × PRICE PER UNIT**

EXAMPLE: Find the cost of leaving a 60 W light bulb on for 30 minutes if one kWh costs 10p.
ANSWER: Energy (in kWh) = Power (in kW) × Time (in hours) = 0.06 kW × ½ hr = 0.03 kWh
Cost = number of units × price per unit = 0.03 × 10p = 0.3p

Off-Peak Electricity is Cheaper

Electricity supplied during the night (off-peak) is sometimes cheaper. Storage heaters take advantage of this — they heat up at night and then release the heat slowly throughout the day. If you can put washing machines, dishwashers, etc. on at night, so much the better.

ADVANTAGES of using off-peak electricity

1) Cost-effective for the electricity company — power stations can't be turned off at night, so it's good if there's a demand for electricity at night.
2) Cheaper for consumers if they buy electricity during the off-peak hours.

DISADVANTAGES of using off-peak electricity

1) There's a slightly increased risk of fire with more appliances going at night but no one watching.
2) You start fitting your routine around the cheap rate hours — i.e. you might stop enjoying the use of electricity during the day.

Watt's the answer — well, part of it...

Get a bit of practice with the equations in those lovely bright red boxes, and try these questions:

1) A kettle draws a current of 12 A from the 230 V mains supply. Calculate its power rating.
2) With 0.5 kWh of energy, for how long could you run the kettle?

Answers on p. 123.

The Greenhouse Effect

The atmosphere keeps us warm by trapping heat.

Some Radiation from the Sun Passes Through the Atmosphere

1) The Earth is surrounded by an atmosphere made up of various gases — the air.
2) The gases in the atmosphere filter out certain types of radiation from the Sun — they absorb or reflect radiation of certain wavelengths (infrared).
3) However, some wavelengths of radiation — mainly visible light and some radio waves — pass through the atmosphere quite easily.

The Greenhouse Effect Helps Regulate Earth's Temperature

1) The Earth absorbs short wavelength EM radiation from the Sun. This warms the Earth's surface up. The Earth then emits some of this EM radiation back out into space — this tends to cool us down.
2) Most of the radiation emitted from Earth is longer wavelength infrared radiation — heat.
3) A lot of this infrared radiation is absorbed by atmospheric gases, including carbon dioxide, methane and water vapour.
4) These gases then re-radiate heat in all directions, including back towards the Earth.
5) So the atmosphere acts as an insulating layer, stopping the Earth losing all its heat at night.

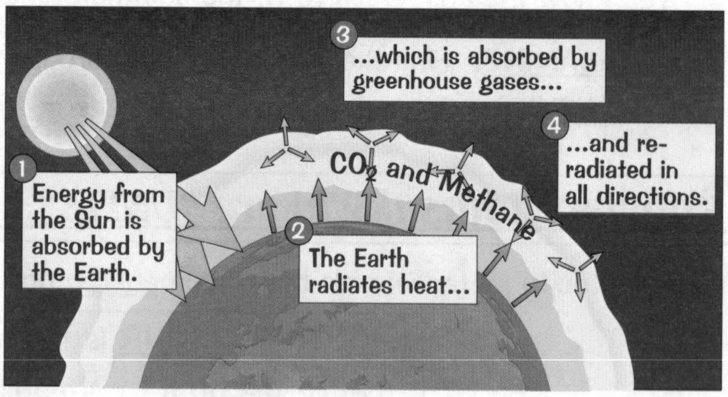

6) This is known as the 'greenhouse effect'. (In a greenhouse, the sun shines in and the glass helps keep some of the heat in.) Without the greenhouse gases (CO_2, methane, water vapour) in our atmosphere, the Earth would be a lot colder.

Humans are Causing an Increase in the Amount of Greenhouse Gases

Over the last 200 years or so, the concentration of greenhouse gases in the atmosphere has been increasing. This is because some of the sources of them are increasing, so more gases are being released:

Carbon Dioxide

People use more energy (e.g. travel more in cars) — which we get mainly from burning fossil fuels, which releases more carbon dioxide.

More land is needed for houses and food and the space is often made by chopping down and burning trees — fewer trees mean less CO_2 is absorbed, and burning releases more CO_2.

CO_2 also comes from natural sources — e.g. respiration in animals and plants, and volcanic eruptions can release it.

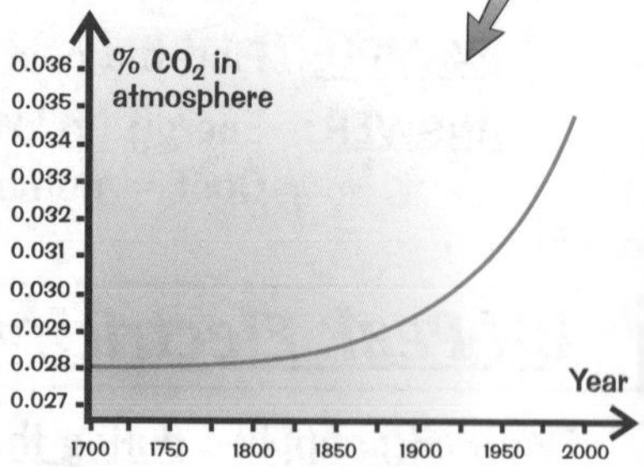

Methane

Cattle farming has increased to feed the growing population — cattle digestion produces methane, so the amount of methane is increasing.

Decaying waste in landfill sites produces methane — the amount of waste is increasing, causing, you guessed it, an increase in methane.

Methane is released naturally by volcanoes, wetlands and wild animals.

You might have to interpret data on greenhouse gases — there's more on interpreting data on pages 6-8.

Water Vapour

Most water vapour comes from natural sources — mainly oceans, seas, rivers and lakes.
As global temperature increases (see next page), so could the amount of water vapour.
Power stations also produce water vapour, which can affect the amount in the local area.

A biologist, a chemist and a physicist walk into a greenhouse...

...it works out badly. You need to know what greenhouse gases are and where they come from. Learn it well.

Global Warming and Climate Change

Without any 'greenhouse gases' in the atmosphere, the Earth would be about 30 °C colder than it is now. So we need the greenhouse effect — just not too much of it...

Upsetting the Greenhouse Effect Has Led to Climate Change

1) Since we started burning fossil fuels, the level of carbon dioxide in the atmosphere has increased (see previous page).
2) The global temperature has also risen during this time (global warming). There's a link between concentration of CO_2 and global temperature.
3) A lot of evidence has been collected that shows the rise in CO_2 is causing global warming by increasing the greenhouse effect.
4) For example, climate models can be used to explain why the climate is changing now. We know that the Earth's climate varies naturally (see below). But climate modelling over the last few years has shown that natural changes don't explain the current 'global warming' — and that the increase in greenhouse gases due to human activity is the cause.
5) So there's now a scientific consensus (general agreement) that humans are causing global warming.
6) Global warming is a type of climate change. But it also causes other types of climate change, e.g. changing weather patterns.

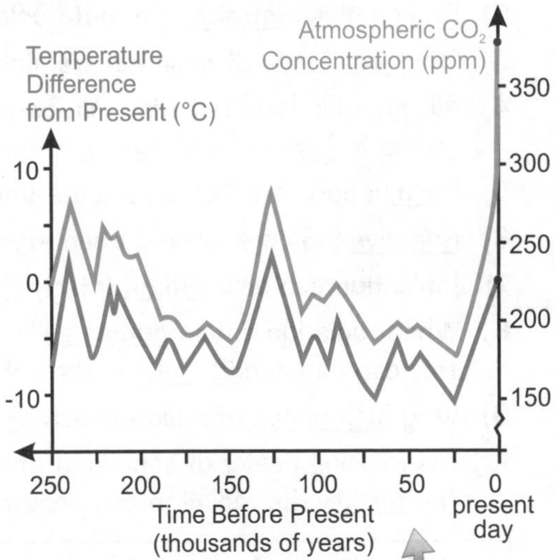

You might be asked to interpret evidence for natural or man-made global warming and climate change in the exam — make sure you look for the evidence and ignore opinions that aren't supported by data. See pages 6-8.

Changes to the Weather can have Human and Natural Causes

1) The climate is very complicated — conditions in the atmosphere, oceans and land all affect one another.
2) Changes in temperature can have large effects on the weather.
3) For example, many regions will suffer more extreme weather because of global warming, e.g. longer, hotter droughts.
4) Hurricanes form over warm water — so with more warm water, you'd expect more hurricanes.
5) Changing weather patterns also affect food production — some regions are now too dry to grow food, some too wet. This will get worse as temperature increases and weather patterns change more.
6) Temperature change, and so changes to the weather, can have both human and natural causes:

HUMAN

1) The rising CO_2 level caused by humans is affecting the greenhouse effect and causing global warming (see above).
2) Soot and gases produced by factories can reflect heat from cities back down to Earth, which can cause increases in local temperature.

NATURAL

1) Ash and gases thrown into the atmosphere by volcanoes can reflect radiation from the Sun back into space, causing the Earth to cool down.
2) Changes in our orbit round the Sun can cause ice ages.

Be a climate model — go on a diet...

Global warming' could mean that some parts of the world cool down. For instance, as ice melts, lots of cold fresh water will enter the sea and this could disrupt ocean currents. This could be bad news for us in Britain — if the nice warm currents we get at the moment weaken, we'll be a lot colder.

Nuclear Radiation

Sometimes the nucleus of an atom can (for no immediately obvious reason) spit out nuclear radiation.

Nuclear Radiation Causes Ionisation

1) When an unstable nucleus decays, it gives off one or more kinds of nuclear radiation.
2) Radioactive materials give out nuclear radiation over time.
3) The three kinds of radiation are alpha (α), beta (β) and gamma (γ).
4) All three kinds of radiation can cause ionisation — the radiation causes atoms to lose or gain electrons, turning those atoms into ions.
5) Positive ions are formed when atoms lose electrons.
6) Negative ions are formed when atoms gain electrons.
7) Ionisation can also initiate (start) chemical reactions between different atoms.
8) When radiation enters human cells it can ionise molecules and damage DNA. This can cause mutations in the cell that could lead to cancer.
9) Very high doses of radiation can kill cells completely.
10) The ionising power of each kind of radiation is linked to how far it can penetrate materials. The further the radiation can penetrate before hitting an atom, the less ionising it is.

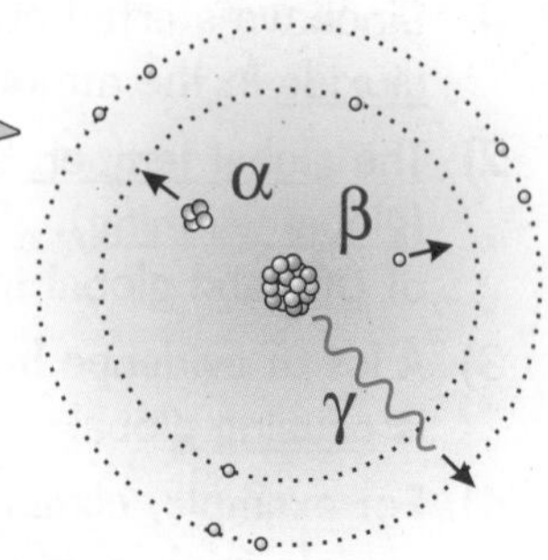

Alpha Particles are Big and Heavy

1) Alpha particles (α) are relatively big, heavy and slow moving (they're 2 protons and 2 neutrons).
2) Because of their size they're stopped quickly — they don't penetrate far into materials. Alpha particles can be stopped by paper or skin.
3) This means they're strongly ionising — they bash into loads of atoms and knock electrons off them before they slow down.

Beta Particles are Electrons

1) Beta particles (β) are just electrons — so they're small, and they move quite fast.
2) Beta particles penetrate moderately (further than α-particles) before colliding, so they're moderately ionising. But they can still be stopped by a thin sheet of metal — a few millimetres of aluminium, say.

Gamma Rays are Very High Frequency Electromagnetic Waves

1) After spitting out an α- or β-particle, the nucleus might need to get rid of some extra energy. It does this by emitting a gamma ray (γ) — a type of EM radiation.
2) Gamma rays have no mass and no charge. They can penetrate a long way into materials without being stopped — meaning they're weakly ionising (they tend to pass through rather than collide with atoms). But eventually they do hit something and do damage.
3) They can be stopped using very thick concrete or a few centimetres of lead.

You can Identify the Type of Radiation by its Penetrating Power

You can tell which kind of radiation you're dealing with by what blocks it. E.g. place a sheet of paper between the radiation source (some radioactive material) and a detector (a Geiger counter): If no radiation reaches the detector, then it must be alpha. If radiation is still reaching the detector then it could be beta or gamma. Swap the paper for aluminium — if no radiation reaches it now, it must be beta. But if radioactivity still gets through, it must be gamma. Simples.

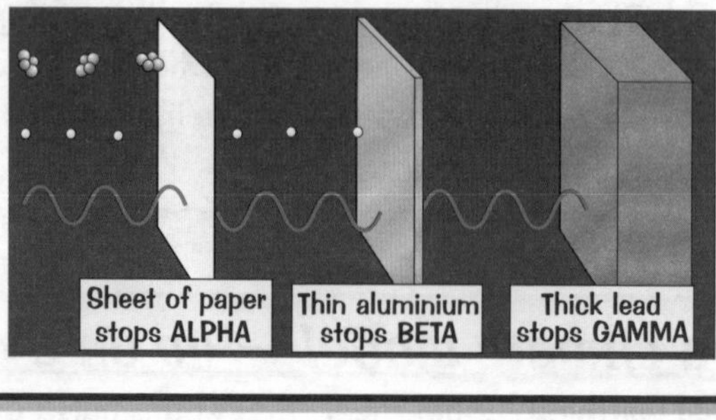

I'm tired out from all this activity...

When an atom spits out alpha or beta radiation it changes into a different type of atom in the process. Neat.

Uses of Nuclear Radiation

Nuclear radiation can be very dangerous. But it can be very useful too. Read on...

Alpha Radiation is Used in Smoke Detectors

1) Smoke detectors have a weak source of α-radiation close to two electrodes.
2) The radiation ionises the air and a current flows between the electrodes.
3) But if there's a fire, the smoke absorbs the radiation — the current stops and the alarm sounds.

Beta Radiation is Used in Tracers and Thickness Gauges

1) Radioactive substances have medical uses as tracers:

   If a radioactive source is injected into a patient (or swallowed), its progress around the body can be followed using an external radiation detector. A computer converts the reading to a TV display showing where the strongest reading is coming from. These 'tracers' can show if the body is working properly.

   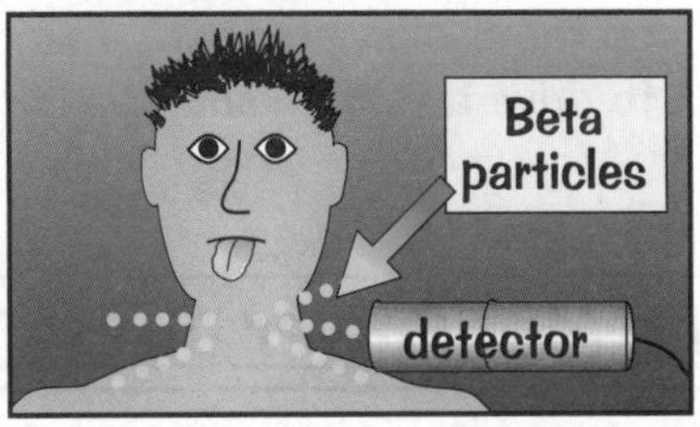

   Doctors use beta or gamma emitters as tracers because this radiation passes out of the body. They also choose things that are only radioactive for a few hours.

2) Beta radiation is also used in thickness control. You direct radiation through the stuff being made (e.g. paper or cardboard), and put a detector on the other side, connected to a control unit.

   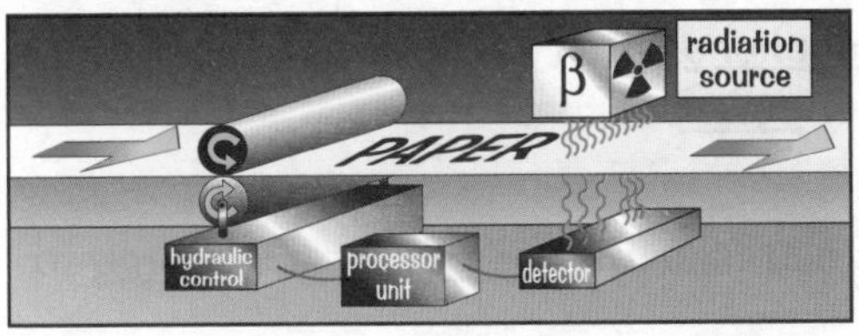

   When the amount of detected radiation goes down, it means the paper is coming out too thick, so the control unit pinches the rollers up to make it thinner. If the reading goes up, the paper's too thin, so the control unit opens the rollers out a bit.

   For this use, your radioactive substance mustn't decay away too quickly, otherwise its strength would gradually fall (and the control unit would keep pinching up the rollers trying to compensate). You need to use a beta source, because then the paper or cardboard will partly block the radiation. If it all goes through (or none of it does), then the reading won't change at all as the thickness changes.

Gamma Radiation Has Medical and Industrial Uses

1) High doses of gamma rays will kill all living cells, so they can be used to treat cancers. The gamma rays have to be directed carefully at the cancer, and at just the right dosage so as to kill the cancer cells without damaging too many normal cells.

2) Gamma rays are also used to sterilise medical instruments — by killing all the microbes. This is better than trying to boil plastic instruments, which might be damaged by high temperatures. You need to use a strongly radioactive source that lasts a long time, so that it doesn't need replacing too often.

   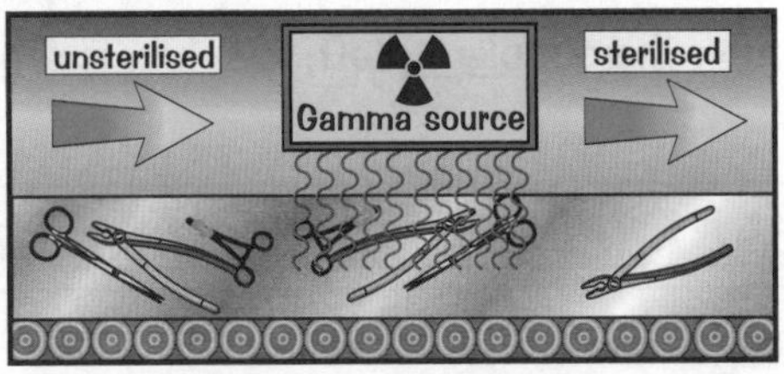

3) Several industries also use gamma radiation to do non-destructive testing. For example, airlines can check the turbine blades of their jet engines by directing gamma rays at them — if too much radiation gets through the blade to the detector on the other side, they know the blade's cracked or there's a fault in the welding. It's so much better to find this out before you take off than in mid-air.

Thickness gauges — they're called 'exams' nowadays...

Knowing the detail is important here. For instance, swallowing an alpha source as a medical tracer would be very foolish — alpha radiation would cause all sorts of chaos inside your body but couldn't be detected outside, making the whole thing pointless. So learn what each type's used for and why.

Nuclear Power

Another use of nuclear radiation — nuclear power. Some people think nuclear power is the best way to reduce CO_2 emissions, but others think it's just too dangerous.

Nuclear Power Uses Uranium as Fuel

1) A nuclear power station is mostly the same as the one on page 34, but with nuclear fission producing the heat to make steam. The difference is in the boiler.
2) In nuclear fission, atoms in the nuclear fuel (e.g. uranium) are split in two, releasing lots of heat energy.
3) Water is used as a coolant to take away the heat produced by the fission process. This heat is used to produce steam to drive a turbine and generator.

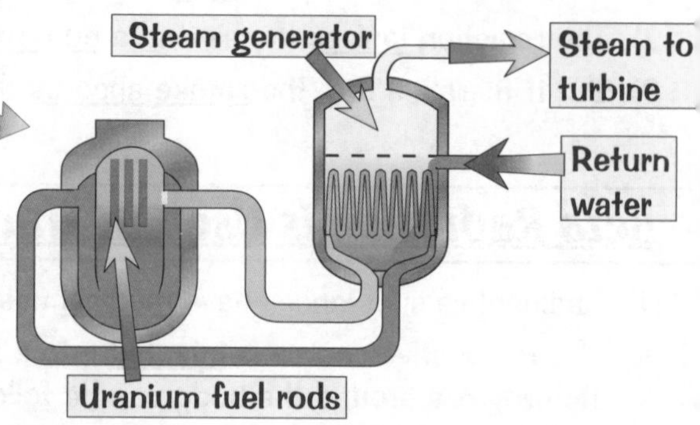

Nuclear Power Doesn't Produce Carbon Dioxide

Time for some advantages and disadvantages of using nuclear power:

ADVANTAGES

1) Nuclear power stations can make lots of energy without releasing lots of CO_2 into the atmosphere (which contributes to global warming — see page 39).
2) Nuclear reactions release a lot more energy than chemical reactions (such as burning), so it takes a lot less uranium to produce the same amount of power as fossil fuel.
3) Nuclear fuel (i.e. uranium) is relatively cheap.
4) There's still plenty of uranium left in the ground (although it can take a lot of money and energy to make it suitable for use in a reactor).

DISADVANTAGES

1) Nuclear power stations are expensive to build and maintain.
2) It takes longer to start up nuclear power stations than fossil fuel power stations.
3) Processing the uranium before you use it causes pollution.
4) And there's always a risk of leaks of radioactive material, or even a major catastrophe like the Chernobyl disaster. (Radioactive material can cause cancer and radiation sickness.)
5) A big problem with nuclear power is the radioactive waste that you always get — it's very dangerous and difficult to reprocess or dispose of.
6) When they're too old and inefficient, nuclear power stations have to be decommissioned (shut down and made safe) — that's expensive too.
7) Although there's plenty left, uranium is a non-renewable resource — so it will eventually run out.

See next page for more about nuclear waste.

Nuclear Fuel is Also Used to Make Nuclear Weapons

1) The used uranium fuel from nuclear power stations can be reprocessed. This is one way of dealing with some of the radioactive waste that would otherwise have to be stored.
2) After reprocessing, you're left with more uranium and a bit of plutonium.
3) You can reuse the uranium in your nuclear power station.
4) The plutonium can be used to make nuclear bombs.

Fission — also the starting orders of a fishing competition...

Current nuclear power stations work because of nuclear fission (where atoms split apart to release energy). In the future it may be possible to use nuclear fusion (where atoms are forced together) to produce power. Nuclear fusion produces more energy and less waste, but so far it's been very hard to get it to work.

Danger from Radioactive Materials

Radioactive stuff certainly has its uses — curing cancer, killing bacteria and generating electricity. But if you don't want to irradiate yourself, you have to know how to handle it safely.

You Should Always Protect Yourself...

1) First things first... don't do anything really stupid — like eating your smoke alarm.
2) Radioactive sources need to be stored safely. They should be kept in a labelled lead box and put back in as soon as you can to keep your exposure time short.
3) If you need to use a radioactive source, always handle it with tongs — never allow skin contact. And keep it at arm's length (so it's as far from the body as possible). Also, keep it pointing away from you and avoid looking directly at it.

...Especially If You Work with Nuclear Radiation

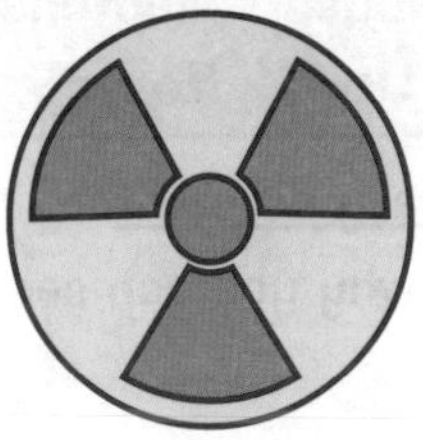

1) Industrial nuclear workers wear full protective suits to prevent tiny radioactive particles being inhaled, or lodging on the skin or under fingernails, etc.
2) Lead-lined suits and lead/concrete barriers and thick lead screens shield workers from gamma rays in highly radioactive areas. (α-radiation and β-radiation are stopped much more easily.)
3) Workers use remote-controlled robot arms to carry out tasks in highly radioactive areas.

Radioactive Waste is Difficult to Dispose of Safely

1) Most waste from nuclear power stations and hospitals is 'low-level' (only slightly radioactive). Low-level waste is things like paper, clothing, gloves, syringes, etc. This kind of waste can be disposed of by burying it in secure landfill sites.
2) High-level waste is the really dangerous stuff — a lot of it stays highly radioactive for tens of thousands of years, and so has to be treated very carefully. It's often sealed into glass blocks, which are then sealed in metal canisters. These could then be buried deep underground.
3) However, it's difficult to find suitable places to bury high-level waste. The site has to be geologically stable (e.g. not be prone to earthquakes), since big movements in the rock could disturb the canisters and allow radioactive material to leak out. If this material gets into the groundwater, it could contaminate the soil, plants, rivers, etc., and get into our drinking water.
4) Even when geologists do find suitable sites, people who live nearby often object. So, at the moment, most high-level waste is kept 'on-site' at nuclear power stations.
5) Not all radioactive waste has to be chucked out though — some of it is reprocessed to reclaim useful radioactive material (see previous page). But even reprocessing leaves some waste behind.
6) Nuclear power stations and reprocessing plants are generally pretty secure — they have high fences and security checks on the people going in and out. But they might still be a target for terrorists — who could use stolen radioactive material to make a 'dirty bomb', or attack the plant directly.
7) There are strict regulations about how waste is disposed of. But the rules could change as we find out more about the dangers of radiation, and the pros and cons of storing waste in different ways. E.g. what's classed as low-level now might be considered high-level in the future.

Radioactive sources — don't put them on your chips...

Most of the UK's nuclear power stations are quite old, and will have to be shut down soon. There's a debate going on over whether we should build new ones. Some people say no — if we can't deal safely with the radioactive waste we've got now, we certainly shouldn't make lots more. Others say that nuclear power is the only way to meet all our energy needs without causing catastrophic climate change.

The Solar System

When I were a lad I was taught that there were nine planets in our Solar System. But in 2006 some pesky astrobods decided that Pluto wasn't really a proper planet, so now there's only eight — for now...

Planets Reflect Sunlight and Orbit the Sun in Ellipses

Our Solar System consists of a star (the Sun) and lots of stuff orbiting it in slightly elongated circles (called ellipses).

Closest to the Sun are the inner planets — Mercury, Venus, Earth and Mars.

Then the asteroid belt — see next page.

Then the outer planets, much further away — Jupiter, Saturn, Uranus, Neptune.

You need to learn the order of the planets, which is made easier by using the little jollyism below:

Mercury,	Venus,	Earth,	Mars,	(Asteroids),	Jupiter,	Saturn,	Uranus,	Neptune
(Mad	Vampires	Eat	Mangoes	And	Jump	Straight	Up	Noses)

1) You can see some planets with the naked eye. They look like stars, but they're totally different.
2) Stars are huge, very hot and very far away. They give out lots of light — which is why you can see them, even though they're very far away.
3) The planets are smaller and nearer and they just reflect sunlight falling on them.
4) Planets often have moons orbiting around them. Jupiter has at least 63 of 'em. We've just got one (see page 46 for more about our Moon).

The Solar System is Held Together by Gravitational Attraction

1) Things only change direction when a force acts on them — if there were no force, they'd move in a straight line (or stay still). Since planets go round and round, there must be a force involved.
2) When it comes to big things in the Solar System and the rest of the Universe (like planets, asteroids, comets, meteors, and so on), there's only really one force it could be — gravity (gravitational attraction).
3) Gravity pulls everything in the Universe towards everything else. The effect is tiny between 'small' things (e.g. between you and a car, or between a house and a hat) — so tiny you don't notice it.
4) But when you're talking about things as big as stars and planets, the pull of gravity can be huge (the bigger the 'thing', the bigger its pull). So it's gravity that makes planets orbit stars, and moons orbit planets. Gravity keeps satellites, comets and asteroids in their orbits, and so on. Get the idea...
5) The pull of an object gets smaller the further away you go. This is why you're pulled strongly towards the Earth and don't hurtle towards the Sun, for example. And this is why the Earth orbits the Sun, rather than some other much bigger star further away.

The pull of gravity is directly towards the Sun...
...but the motion of the Earth is around the Sun.

6) If the Earth wasn't already moving, it would be pulled by gravity directly towards the Sun. But what gravity normally does is make things that are already moving change their course — often into circular or elliptical orbits.

> Circular motion is always caused by a force (pull) towards the centre of the circle.
> For planets, moons, etc. in an orbit, this force is provided by gravity.
> A force that causes a circular motion is called a centripetal force.

Pull yourself together — get this stuff learnt...

Brilliantly, the moons of some planets in our Solar System are so small that although there is enough gravity to keep you standing on them, if you jumped hard you'd fly off into outer space and never come back down. Head to Deimos (orbiting Mars) next time you're passing and give it a go. Weeeee...

Asteroids and Comets

There's more than planets out there in the Solar System — aliens, space probes, but mostly just other rocks.

There's a Belt of Asteroids Orbiting Between Mars and Jupiter

1) When the Solar System was forming, the rocks between Mars and Jupiter didn't form a planet — the large gravitational attraction of Jupiter kept interfering.
2) This left millions of asteroids — piles of rubble and rock measuring up to about 1000 km in diameter. They orbit the Sun between the orbits of Jupiter and Mars.
3) Asteroids usually stay in their orbits but sometimes they're pushed or pulled into different ones...

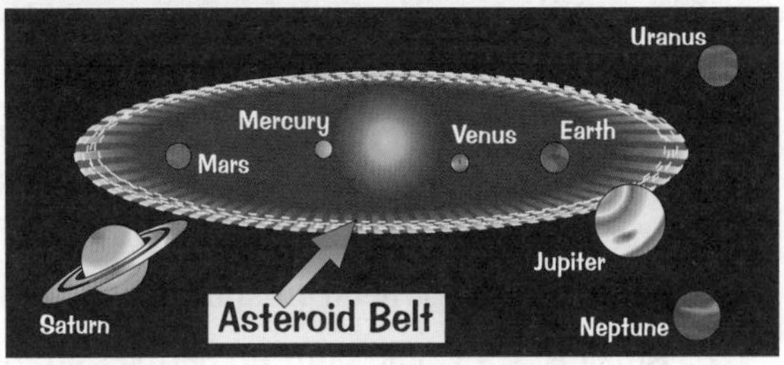

Not to scale.

Meteorites are Rocks That Have Crashed Down to Earth

1) Meteors are rocks or dust that enter the Earth's atmosphere. As they pass through the atmosphere they burn up, and we see them as 'shooting stars'.
2) Sometimes, not all of the meteor burns up and part of it crashes into the Earth's surface as a meteorite. This only happens rarely, but when large meteors do hit us, they can cause havoc...
3) They can start fires, and throw loads of hot rocks and dust into the air. They also make big holes in the ground (craters, if we're being technical).

4) The dust and smoke from a large impact can block out the sunlight for many months, causing climate change — which in turn can cause species to become extinct.
5) For example, about 65 million years ago an asteroid about 10 km across struck the Yucatán peninsula in Mexico. The dust it kicked up caused global temperatures to plummet, and over half the species on Earth subsequently died out (including maybe the last of the dinosaurs).
6) We can tell that asteroids have collided with Earth in the past. There are the big craters, but also:
   - layers of unusual elements in rocks — these must have been 'imported' by an asteroid,
   - sudden changes in fossil numbers between adjacent layers of rock, as species suffer extinction.

Comets Orbit the Sun in Very Elliptical Orbits

1) Comets are balls of rock, dust and ice which orbit the Sun in very elongated ellipses, often in different planes from the planets.
2) They come from objects orbiting the Sun way beyond the planets.
3) As a comet approaches the Sun, its ice melts, leaving a bright tail of gas and debris which can be millions of kilometres long. This is what we see from the Earth.
4) Comets speed up as they approach the Sun, because the Sun's gravitational pull increases as you get closer.

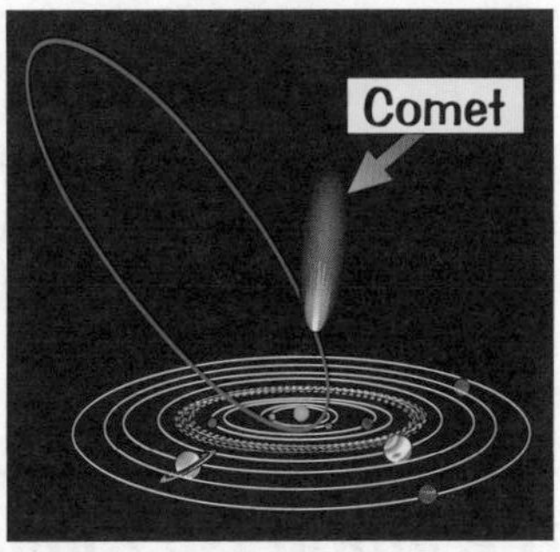

Comet in an elliptical orbit (red line).

I remember that asteroids looked different in 1979...

They were definitely more angular and collisions could be solved simply by shooting them or 'warping' to another part of space*. Comets looked the same in 1066 though — Halley's comet is shown on the Bayeux tapestry.

*computer game history lesson no. 4

NEOs and the Moon

As you read this, there are thousands of hefty lumps of rock just whizzing about in space — and one of them might be coming straight at you.

Near-Earth Objects (NEOs) Could Collide with Earth

1) Near-Earth objects (NEOs) are asteroids or comets which might be on a collision course with Earth.
2) Astronomers use powerful telescopes and satellites to search for and monitor NEOs.
3) When they find one they can calculate the object's trajectory (the path it's going to take) and find out if it's heading for us.
4) NEOs can be difficult to spot because they're small, dark and may have unusual orbits.
5) Small NEOs would burn up harmlessly in the atmosphere if they hit the Earth, but larger ones could cause explosions more powerful than nuclear weapons.
6) If we got enough warning about an NEO coming our way, we could try to deflect it before it hit us.
7) If you exploded a bomb really close to (or on or in) the NEO when it was far away from us, you might 'nudge' it off course. (That'd probably make quite a good plot for a film.)

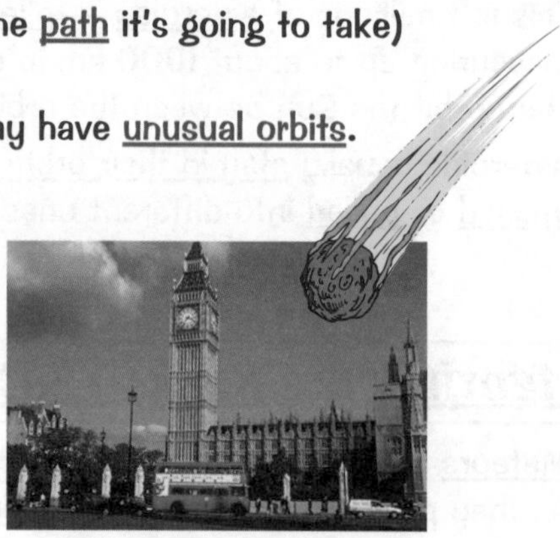

Even Bruce Willis gets it wrong sometimes.

The Moon May Have Come from a Colliding Planet

Scientists can use what they know about the Earth and the Moon to come up with believable theories about where the Moon came from in the first place.
It's pretty amazing.

1) Scientists think that 'our' Moon was formed when another planet collided side-on with Earth.
2) The theory is that some time after the Earth was formed, a smaller Mars-sized object crashed into it.
3) In the heat of the collision, the dense iron cores of these two planets merged to form the Earth's core.
4) The less dense material was ejected as really hot dust and rocks — which orbited around the Earth for a while and eventually came together to form the Moon.
5) There's quite a bit of evidence for this theory. For example:

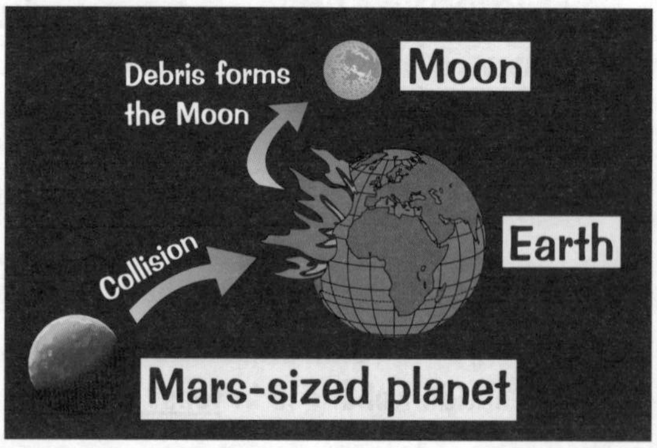

A chocolate-bar sized planet collides with Earth and forms the Moon.

- The Moon has a lower density than the Earth and doesn't have a big iron core, whereas Earth does.
- Moon rocks contain few substances which evaporate at low temperatures — suggesting that the Moon formed from hot material (all the water, etc. was boiled away, as would happen in a collision).

Sadly the Moon isn't made of cheese...

Time for some exciting Moon facts — don't say I never treat you... There's no evidence of mice (or other life) on the Moon. Sad. When humans landed on the Moon they were worried that the surface wouldn't be solid enough and the landing craft would sink — not because they actually thought it was made of cheese though.
The Moon is also known as Luna, after the Roman goddess of the Moon. Astrobods call the planet that hit the Earth 'Theia' after the mother of the ancient Greek moon goddess Selene.

Beyond the Solar System

There's all sorts of exciting stuff out there... Our whole Solar System is just part of a huge galaxy. And there are billions upon billions of galaxies. You should be realising now that the Universe is huge...

We're in the Milky Way Galaxy

1) Our Sun is just one of many billions of stars which form the Milky Way galaxy. Our Sun is about halfway along one of the spiral arms of the Milky Way.
2) The distance between neighbouring stars in the galaxy is usually millions of times greater than the distance between planets in our Solar System.
3) The force which keeps the stars together in a galaxy is gravity, of course. And like most things in the Universe, galaxies rotate — a bit like a Catherine wheel.

The Whole Universe Has More Than a Billion Galaxies

1) Galaxies themselves are often millions of times further apart than the stars are within a galaxy.
2) So even the slowest among you will have worked out that the Universe is mostly empty space and is really really BIG.

Scientists Measure Distances in Space Using Light Years

1) Once you get outside our Solar System, the distances between stars and between galaxies are so enormous that kilometres seem pathetically small for measuring them.
2) For example, the closest star to us (after the Sun) is about 40 000 000 000 000 kilometres away (give or take a few hundred billion kilometres). Numbers like that soon get out of hand.
3) So scientists use light years instead — a light year is the distance that light travels through a vacuum (like space) in one year. Simple as that.
4) If you work it out, 1 light year is equal to about 9 460 000 000 000 kilometres. Which means the closest star after the Sun is about 4.2 light years away from us.
5) Just remember — a light year is a measure of DISTANCE (not time).

Stars Can Explode — and They Sometimes Leave Black Holes

1) When a really big star has used up most of its fuel, it explodes. What's usually left after the explosion is really dense — sometimes so dense that nothing can escape its strong gravitational attraction. It's now called a black hole.
2) Black holes have a very large mass, small volume and a very high density.
3) They're not visible — even light can't escape their gravitational pull (that's why it's 'black', d'oh).
4) Astronomers have to detect black holes in other ways — e.g. they can observe X-rays emitted by hot gases from other stars as they spiral into the black hole.

See p. 50 for more about the death of stars.

Spiral arms — would you still need elbows...

A lot of people say it's a small world. I'm not sure... it's always seemed pretty big to me. Anyway... you never hear anybody say the Universe is small. Not nowadays, anyway. Weirdly though, the Universe used to be tiny (see p. 49). That was a while ago now though. Before my time.

Exploring the Solar System

If you want to know what it's like on another planet, you have three options — peer at it from a distance, send a robot to have a peek, or get in a spaceship and go there yourself...

We Can Explore Space Using Manned Spacecraft...

1) The Solar System is big — so big that even radio waves (which travel at 300 000 000 m/s) take several hours to cross it. Even from Mars, radio signals take at least three minutes.
2) But sending a manned spacecraft to Mars would take at least a couple of years (for a round trip).
3) The spacecraft would need to carry a lot of fuel, making it heavy — and expensive.
4) And it would be difficult keeping the astronauts alive and healthy for all that time...
   - the spacecraft would have to carry loads of food, water and oxygen (or recycle them),
   - you'd need to regulate the temperature and remove toxic gases from the air,
   - the spacecraft would have to shield the astronauts from radiation in space,
   - long periods in low gravity causes muscle wastage and loss of bone tissue,
   - spending ages in a tiny space, with the same people, is psychologically stressful.

Space travel can be very stressful.

...but Sending Unmanned Probes is Much Easier

First, build a spacecraft. Then build and program loads of instruments — to record data and send it back to Earth (probably by radio). Finish the job by packing the instruments on board, turning on the computer and launching your probe. Like I said... easy.

1) 'Fly-by' missions are simplest — the probe passes close by an object but doesn't land. It can gather data on loads of things, including temperature, magnetic and gravitational fields and radiation levels.
2) Sometimes a probe is programmed to enter a planet's atmosphere. It might be designed to burn up after a while, having already sent back lots of data.
3) Some probes are designed to land on other planets (or moons, asteroids...). They often carry exploration rovers that can wander about, taking photos and sample, etc.

Advantages of Unmanned Probes

- They don't have to carry food, water and oxygen.
- They can withstand conditions that would be lethal to humans (e.g. extreme heat, cold or radiation levels).
- With no people taking up room and weighing the probe down, more instruments can be fitted in.
- They're cheaper — they carry less, they don't have to come back to Earth, and less is spent on safety.
- If the probe does crash or burn up unexpectedly it's a bit embarrassing, and you've wasted lots of time and money, but at least no one gets hurt.

Disadvantages of Unmanned Probes

- Unmanned probes can't think for themselves (whereas people are very good at overcoming simple problems that could be disastrous).
- A spacecraft can't do maintenance and repairs — people can (as the astronauts on the Space Shuttle 'Discovery' had to do when its heat shield was damaged during take-off).

The Information Collected Needs to be Sent Back to Earth

Whether a spacecraft is manned or unmanned, the information it collects needs to be sent back to Earth. How it's sent back depends on how far it's travelled and the type of information (e.g. samples or data).

1) Distant objects (e.g. further away than Mars) — data needs to be 'beamed' back (e.g. using radio waves) as it would take too long (or be too difficult) for the spacecraft itself to travel back to Earth.
2) Nearer objects — probes or people could collect samples and physically bring them back to Earth.

Probes — a popular feature of alien abduction stories...

The first ever space probe was called Sputnik 1, which orbited the Earth for 3 months and went 'beeeeeeep'.

The Origin of the Universe

How did it all begin... Well, once upon a time, there was a really Big Bang.
(That's the most convincing theory we've got for how the Universe started.)

The Universe Seems to be Expanding

As big as the Universe already is, it looks like it's getting even bigger.
All its galaxies seem to be moving away from each other. There's good evidence for this...

Light from Distant Galaxies is Red-Shifted

1) When we look at light from distant galaxies we find that the frequencies are all lower than they should be — they're shifted towards the red end of the spectrum.
2) This red-shift is the same effect as a car horn sounding lower-pitched when the car is travelling away from you. The sound drops in frequency.
3) Measurements of the red-shift suggest that all the distant galaxies are moving away from us very quickly — and it's the same result whichever direction you look in.

More Distant Galaxies Have Greater Red-Shifts

1) More distant galaxies have greater red-shifts than nearer ones.
2) This means that more distant galaxies are moving away faster than nearer ones. The inescapable conclusion appears to be that the whole Universe is expanding.

There's Microwave Radiation from All Directions

This is another observation that scientists made. It's not interesting in itself, but the theory that explains all this evidence definitely is.

1) Scientists can detect low frequency microwave radiation coming from all directions and all parts of the Universe.
2) It's known as the cosmic background radiation.
3) For complicated reasons this background radiation is strong evidence for an initial Big Bang (see below). As the Universe expands and cools, this background radiation 'cools' and drops in frequency.

This Evidence Suggests the Universe Started with a Bang

So all the galaxies are moving away from each other at great speed — suggesting something must have got them going. That 'something' was probably a big explosion — the Big Bang. Here's the theory...

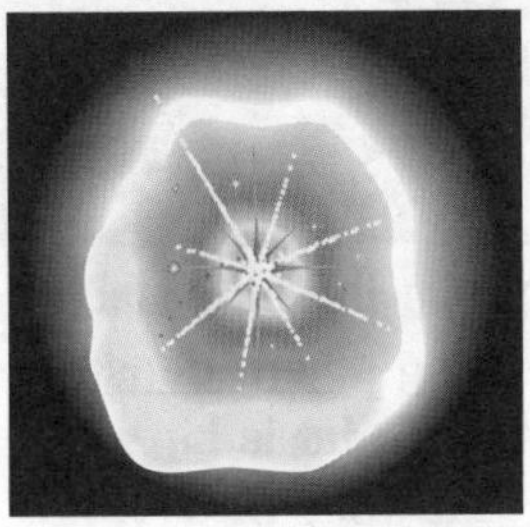

1) Initially, all the matter in the Universe occupied a very small space (that's all the matter in all the galaxies squashed into a space much much smaller than a pinhead — wowzers). Then it 'exploded' — the space started expanding, and the expansion is still going on.
2) The Big Bang theory lets us guess the age of the Universe. From the current rate of expansion, we think the Universe is about 14 billion years old.
3) But estimates of the age of the Universe are very difficult because it's hard to tell how much speed of the expansion has changed since the Big Bang.

In the beginning, there were — no exams...

'How it all began' is quite a tricky problem. Some religious people say that God created the world. Among scientists, the theory of a 'big bang' to get things started is now generally accepted, because that's what the evidence suggests. But we're still rather hazy about if/when/how it's all going to end...

The Life Cycle of Stars

Stars go through many traumatic stages in their lives — just like teenagers.

Clouds of Dust and Gas

1) Stars initially form from clouds of DUST AND GAS.

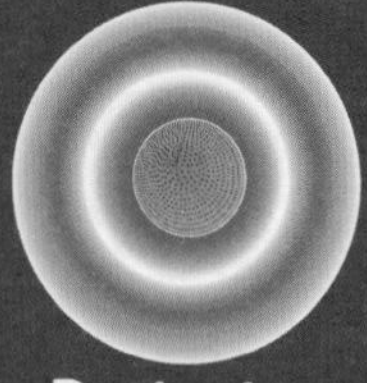

Protostar

2) The force of gravity makes the gas and dust spiral in together to form a protostar. Gravitational energy has been converted into heat energy, so the temperature rises.

Main Sequence Star

3) When the temperature gets high enough, hydrogen nuclei undergo thermonuclear fusion to form helium nuclei and give out massive amounts of heat and light. A star is born. It immediately enters a long stable period where the heat created by the nuclear fusion provides an outward pressure to balance the force of gravity pulling everything inwards. In this stable period it's called a MAIN SEQUENCE STAR and it typically lasts several billion years. (The Sun is in the middle of this stable period — or to put it another way, the Earth has already had half its innings before the Sun engulfs it!)

4) Eventually the hydrogen begins to run out and the star then swells into a RED GIANT (it becomes red because the surface cools).

Small stars

planetary nebula.... and a White Dwarf

5) A small-to-medium-sized star like the Sun then becomes unstable and ejects its outer layer of dust and gas as a planetary nebula.

6) This leaves behind a hot, dense solid core — a WHITE DWARF, which just cools down and eventually fades away. (That's going to be really sad.)

Big stars
Red supergiant

Supernova

Neutron Star...

...or Black Hole

7) Big stars, however, form red supergiants — they start to glow brightly again as they undergo more fusion and expand and contract several times, forming heavier elements in various nuclear reactions. Eventually they'll explode in a SUPERNOVA.

8) The exploding supernova throws the outer layers of dust and gas into space, leaving a very dense core called a NEUTRON STAR. If the star is big enough this will become a BLACK HOLE (see p. 47).

Red Giants, White Dwarfs, Black Holes, Green Ghosts...

Erm. Now how do they know that exactly... Anyway, now you know what the future holds — our Sun is going to fizzle out, and it'll just get very very cold and very very dark. Great. On a brighter note, the Sun's got a good few years in it yet, so it's still worth passing those exams.

Galileo and Copernicus

We're pretty sure we know what the Solar System is like now, but we haven't always thought it was like this...

Ancient Greeks Thought the Earth was the Centre of the Universe

1) Most ancient Greek astronomers believed that the Sun, Moon, planets and stars all orbited the Earth in perfect circles — this is known as the geocentric model or Ptolemaic model.
2) The Ptolemaic model was the accepted model of the Universe from the time of the ancient Greeks until the 1500s. It was only in the 1600s that it began to be replaced by the Copernican model...

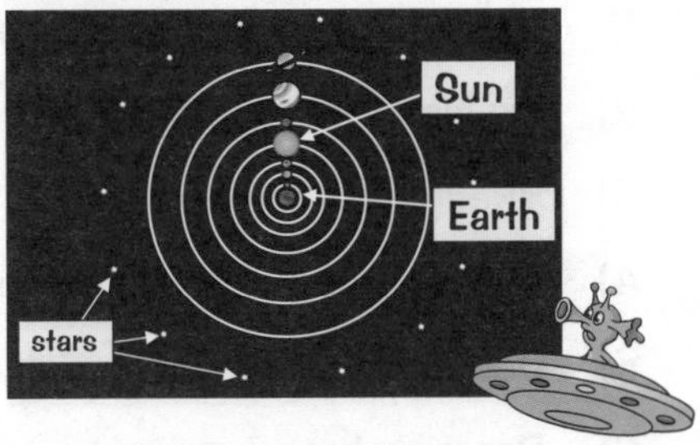

Copernican Model — Sun at the Centre

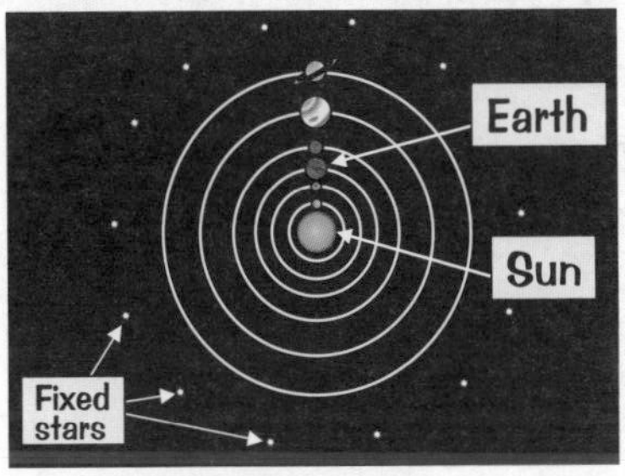

The Copernican model.

1) The Copernican model states that the Earth and planets all orbit the Sun, which is at the centre of the Universe, in perfect circles.
2) The idea had already been around for 2000 years, but the model was first introduced in a book by Copernicus in 1543. This book showed astronomical observations could be explained without having the Earth at the centre of the Universe.
3) The Copernican model is also a heliocentric model (Sun at the centre).
4) Galileo found one of the best pieces of evidence for this theory:

> Around 1610, Galileo was observing Jupiter using a telescope (a new invention at the time) when he saw some stars in a line near the planet. When he looked again, he saw these stars never moved away from Jupiter and seemed to be carried along with the planet — which suggested they weren't stars, but moons orbiting Jupiter.
> This showed not everything was in orbit around the Earth — evidence that the Ptolemaic model was wrong.
>
> Theories change with technological advances — like the invention of the telescope.

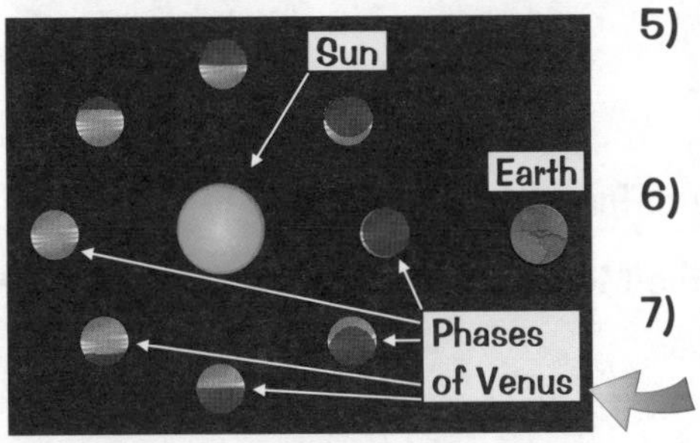

The phases of Venus as it orbits the Sun, as seen from Earth.

5) In the autumn of 1610, Galileo noticed that Venus has phases — where the amount of the planet that's lit by the Sun seems to change over time.
6) If the Ptolemaic model was right then these changes would be very small because Venus would always be in front of the Sun.
7) But if the Copernican model was right, Venus could move in front of and behind the Sun and so the changes in the amount Venus was lit would be really big — just like Galileo saw.
8) Copernicus' ideas weren't very popular at that time because the current models had been around for a long time.
9) The model was also condemned by the church. They claimed that the model went against the Bible, which said the Earth was at the centre of the Universe.
10) Gradually, evidence for the Copernican model increased thanks to more technological advances.
11) The current model still says that the planets in our Solar System orbit the Sun — but that these orbits are actually elliptical rather than circular and the Sun isn't really at the centre of the Universe.

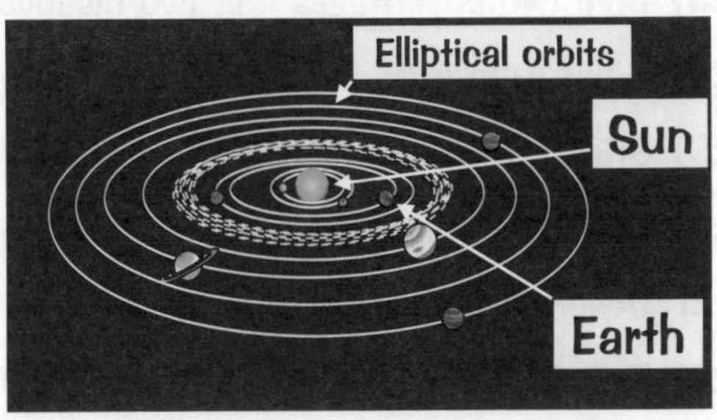

Our current view of the Solar System.

Copernicus — not a brand of metal underwear...

It's taken thousands of years for us to reach our current model of the Solar System. Although these models turned out to be wrong, they played a really important part in helping us reach the model we have today. And unsurprisingly, there's loads and loads that scientists still don't know about our Solar System.

Revision Summary for Module P2

Just what you were waiting for — a whole list of lovely questions to have a go at. Try the questions, then look back and see what you got right and what you got wrong. If you did get any wrong, you're not ready for the exam — so do more revision and then try the questions again.

1) Give one advantage and one disadvantage of using photocells to generate electricity.
2) Explain how wind turbines convert energy from the Sun into electricity.
3) Briefly describe how a typical power station works.
4) Give one advantage and one disadvantage of using: a) fossil fuels; b) biomass, to generate power.
5) Define electromagnetic induction. What factors affect the size of the induced voltage and current?
6) Describe how a generator works.
7) Explain why a very high electrical voltage is used to transmit electricity in the National Grid.
8) Write down the formula for calculating the efficiency of power stations.
9) *a) How many units of electricity (in kWh) would a kettle of power 2500 W use in 3 minutes?
   *b) How much would that cost, if one unit of electricity costs 12p?
10) Briefly describe how the greenhouse effect keeps the Earth warm.
11) How has human activity affected weather patterns?
12) Name the three types of radiation and describe their ionising powers.
13) Explain which types of nuclear radiation are used, and why, in each of the following:
    a) medical tracers, b) treating cancer, c) smoke detectors.
14) Give one advantage and one disadvantage of nuclear power.
15) Describe the precautions you should take when handling radioactive sources in the laboratory.
16) Briefly explain why it's difficult to dispose of high-level radioactive waste safely.
17) What shape are the orbits of the planets in the Solar System?
18) What force keeps planets and satellites in their orbits?
19) What are asteroids and where are they found? How are they different to meteorites?
20) Briefly describe the evidence that led scientists to think that the Moon may be the result of another planet colliding with Earth.
21) What's a light year?
22) Briefly describe the problems with sending a group of astronauts to Neptune.
23) Give two advantages and two disadvantages of manned space travel.
24) What type of radiation is found everywhere in the Universe?
25) Briefly describe the 'Big Bang' theory for the origin of the Universe.
26) List the steps that lead to the formation of a main sequence star (like our Sun).
27) Describe Copernican's model of the Universe.
28) Explain the evidence that Galileo produced that supported Copernicus' theory.

*Answers on p. 123.

Speed and Distance

Reckon you can speed on through this module? On your marks. Get set. Go...

Speed is Just the Distance Travelled in a Certain Time

1) To find the speed of an object, you need to measure the distance it travels (in metres or km) and the time it takes (in seconds or hours). Then the speed is calculated in metres per second (m/s) or kilometres per hour (km/h).
2) The greater the speed of an object, the further the distance it can travel in a certain time, or the shorter the time it takes to go a certain distance.
3) Speed, distance and time are related by the formula: Distance = Speed × Time
4) If an object is speeding up (or slowing down) then you might need to find the average of its speed over the journey: $\text{Average Speed} = \frac{(u + v)}{2}$
5) If you put these equations together you get:

$$\text{Distance} = \text{Average Speed} \times \text{Time} = \frac{(u + v)}{2} \times t$$

u is the speed at the start
v is the speed at the end

(You need to get pretty slick at using this formula.)

EXAMPLE: A ferret speeds up from 0 to 60 km/h in a time of half an hour. What distance does it cover in this time?

ANSWER: u = 0 km/h and v = 60 km/h, t = 0.5 h,
so, distance = ((0 + 60) ÷ 2) × 0.5 = 30 × 0.5 = 15 km.

6) You might need to change the units:

EXAMPLE: A swimmer takes 8 hours to swim across the English Channel. She starts swimming at a speed of 2 m/s and gradually slows down to a speed of 0.5 m/s. How far did she swim? Give your answer in km.

ANSWER: u = 2 m/s, v = 0.5 m/s, t = 8 h, but t needs to be in seconds,
so 8 × 3600 = 28 800 s. Distance = ((2 + 0.5) ÷ 2) × 28 800
= 1.25 × 28 800 = 36 000 m. Give answer in km = 36 000 ÷ 1000 = 36 km.

Distance-Time Graphs

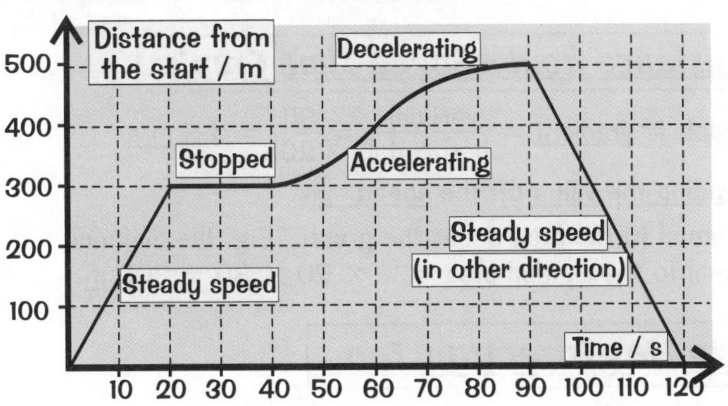

Very Important Notes:

1) GRADIENT = SPEED.
2) Flat sections are where it's stopped.
3) The steeper the gradient, the faster it's going.
4) 'Downhill' sections (negative gradient) mean it's changed direction and is coming back toward its starting point.
5) Curves represent acceleration or deceleration.
6) A steepening curve means it's speeding up (increasing gradient).
7) A levelling off curve means it's slowing down (decreasing gradient).

Calculating Speed from a Distance-Time Graph — It's Just the Gradient

For example, the speed of the return section of the graph is:

$$\text{Speed} = \text{gradient} = \frac{\text{vertical}}{\text{horizontal}} = \frac{500}{30} = 16.7 \text{ m/s}$$

Don't forget that you have to use the scales of the axes to work out the gradient. Don't measure in cm.

Miles (of revision) to go before I sleep...

You might have to draw graphs in an exam too, so have a peak at page 7 for a bit more on how to go about it.

Speed and Acceleration

Speed-time graphs allow you to calculate acceleration (which is how fast the speed is changing). Fun times.

Acceleration is How Quickly You're Speeding Up

1) Acceleration is how quickly the speed is changing.
2) You also accelerate when you change direction, with or without changing speed.
3) A decrease in speed is a deceleration — a negative acceleration.
4) The units of acceleration (or deceleration) are m/s^2.

The 'Δv' means 'change in speed'.

$$\text{Acceleration} = \frac{\text{Change in Speed}}{\text{Time Taken}}$$

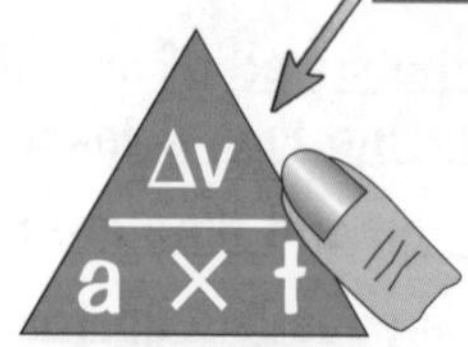

EXAMPLE: A skulking cat decelerates at $0.5\ m/s^2$ for 5.6 s until it reaches a speed of 2.5 m/s. Find its initial speed before it started to decelerate.

ANSWER: Find change in speed using the formula triangle: $\Delta v = a \times t = 0.5\ m/s^2 \times 5.6\ s = 2.8\ m/s$.
Because the cat decelerated, its initial speed must be 2.8 m/s MORE than its end speed.
So initial speed = 2.5 m/s + 2.8 m/s = 5.3 m/s.

Speed-Time Graphs

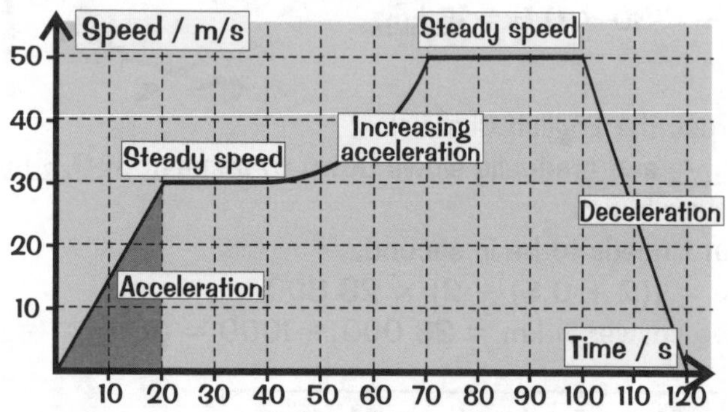

Very Important Notes:

1) GRADIENT = ACCELERATION.
2) Flat sections represent steady speed.
3) The steeper the gradient, the greater the acceleration or deceleration.
4) Uphill sections (/), +ve gradient, are acceleration.
5) Downhill sections (\), –ve gradient, are deceleration.
6) The area under any section of the graph is the distance travelled in that time interval.
7) A curve means non-uniform (changing) acceleration or deceleration.

Calculating Acceleration, Speed and Distance from a Speed-Time Graph

1) The acceleration in the first section of the graph = gradient = $\frac{\text{vertical}}{\text{horizontal}} = \frac{30}{20} = 1.5\ m/s^2$
2) The speed at any point is simply found by reading the value off the speed axis.
3) The distance travelled in any time interval is equal to the area under the graph. E.g. the distance travelled in the first acceleration period is equal to the shaded area = $\frac{1}{2} \times 20 \times 30 = 300$ m.

Speed is Just a Number, but Velocity Has Direction Too

1) The speed of an object is just how fast it's going — the direction isn't important. E.g. speed = 30 mph.
2) Velocity describes both the speed and direction of an object. E.g. velocity = 30 mph due north.
3) You can have negative velocities. If a car travelling at 20 m/s then turns around to go in the opposite direction, the speed is still 20 m/s but the velocity becomes –20 m/s.
4) If two objects are moving parallel to each other, their relative velocity is the difference in their velocities. E.g. two cars travelling at speeds of 30 m/s in opposite directions have a relative velocity of 60 m/s — because the difference between their velocities (30 and –30) is 60.

Speed-time graphs — more fun than gravel (just)...

The tricky thing about graphs is that they can look the same but show totally different things. Make sure you can calculate both speed and acceleration, as well as being able to rearrange the formulas to calculate other things.

Mass, Weight and Gravity

Gravity attracts everything with mass, but you only notice it when one of the masses is really really big, like a planet. The weight of something depends on its mass, and how much gravity there is pulling it down.

Gravity is the Force of Attraction Between All Masses

1) On the surface of a planet, gravity makes all things accelerate towards the ground, all with the same acceleration, g.
2) So g is the acceleration due to gravity and it's also known as the gravitational field strength.
3) The value of g is about 10 m/s^2 (or 10 N/kg) on Earth. It's different on other planets though, and can even vary slightly in different places on Earth (e.g. g will be slightly different down a mineshaft compared to on top of a mountain). It's not affected by changes in the atmosphere though.
4) Gravity gives an object its weight — which is different from its mass.
5) Mass is just the amount of 'stuff' in an object. For any given object this will have the same value anywhere in the Universe.

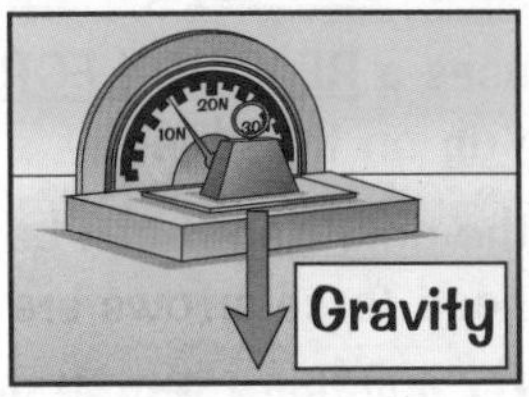

6) Weight is caused by the pull of gravity.
7) Weight is a force measured in newtons (N). Mass is not a force. It's measured in kilograms.
8) An object has the same mass whether it's on Earth or on the Moon — but its weight will be different. A 1 kg mass will weigh less on the Moon (about 1.6 N) than it does on Earth (about 10 N), simply because the force of gravity pulling on it is less (see below).

The Very Important Formula Relating Mass, Weight and Gravity

1) You need to know how to use this hideously easy formula:

weight = mass × gravitational field strength

$$W = m \times g$$

EXAMPLE: What is the weight, in newtons, of a 5 kg chicken, both on Earth ($g = 10$ m/s^2) and on the Moon ($g = 1.6$ m/s^2)?

ANSWER: $W = m \times g$
On Earth: Weight $= 5 \times 10 =$ 50 N
On the Moon: Weight $= 5 \times 1.6 =$ 8 N

2) You need to know how to rearrange it too:

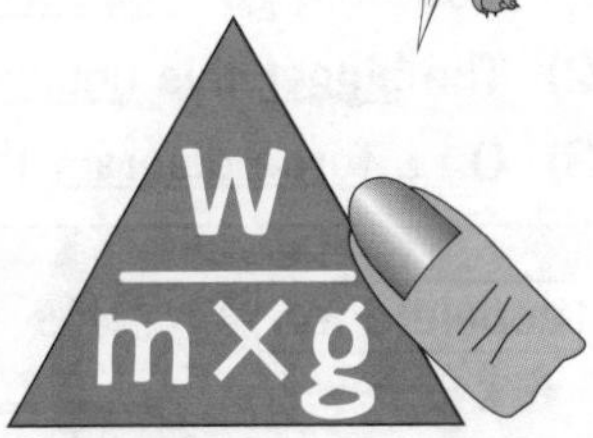

EXAMPLE: The 5 kg chicken has a weight of 20 N on a mystery planet. What is the gravitational field strength of the planet?

ANSWER: Using the formula triangle: $g = W \div m$
So gravitational field strength $= 20 \div 5 =$ 4 m/s^2
(Remember — g is a measure of acceleration, so the units are m/s^2. Or you can use N/kg.)

Learn about gravity now — no point in "weighting" around...

Often the only way to "understand" something is learn all the facts about it. And that's certainly true here. "Understanding" the difference between mass and weight is no more than learning all the facts about them. When you've learnt all those facts properly, you'll understand it. And make sure you can use that formula too.

Forces

A force is simply a push or a pull. There are only six different forces for you to know about:

1) GRAVITY or WEIGHT (see previous page) always acting straight downwards.
2) REACTION FORCE from a surface, usually acting straight upwards.
3) THRUST or PUSH or PULL due to an engine or rocket speeding something up.
4) DRAG or AIR RESISTANCE or FRICTION which is slowing the thing down.
5) LIFT due to an aeroplane wing.
6) TENSION in a rope or cable.

And there are basically only five different force diagrams:

1) Stationary Object — All Forces in Balance

1) The force of GRAVITY (or weight) is acting downwards.
2) This causes a REACTION FORCE from the surface pushing up on the object.
3) This is the only way it can be in BALANCE — balanced force arrows are equal in size.
4) Without a reaction force, it would accelerate downwards due to the pull of gravity.
5) Any HORIZONTAL forces must be equal and opposite otherwise the object will accelerate sideways.

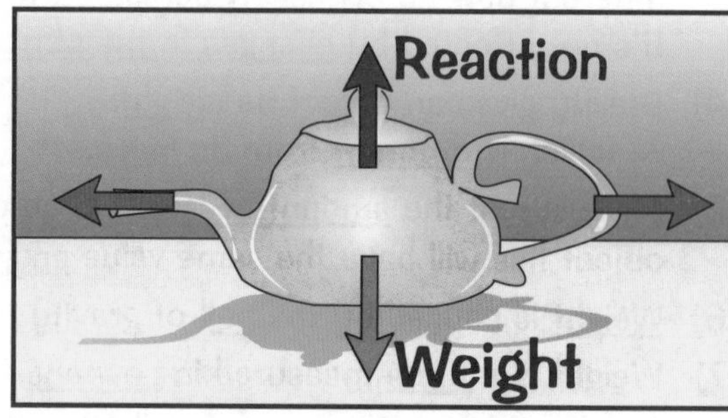

2) Steady Horizontal Speed — All Forces in Balance!

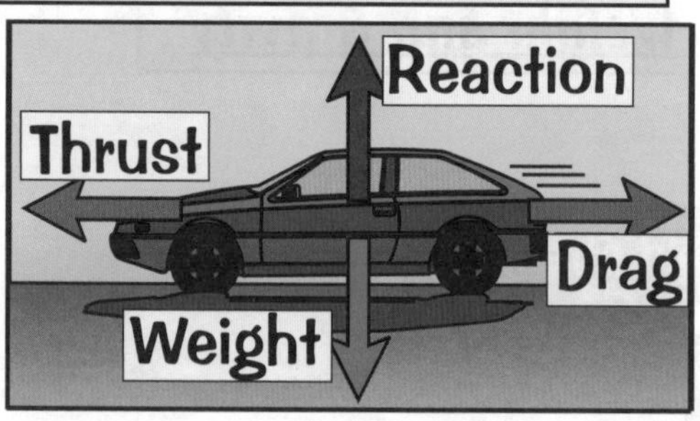

3) Steady Vertical Speed — All Forces in Balance!

This skydiver is free-falling at 'terminal speed' (see next page).

Take note — to move with a steady speed the forces must be in balance.
If there is an unbalanced force then you get acceleration, not steady speed. That's rrrreally important.

4) Horizontal Acceleration — Unbalanced Forces

5) Vertical Acceleration — Unbalanced Forces

1) You only get acceleration with an overall resultant (unbalanced) force.
2) The bigger this unbalanced force, the greater the acceleration.
3) On a force diagram the arrows will be unequal.

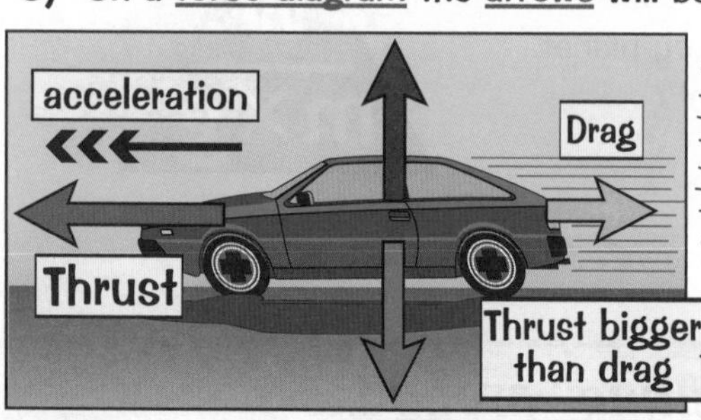

Note that the forces in the other direction (up and down) are still balanced (equal).

If drag was bigger than thrust you'd get deceleration.

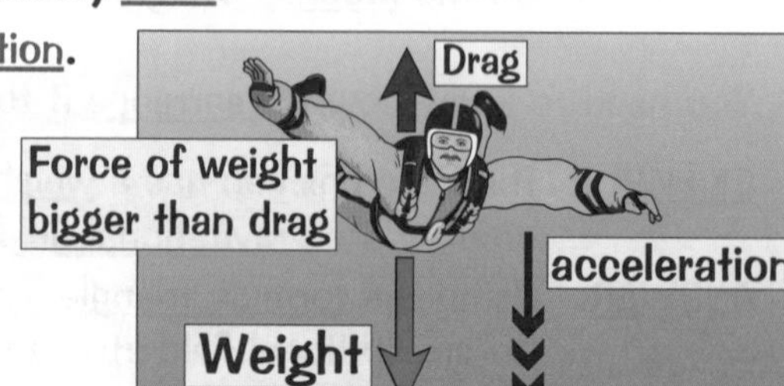

Just after dropping out of the plane, the skydiver accelerates — see next page.

Accelerate your learning — force yourself to revise...

So, things only accelerate in a particular direction if there's an overall force in that direction. Simple.

Friction Forces and Terminal Speed

Imagine a world without friction — you'd be sliding around all over the place. Weeeeeeeee.... Ouch.

Friction Will Slow Things Down

1) When an object is moving (or trying to move) friction acts in the direction that opposes movement.
2) The frictional force will match the size of the force trying to move it, up to a point — after this the friction will be less than the other force and the object will move.
3) Friction will act to make the moving object slow down and stop.
4) So to travel at a steady speed, things always need a driving force to overcome the friction.
5) Friction occurs in three main ways:

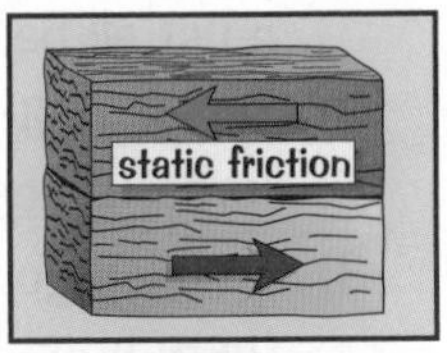

a) FRICTION BETWEEN SOLID SURFACES WHICH ARE GRIPPING (static friction)

b) FRICTION BETWEEN SOLID SURFACES WHICH ARE SLIDING PAST EACH OTHER

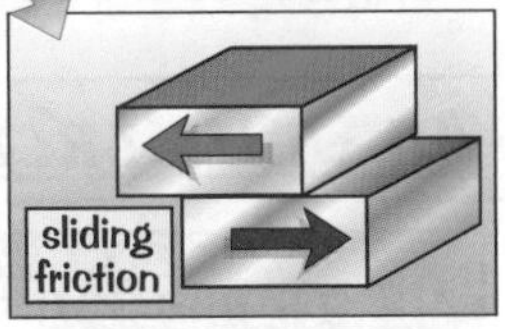

c) RESISTANCE OR "DRAG" FROM FLUIDS (LIQUIDS OR GASES, e.g. AIR)

The larger the area of the object, the greater the drag. So, to reduce drag, the area and shape should be streamlined and reduced, like wedge-shaped sports cars. Roof boxes on cars spoil this shape and so slow them down. Driving with the windows open also increases drag.

Something that's designed to reduce your speed, e.g. a parachute, often has a large area to give a high drag to slow you down. For a given thrust, the higher the drag, the lower the top speed (see below).

In a fluid: FRICTION (DRAG) ALWAYS INCREASES AS THE SPEED INCREASES — and don't forget it.

Moving Objects Can Reach a Terminal Speed

1) When objects first set off they have much more force accelerating them than resistance slowing them down.
2) As the speed increases, the resistance increases as well.
3) This gradually reduces the acceleration until the resistance force (friction or drag) is equal to the accelerating force (weight or thrust) so it can't accelerate any more. The forces are balanced.
4) It will have reached its maximum speed or terminal speed.

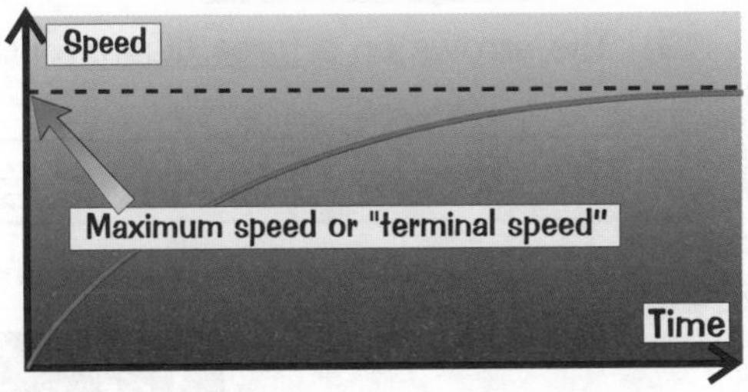

The Terminal Speed of Moving Objects Depends on Their Drag

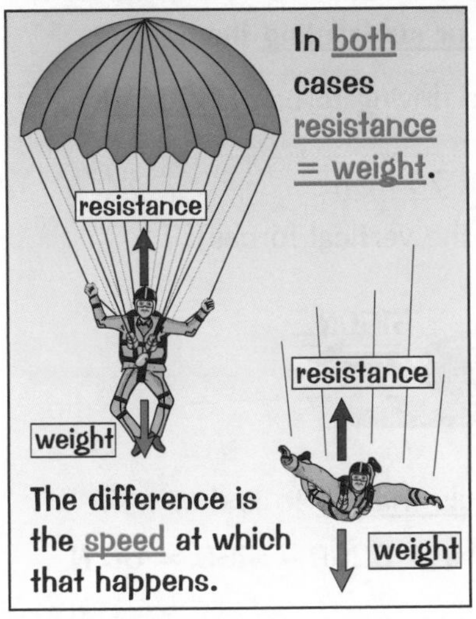

In both cases resistance = weight.
resistance
resistance
weight
weight
The difference is the speed at which that happens.

1) The terminal speed of any moving object depends on its drag compared to its driving force (weight for a falling object, thrust for, e.g. a car).
2) The greater the drag, the lower the terminal speed of the object, and the drag depends on its shape and area.
3) For example, think about a skydiver falling to Earth — the driving (accelerating) force acting on all falling objects is gravity and the drag (air resistance) depends on the skydiver's shape and area.
4) Without his parachute open, a skydiver's area is quite small. His terminal speed is about 120 mph.
5) But with the parachute open, there's much more air resistance (at any given speed) but the same force (his weight) pulling him down.
6) This means his terminal speed comes right down to about 15 mph, which is a safe speed to hit the ground at.

In space, where there's no air, everything falls at the same speed.

Air resistance — it can be a real drag...

Without friction, you wouldn't be able to walk or run or skip or write... hmm, not all bad then.

Forces and Acceleration

Things only accelerate or change direction if you give them a push. Makes sense.

A Balanced Force Means Steady Speed and Direction

If the forces on an object are all BALANCED, then it'll keep moving at the SAME SPEED in the SAME DIRECTION (so if it starts off still, it'll stay still).

1) When an object is moving at a constant speed, without changing direction, then the forces on it must all be balanced (arrows are equal).
2) Things definitely DON'T need a constant overall force to keep them moving — NO NO NO NO!
3) To keep going at a steady speed, there must be zero resultant (overall) force.

An Unbalanced Force Means Acceleration

If there is an UNBALANCED FORCE, the object will ACCELERATE in the direction of the force. The size of the acceleration is decided by: F = ma. This is NEWTON'S 2ND LAW OF MOTION.

1) An unbalanced force will always produce acceleration (or deceleration).
2) This 'acceleration' can take five different forms: starting, stopping, speeding up, slowing down and changing direction.
3) The arrows on a force diagram will be unequal:

The Overall Unbalanced Force is Often Called the Resultant Force

1) Any resultant force will produce acceleration and this is the formula for it:

Force = mass × acceleration

F is always the resultant force

2) In most real situations there are at least two forces acting on an object along any direction.
3) If the forces are parallel, the resultant force is found by just adding or subtracting them.

EXAMPLE: A car with a mass of 1750 kg has an engine which provides a driving force of 5200 N. At 70 mph the drag force acting on the car is 5150 N. Find its acceleration a) when first setting off from rest b) at 70 mph.

ANSWER: First draw a force diagram for both cases (no need to show the vertical forces):

Remember — force is measured in newtons (N).

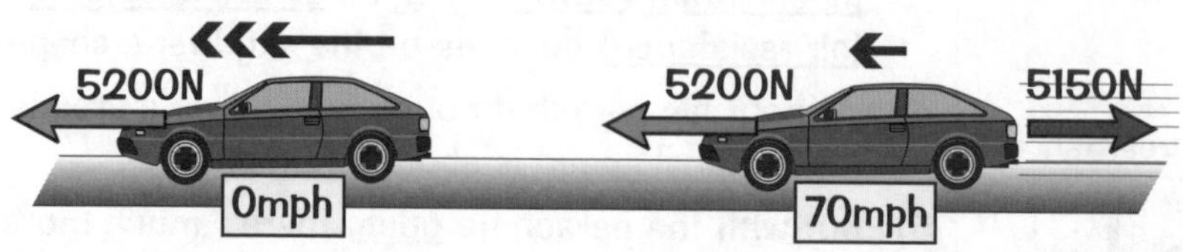

Work out the resultant force in each case, and use the formula triangle to find a.

a) Resultant force = 5200 N
$a = F \div m$
$= 5200 \div 1750 = 3.0\ m/s^2$

b) Resultant force = 5200 – 5150 = 50 N
$a = F \div m$
$= 50 \div 1750 = 0.03\ m/s^2$

Resultant force... I'm pretty sure that's a Steven Seagal film...

A 70 kg runner accelerates at $1.2\ m/s^2$. 8 N of drag are acting on the runner. Find the runner's driving force*.

* Answer on page 123.

Stopping Distances

The stopping distance of a car is the distance covered in the time between the driver first spotting a hazard and the car coming to a complete stop. Examiners are pretty keen on this stuff, so make sure you learn it.

Many Factors Affect Your Total Stopping Distance

The longer it takes to stop after spotting a hazard, the higher the risk of crashing into whatever's in front. The distance it takes to stop a car is divided into the THINKING DISTANCE and the BRAKING DISTANCE:

STOPPING DISTANCE = THINKING DISTANCE + BRAKING DISTANCE

1) Thinking Distance

"The distance the car travels in the time between the driver noticing the hazard and applying the brakes."

It's affected by TWO MAIN FACTORS:

a) **How FAST you're going** — obviously. Whatever your reaction time, the faster you're going, the further you'll go.

b) **How DOPEY you are** — This is affected by tiredness, drugs, alcohol, distractions, a lack of concentration and a careless blasé attitude.

2) Braking Distance

"The distance taken to stop once the brakes have been applied."

It's affected by FOUR MAIN FACTORS.
These are all to do with changes in speed, mass, braking force and friction:

a) **How FAST you're going** — The faster you're going, the further it takes to stop (see next page).

b) **How HEAVILY LOADED the vehicle is** — With the same brakes, the heavier the vehicle the longer it takes to stop. E.g. a car won't stop as quickly when it's full of people and luggage and towing a caravan.

c) **How good your BRAKES are** — Braking depends on how much force you apply — a little tap won't slow you down as much as if you put your foot down hard. Brakes must be checked and maintained regularly. If your brakes are worn or faulty you won't be able to brake with as much force, which will let you down catastrophically just when you need them the most, i.e. in an emergency.

d) **How good the GRIP is** — This depends on THREE THINGS:

1) Road surface — Leaves and diesel spills and muck on t'road are serious hazards.
2) Weather conditions — Wet or icy roads are always much more slippy than dry roads, but often you only discover this when you try to brake hard!
3) Tyres — By law, tyres should have a minimum tread depth of 1.6 mm. This is essential for getting rid of the water in wet conditions. A tyre without tread (i.e. a bald tyre) will simply ride on a layer of water and skid very easily. This is called 'aquaplaning' and isn't nearly as cool as it sounds.

Whatever the reason, if there's less friction between the car and the road then it takes longer to stop and the braking distance increases.

Bad visibility can also be a major factor in accidents — lashing rain, thick fog, bright oncoming lights, etc. might mean that a driver doesn't notice a hazard until they're quite close to it — so they have a much shorter distance available to stop in.

Stop right there — and learn this page...

Makes you think, doesn't it. Learn the details and write yourself a mini-essay to see how much you really know.

More on Stopping Distances

So now you know what affects stopping distances, let's have a look at the facts and figures.

Leave Enough Space to Stop

1) The figures below for typical stopping distances are from the Highway Code. It's frightening to see just how far it takes to stop when you're going at 70 mph.

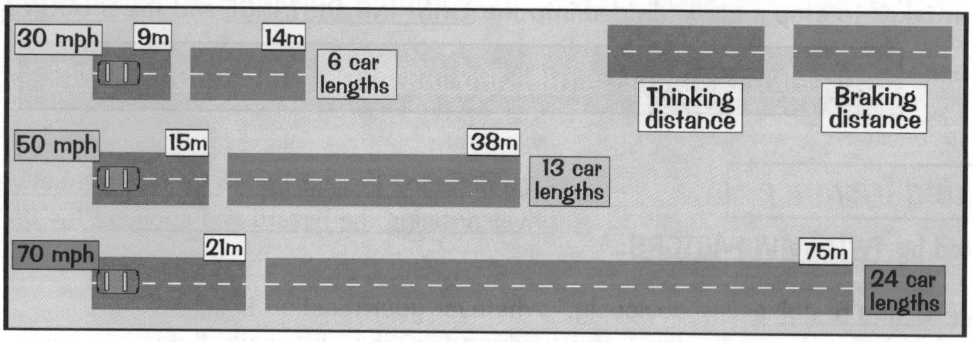

2) To avoid an accident, drivers need to leave enough space between their car and the one in front so that if they had to stop suddenly they would have time to do so safely. 'Enough space' means the stopping distance for whatever speed they're going at.
3) So even at 30 mph, you should drive no closer than 6 or 7 car lengths away from the car in front — just in case.
4) Speed limits are really important because speed affects the stopping distance so much — some residential areas are now 20 mph zones.

Don't forget — things like bad weather and road conditions will make stopping distances even longer (see previous page).

Speed Affects Braking Distance More Than Thinking Distance

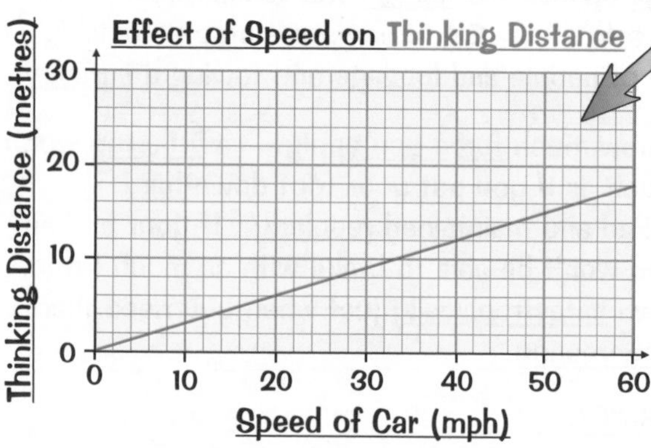

1) As a car speeds up, the thinking distance increases at the same rate as speed. The graph is linear (a straight line).
2) This is because the thinking time (how long it takes the driver to apply the brakes) stays pretty constant — but the higher the speed, the more distance you cover in that same time.

3) Braking distance, however, increases faster the more you speed up.
4) The relationship between speed and braking distance is a squared relationship.
5) This means as speed doubles, braking distance increases 4-fold (2^2). And if speed trebles, braking distance increases 9-fold (3^2). Why is explained on p. 64.

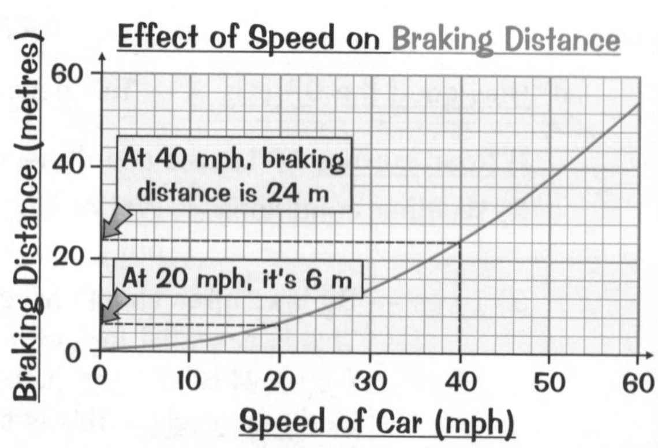

If you live life in the fast lane — leave plenty of space in front...

There's a little rhyme that goes: "Only a fool breaks the two second rule". It's a handy way of making sure you leave enough space when driving. When the car in front goes past a street light or a tree, count the seconds until you pass the same thing. If it's less than two seconds you're too close, so you need to ease up a bit. And if you're going faster than about 50 mph then you need to leave even more space. If only there was a little rhyme like that to help you pass your exams... Learning this page should do the trick though, so get a move on.

Momentum

A large rugby player running very fast is going to be a lot harder to stop than a scrawny one out for a Sunday afternoon stroll — that's momentum for you.

Momentum = Mass × Velocity

1) The greater the mass of an object and the greater its velocity, the more momentum the object has. They're linked by this equation:

Momentum (kg m/s) = Mass (kg) × Velocity (m/s)

$$\frac{\text{momentum}}{\text{mass} \times \text{velocity}}$$

EXAMPLE: A 65 kg kangaroo is moving in a straight line at 10 m/s. Calculate its momentum.

ANSWER: Momentum = mass × velocity = 65 × 10 = 650 kg m/s.

2) Momentum has size and direction — like velocity (but not speed).

Forces Cause Changes in Momentum

1) When a force acts on an object, it causes a change in momentum.

$$\text{Force acting (N)} = \frac{\text{Change in momentum (kg m/s)}}{\text{Time taken for change to happen (s)}}$$

$$\frac{\Delta M}{F \times t}$$

2) You can use Newton's 2nd Law of motion (force = mass × acceleration — see p. 58) to explain this:
   - Any force applied to an object increases its acceleration, $F = m \times a$.
   - And acceleration is just change in velocity over time, $a = \Delta v/t$ (see p. 54).
   - So a force applied to an object changes its velocity over time, $F = m \times \Delta v/t$.
   - A change in momentum can be caused by a change in velocity ($\Delta M = m \times \Delta v$), so any force applied to an object over a certain time causes a change in momentum, $F = \Delta M \div t$.

EXAMPLE: A rock with mass 1 kg is travelling through space at 15 m/s. A comet hits the rock, giving it a resultant force of 2500 N for 0.7 seconds. Calculate a) the rock's initial momentum, and b) the change in its momentum resulting from the impact.

ANSWER: a) Momentum = mass × velocity = 1 × 15 = 15 kg m/s
b) Using the formula triangle, Change of momentum = force × time = 2500 × 0.7 = 1750 kg m/s.

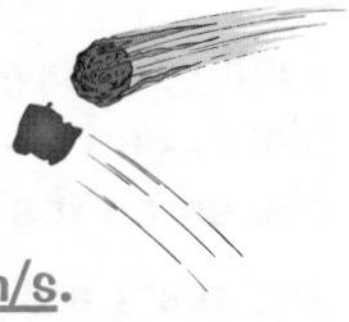

3) It's the amount of time taken for a change in momentum that determines how big or small the force is. If the change in momentum stays the same and t is small, F will be big, but if t is big, F will be small.
4) So if someone's momentum changes very quickly (like in a car crash), the forces on the body will be very large, and more likely to cause injury.
5) This is why cars are designed to slow people down over a longer time when they have a crash — the longer it takes for a change in momentum, the smaller the force, which reduces the injuries (see next page).

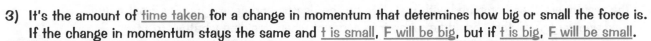

> You can also think of a car crash as being a very fast deceleration (just a negative acceleration, remember). Because F = ma, any large deceleration causes a large force, which can lead to injury.

Learn this stuff — it'll only take a moment... um...

Momentum's a pretty fundamental bit of Physics — so make sure you learn it properly. Momentum depends on mass and velocity, and a force can result in a change in momentum (because of Newton's 2nd Law of motion). Safety features on cars work by slowing down the change in momentum — there's more on this over the page.

Car Safety

Cars have many safety features that are designed to reduce the forces acting on people involved in an accident. Smaller forces can mean less severe injuries.

Car Safety Features Reduce the Forces Acting in Accidents

1) In a collision, the force on an object can be lowered by slowing the object down over a longer time. This is because the longer it takes for a change in momentum, the smaller the forces acting (see previous page). Some injuries are caused by a rapid deceleration of parts of the body. Increasing the collision time reduces deceleration too (because $a = \Delta v \div t$).
2) These safety features increase the collision time to reduce the forces and deceleration to try and reduce injury.
3) These safety features also change shape during a crash, which helps absorb some of the kinetic energy of the moving car.
4) They can also reduce injuries by stopping people hitting hard surfaces inside the car.

- CRUMPLE ZONES crumple and change shape on impact, increasing the time taken for the car to stop.
- SEAT BELTS stretch slightly, increasing the time taken for the wearer to stop. This reduces the forces acting on the chest. (They need to be replaced after a crash though — they're not as strong once they've been stretched.)
- AIR BAGS also slow you down more gradually.

5) Roads can also be made safer by placing structures like crash barriers and escape lanes in dangerous locations (like on sharp bends or steep hills). These structures are designed to increase the time and distance of any collision — which means the collision force is reduced.

ABS Brakes Help Drivers Take Control in an Emergency

1) ABS (anti-lock braking system) brakes help drivers keep control of the car's steering when braking hard.
2) When a driver brakes hard (e.g. to avoid a hazard), ordinary brakes lock the wheels so they can't turn, which can cause the car to skid.
3) ABS brakes automatically pump on and off to stop the wheels locking and preventing skidding.
4) They can also give the car a shorter braking distance which could prevent a collision with a car in front.

Safety Features Save Lives

1) Safety features are rigorously tested to see how effectively they save lives or stop injuries in an accident.
2) Testing involves crashing cars containing crash test dummies, both with and without the safety feature in place, and watching slow motion film footage to see the results. The dummies have sensors at different places on their 'bodies' to show where a real person would be injured, and how bad the injury would be.
3) The tests are repeated using different cars, at different speeds, and using different sized dummies.
4) The results are then compared with real data on the deaths and severe injuries from actual road accidents. All this should be taken into account when deciding whether to fit or use a particular safety feature (although seatbelts are required by law).
5) Crash tests have shown that wearing a seat belt reduces the number of fatalities (deaths) in car accidents by about 50% and that airbags reduce the number of fatalities by about 30% — so they're well worth using.
6) The Department for Transport produce reports each year on road traffic accidents in the UK. They show a significant reduction in the number of deaths and serious injuries since the 1980s — probably due to the wide range of safety features found in cars since then.

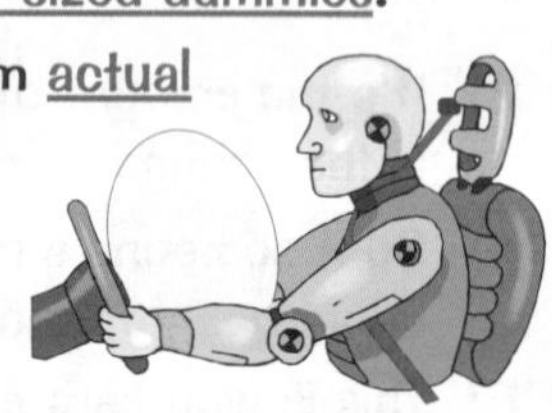

You might have to evaluate the effectiveness of different safety features. Think about the pros and cons and use any data you're given (see pages 6-8 for data analysis).

Belt up and start revising...

Back seat passengers who don't wear a seat belt will hit the front seat with a force of between 30 to 60 times their body's weight in an accident at 30 mph — this is like the force you'd feel if you were sat on by an elephant.

Work Done and Gravitational Potential Energy

Time to get some work done on... er... work done. You'll need to muster up some energy too.

Work is Done When a Force Moves an Object

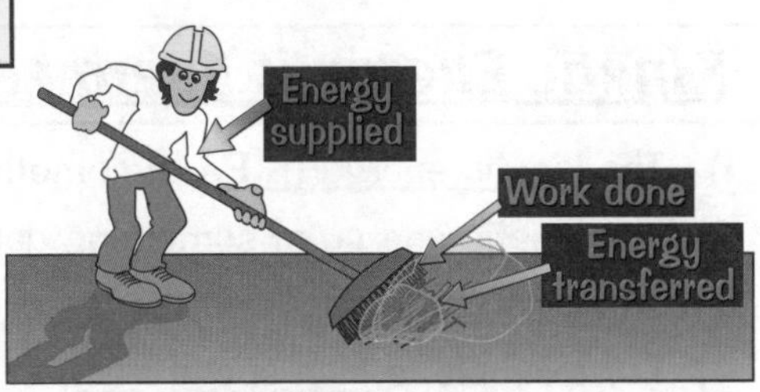

When a FORCE makes an object MOVE, ENERGY IS TRANSFERRED and WORK IS DONE.

1) Whenever something moves, something else is providing some sort of 'effort' to move it.
2) The thing putting the effort in needs a supply of energy (like fuel or food or electricity etc.).
3) It then does 'work' by moving the object — and transfers the energy it receives (as fuel) into other forms.
4) Whether this energy is transferred 'usefully' (e.g. by lifting a load) or is 'wasted' (e.g. lost as heat through friction), you can still say that 'work is done'. Just like Batman and Bruce Wayne, 'work done' and 'energy transferred' are indeed 'one and the same'. (And they're both given in joules.)
5) The formula to calculate the amount of work done is:

Work Done = Force × Distance

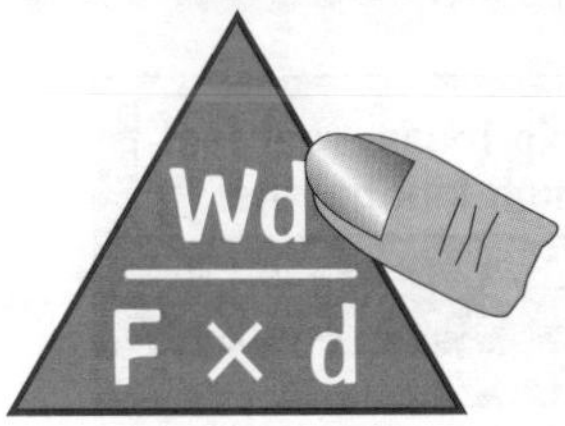

EXAMPLE: Some hooligan kids drag an old tractor tyre 5 m over rough ground. They pull with a total force of 340 N. a) Find the energy transferred dragging the tyre. b) How far could they pull the tyre using the same force but using 5100 J of energy?

ANSWER: a) Wd = F × d = 340 × 5 = 1700 J.
b) Using the formula triangle, d = Wd ÷ F,
so d = 5100 ÷ 340 = 15 m.

Gravitational Potential Energy is Energy Due to Height

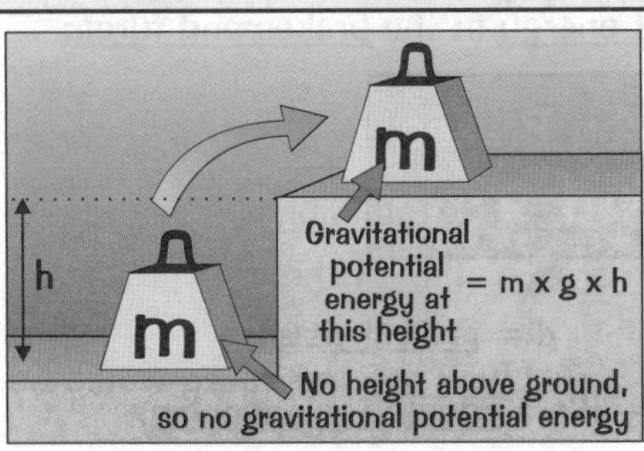

1) Gravitational potential energy (G.P.E.) is the energy that something has because of its height above the ground. The energy used to raise it is 'stored', and can be changed to kinetic energy if it falls.
2) For example, a lift has a lot more G.P.E. on the top floor than it does at lower floors, because it is higher above the ground.
3) There are other types of potential energy too — e.g. elastic and chemical. G.P.E. is all about height.
4) G.P.E. can be found using this formula: **G.P.E. = mass × g × height**

5) The g in the formula is gravitational field strength (see p. 55). On Earth, g is about 10 m/s^2 (or 10 N/kg).

EXAMPLE: A sheep of mass 47 kg is slowly raised through 6.3 m. Find its gain in gravitational potential energy.

ANSWER: Just plug the numbers into the formula:
G.P.E. = mgh = 47 × 10 × 6.3 = 2961 J.
(Joules because it's energy.)

Revise work done — what else...

Remember "energy transferred" and "work done" are the same thing. If you need a force to make something speed up (p. 58), all that means is that you need to give it a bit of energy. Makes sense.

Kinetic Energy

Anything that's moving has kinetic energy. There's a slightly tricky formula for it, so you have to concentrate a little bit harder for this one. But hey, that's life — it can be real tough sometimes.

Kinetic Energy is Energy of Movement

1) The kinetic energy (K.E.) of something is the energy it has when moving.
2) The kinetic energy of something depends on both its mass and speed.
3) The greater its mass and the faster it's going, the bigger its kinetic energy will be.
4) For example, a high-speed train, or a speedboat, will have lots of kinetic energy — but your gran doing the weekly shop on her little scooter will only have a little bit.
5) You need to know how to use the formula:

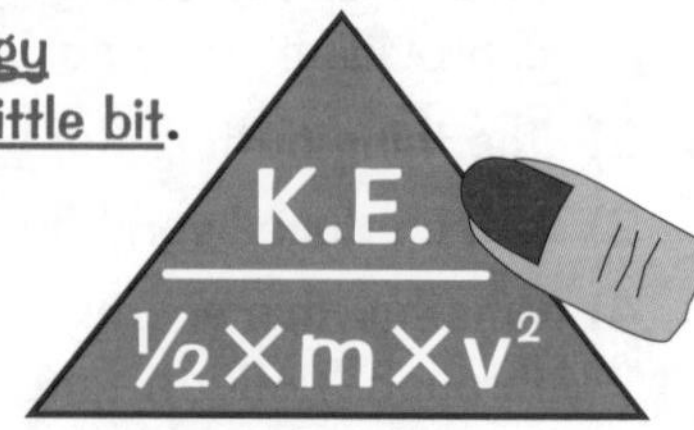

$$\text{Kinetic Energy} = \tfrac{1}{2} \times \text{mass} \times \text{speed}^2$$

EXAMPLE: A car of mass 1450 kg is travelling at 28 m/s. Calculate its kinetic energy.

ANSWER: It's pretty easy. You just plug the numbers into the formula — but watch the 'v^2'!
K.E. = $\frac{1}{2}mv^2 = \frac{1}{2} \times 1450 \times 28^2$ = 568 400 J. (Joules because it's energy.)

6) If you double the mass, the K.E. doubles. If you double the speed, though, the K.E. quadruples (increases by a factor of 4) — it's because of the 'v^2' in the formula.

Stopping Distances Increase Alarmingly with Extra Speed — Mainly Because of the v^2 Bit in the K.E. Formula

1) To stop a car, the kinetic energy, $\frac{1}{2}mv^2$, has to be converted to heat energy at the brakes and tyres:

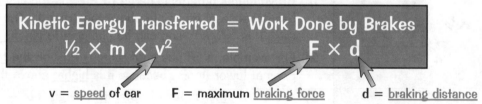

$$\text{Kinetic Energy Transferred} = \text{Work Done by Brakes}$$
$$\tfrac{1}{2} \times m \times v^2 = F \times d$$

v = speed of car   F = maximum braking force   d = braking distance

2) The braking distance (d) increases as speed squared (v^2) increases — it's a squared relationship.
3) This means if you double the speed, you double the value of v, but the v^2 means that the K.E. is then increased by a factor of four.
4) Because 'F' is always the maximum possible braking force (which can't be increased), d must increase by a factor of four to make the equation balance.
5) In other words, if you go twice as fast, the braking distance must increase by a factor of four to convert the extra K.E.
6) Increasing the speed by a factor of 3 increases the K.E. by a factor of 3^2 (= 9), so the braking distance becomes 9 times as long.
7) Doubling the mass of the object doubles the K.E. it has — which will double the braking distance. So a big heavy lorry will need more space to stop than a small car.

Look back at pages 59-60 for more on braking distances.

Kinetic energy — just get a move on and learn it, OK...

So that's why braking distance goes up so much with speed. Bet you've been dying to find that out — and now you know. What you probably don't know yet, though, is that rather lovely formula at the top of the page. I mean, gosh, it's got more than two letters in it. So I'd hurry up and get it learnt if I were you.

Falling Objects and Roller Coasters

What goes up must come down — and transfer its gravitational potential energy to kinetic energy on the way.

Falling Objects Convert G.P.E. into K.E.

1) When something falls, its gravitational potential energy (G.P.E) is converted into kinetic energy (K.E.).
2) So the further it falls, the faster it goes.
3) You just need to remember this simple and really quite obvious formula:

Kinetic Energy gained = Gravitational Potential Energy lost

$$\frac{1}{2}mv^2 = mgh$$

EXAMPLE: A sheep of mass 52 kg falls from the top of a building 30 m high. Find the speed it hits the ground at (ignoring air resistance).

ANSWER: $\frac{1}{2}mv^2 = mgh$, so $\frac{1}{2} \times 52 \times v^2 = 52 \times 10 \times 30$
$26v^2 = 15\,600$, so $v^2 = 15\,600 \div 26 = 600$,
so $v = \sqrt{600} = 24.5$ m/s.

Remember g is about 10 m/s^2.

4) When a falling object reaches terminal speed (see p. 57) its speed can't increase anymore, so its K.E. doesn't increase. Instead, the G.P.E. is transferred to internal energy of the object, or it's used heating up the air particles through friction — so it's turned into thermal energy. (This can happen even if it's not at terminal speed, but you're usually told to ignore air resistance in the exam question — so always use the formula above).
5) The formula can be rearranged to give: $h = v^2 \div 2g$ which will work for most things falling to Earth. As long as the mass of the object doesn't change while it's falling, the 'm' on both sides of the equation will cancel out, leaving you with $\frac{1}{2}v^2 = gh$. Then divide both sides by g to get $h = v^2 \div 2g$.
6) This version can be used to easily find the height something needs to fall from to reach a certain speed, e.g. when designing a roller coaster (see below).

Roller Coasters Transfer Energy

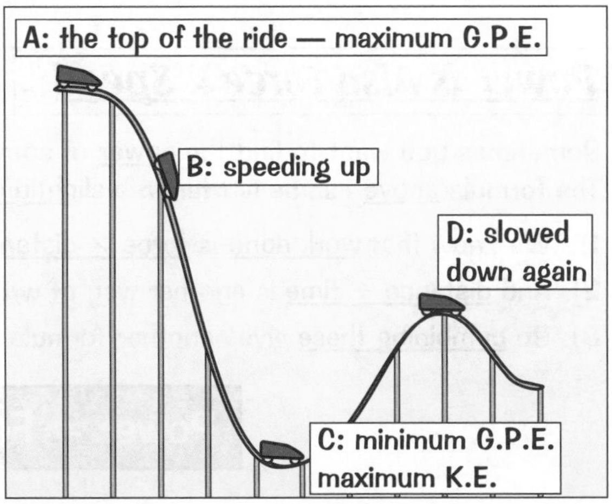

1) At the top of a roller coaster (position A) the carriage has lots of gravitational potential energy.
2) As the carriage descends to position B, G.P.E. is transferred to kinetic energy and the carriage speeds up.
3) Between positions B and C the carriage keeps accelerating as its G.P.E. is converted into K.E.
4) If you ignore any air resistance or friction between the carriage and the track, then the carriage will have as much energy at C as it did at A. That energy must have been converted from G.P.E. to K.E. So at C the carriage has minimum G.P.E. and maximum K.E.
5) In a real roller coaster (that does have friction to deal with), the carriage has to have enough kinetic energy at point C to carry it up the hill again to D.

Life is a roller coaster — just gotta ride it...

Now then, who said physics couldn't be fun? This has been a pretty adrenaline-fuelled section so far — I hope you're enjoying the ride. Even if you're not, you still need to know all this stuff for the exam, so get learning.

Power

Whenever I think of '<u>power</u>', I have to stop myself saying things like 'mua haa haaarrr' and furtively plotting world domination whilst stroking a cat. It's hard being an evil genius (sigh).

Power is the 'Rate of Doing Work' — i.e. How Much per Second

<u>POWER</u> is <u>not</u> the same thing as <u>force</u>, nor <u>energy</u>. Power is a measure of <u>how quickly work</u> is being <u>done</u>.

A <u>powerful</u> machine is not necessarily one which can exert a strong <u>force</u> (though it usually ends up that way).

A <u>POWERFUL</u> machine is one which transfers <u>A LOT OF ENERGY IN A SHORT SPACE OF TIME</u>.

This is the <u>very easy formula</u> for power:

You might need to be able to answer questions where you have to calculate the <u>work done</u> <u>first</u>, so make sure you know how — see page 63.

$$\text{Power} = \frac{\text{Work done}}{\text{Time taken}}$$

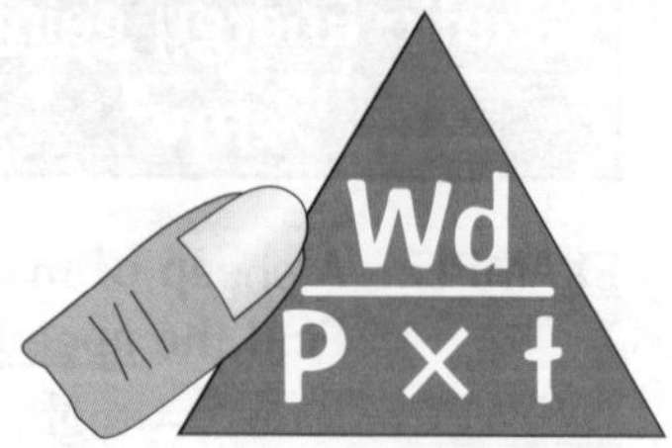

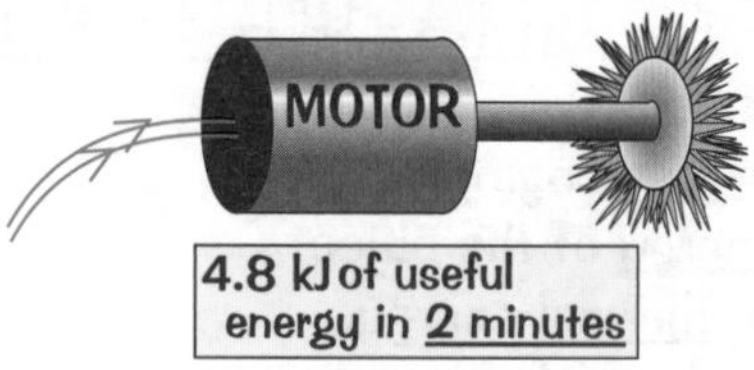

<u>EXAMPLE</u>: A motor transfers <u>4.8 kJ</u> of useful energy in <u>2 minutes</u>. Find:
a) its <u>power</u> output, and b) how much <u>work</u> it could do in an <u>hour</u>.

<u>ANSWER</u>: a) 4.8 kJ = 4800 J, and 2 mins = 120 s. So
P = Wd / t = 4800/120 = <u>40 W</u> (or 40 J/s — see below).
b) Using the formula triangle, Wd = P × t
P is 40 W (from a) and t = 1 h = 3600 s, so
Wd = 40 × 3600 = <u>144 000 J</u>.

Power is Measured in Watts (or J/s)

The proper unit of power is the <u>watt</u> (<u>W</u>). <u>1 W = 1 J of energy transferred per second</u>.
<u>Power</u> means 'how much energy <u>per second</u>', so <u>watts</u> are the same as '<u>joules per second</u>' (J/s).

Don't ever say 'watts per second' — it's <u>nonsense</u>.

Power is Also Force × Speed

Sometimes you want to find the <u>power</u> of something based on <u>force</u> and <u>speed</u>.
The formula <u>above</u> can be written in a <u>slightly different way</u> to allow for this:

1) We know that <u>work done</u> is <u>force × distance moved</u> (see p. 63).
2) And <u>distance ÷ time</u> is another way of writing <u>speed</u> (see p. 53).
3) So <u>combining these</u> gives another formula for <u>power</u>:

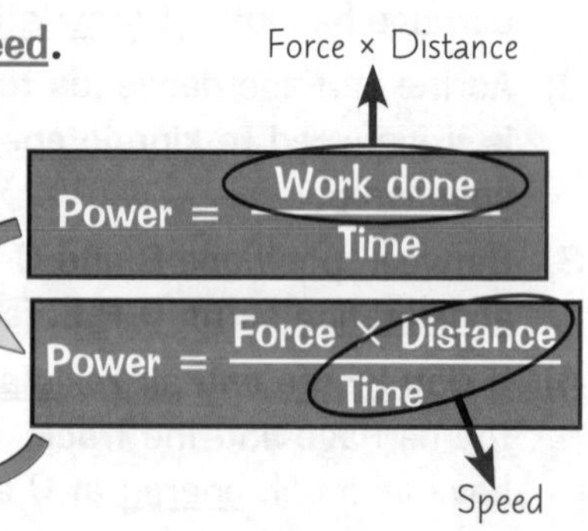

$$\text{Power} = \text{Force} \times \text{Speed}$$

<u>EXAMPLE</u>: A car's engine exerts a driving force of <u>1900 N</u> when travelling at a speed of <u>25 m/s</u>. Find its <u>power</u> output.

<u>ANSWER</u>: Power = Force × Speed = 1900 × 25 = <u>47 500 W</u> (= <u>47.5 kW</u>).

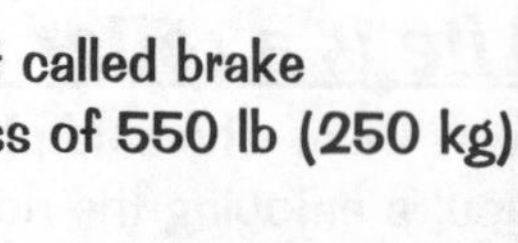

Watt are you waiting for — revise this stuff now...

The power of a car isn't always measured in watts — sometimes you'll see it in a funny unit called brake horsepower. James Watt defined 1 horsepower as the work done when a horse raises a mass of 550 lb (250 kg) through a height of 1 ft (0.3 m) in 1 second... as you do. I'd stick to <u>watts</u> if I were you.

Fuel Consumption and Emissions

A lot of us use cars to get us around and about, and lorries transport stuff around the country — but these forms of transport would be pretty useless if they didn't have any fuel to get them moving...

Fuel Consumption is All About the Amount of Fuel Used

1) The size and design of car engines determine how powerful they are.
2) The larger or more powerful an engine, the more energy it transfers from its fuel every second, so (usually) the higher the fuel consumption.
3) The fuel consumption of a car is usually stated as the distance travelled using a certain amount of fuel. Fuel consumption is often given in miles per gallon (mpg) or litres per 100 km (l/100 km) — e.g. a car with a fuel consumption of 5 l/100 km will travel 100 km on 5 litres of fuel.
4) Cars that use a lot of fuel compared to other cars are more expensive to run, because fuel costs money.
5) They're also more damaging to the environment, because fossil fuels pollute — see below and next page.
6) You might have to interpret data on fuel consumption — watch out for the units. A car with a low value for 'l/100 km' has a low fuel consumption — it doesn't need much fuel to travel 100 km. But a car with a low value for 'mpg' has a high fuel consumption — it means it won't travel very far on a gallon of fuel.

Different Things Can Affect Fuel Consumption

1) A car's fuel consumption depends on many different things — e.g. the size of the engine, how the car is driven, the mass of the car, the speed it's driven at, the road conditions etc.
2) To move a car, the energy from the fuel needs to be changed into kinetic energy (K.E.). Since K.E. = $\frac{1}{2}mv^2$ (see p. 64), the higher the mass of the car (m) or the higher the speed you want it to go (v), the higher the K.E. will be — and so the more energy you need from fuel to give it that K.E.
3) So, in general, heavy cars have a higher fuel consumption than lighter cars, and the faster you drive the car the greater the fuel consumption too.
4) Cars work more efficiently at some speeds compared to others though — the most efficient speed is usually between 40 and 55 mph.
5) Driving style will also affect the fuel consumption — faster accelerations need more energy and so use more fuel. Frequent braking and acceleration (e.g. when driving in a town) will increase the fuel consumption. Driving in different road conditions can affect how much you need to brake too.
6) The energy from the fuel is also needed to do work against friction — e.g. between the tyres and the road, and between the car itself and the air around it. So, things like opening the windows or having a roof box will increase a car's fuel consumption because it increases air resistance and drag (see p. 57).
7) Cars are now designed to be more fuel efficient — e.g. more efficient engines, more streamlined.

When Cars Burn Fuel they Release Emissions

1) As fossil fuels are burnt they release emissions — gases like CO_2, nitrogen dioxide (NO_2) and water vapour.
2) These emissions can cause environmental problems like acid rain and global warming.
3) In general, the higher the fuel consumption, the greater the emissions, and the worse for the environment.
4) But car manufacturers are changing the design of car engines to try and reduce emissions. Older cars often have worse fuel consumption and/or emission figures.
5) If you have to interpret data on emissions make sure you carefully read all the data given and check the units (there are lots of different ones that could be used, e.g. grams per unit distance like g/mile or g/km).

I bet this page has fuelled your enthusiasm...

You might get asked how to reduce the fuel consumption of a car, so it's important that you remember the different things that can affect fuel consumption — e.g. speed, friction, mass, driving style and conditions etc.

Fuels for Cars

We can't keep filling our fuel tanks with petrol and diesel forever.
Not only are they running out fast, but they're also bad for the environment. Eeep!

Most Cars Run on Fossil Fuels

1) All vehicles need a fuel to make them move — e.g. most cars and lorries use petrol or diesel.
2) Petrol and diesel are fuels that are made from oil, which is a fossil fuel. The emissions released when these fuels are burnt can cause environmental problems like acid rain and climate change.
3) Climate change is linked to an increase in greenhouse gases, such as carbon dioxide (CO_2), in the atmosphere. Fossil fuels produce a lot of carbon dioxide when they're burnt.
4) Fossil fuels are also non-renewable, so one day they'll run out — not good news if your car runs on them.
5) In the future we may have to rely on renewable sources of energy such as biofuels or solar power to power our vehicles (see below).

You learnt about this in P2 — see p. 39.

Some Cars Run On Biofuels

1) To get around some of the problems with petrol and diesel fuels, scientists are developing engines that run on alternative types of fuel, such as biofuels.
2) Biofuels are made from plants and organic waste, and are renewable — they won't run out because we can keep growing more.
3) Like fossil fuels, biofuels give off carbon dioxide when they're burnt. BUT because plants (grown to make the biofuel) also take in CO_2 when they're growing there is no overall increase in the amount of CO_2 in the atmosphere when the biofuels are burnt. So if we switch from fossil fuels to biofuels, the overall CO_2 emissions could be reduced.
4) Burning biofuels when driving the cars doesn't produce as much other pollution (pollution at the point of use) as burning fossil fuels either.
5) BUT the cars themselves still have to be produced though and pollution is created in their production.

Electric Cars Need To Be Recharged

1) A few vehicles use large batteries to power electric motors.
2) These vehicles don't release any pollution at the point of use when they're driven, but their batteries need to be charged using electricity.
3) This electricity is likely to come from power stations that do pollute though — most power stations currently just burn fossil fuels to produce electricity.
4) One way around this is to use solar power — vehicles can have solar panels which change the energy from the sun into electricity to power the motor.
5) Solar-powered vehicles produce no pollution at the point of use, and there's also no pollution from making the electricity in this way. So solar panels could reduce overall CO_2 emissions from vehicles.
6) But electric cars and solar panels are expensive to make and buy, and pollution is created during their production too.
7) Currently, electric cars have limited performance compared to ordinary fossil fuel cars. But that is changing — newer, better designs are coming out all the time.

Make sure you can describe arguments for and against electrically-powered cars.

"I pity the fuel" — Mr T, campaigner for electric vehicles...

Almost done for another section — just one lovely little page of questions to go. Make sure you learn this page first though. You need to know about the ways we can power our cars without fossil fuels — biofuels, batteries and solar panels — and how they can reduce pollution. Of course, the humble bicycle is always an option too...

Revision Summary for Module P3

Well done, you've made it to the end of this section. There are loads of bits and bobs about forces, motion and fast cars which you definitely have to learn — and the best way to find out what you know is to get stuck in to these lovely revision questions, which you're going to really enjoy (honest)...

1)* A partly chewed mouse starting from rest reaches a speed of 0.08 m/s in 35 seconds. How far does it travel in that time?

2) Explain how to calculate speed from a distance-time graph.

3)* What's the acceleration of a soggy pea flicked from rest to a speed of 14 m/s in 0.4 seconds?

4) Explain how to find speed, distance and acceleration from a speed-time graph.

5) Explain the difference between mass and weight. What's the formula for weight?

6) Draw and label a diagram to show the forces acting on a stationary owl sat on a (stationary) rock.

7) Describe the effect on the top speed of a car of adding a roof box. Explain your answer.

8) Describe how air resistance is affected by speed.

9) What is "terminal speed"? What two main factors affect the amount of drag on a falling object?

10) If an object has zero resultant force on it, can it be moving? Can it be accelerating?

11)* A force of 30 N pushes a trolley of mass 4 kg. What will be its acceleration?

12) What are the two different parts of the overall stopping distance of a car?

13) List all the factors which affect each of the two parts of the stopping distance.

14) How does thinking distance change as speed increases?

15) If speed doubles, what happens to the braking distance?

16)* A 6 kg ferret has a momentum of 45 kg m/s. What is its velocity?

17)* The same ferret is hit by a speeding vole with a force of 70 N for 0.5 s. Calculate the ferret's change in momentum.

18) Explain how seat belts, crumple zones and air bags are useful in a crash.

19) How do ABS brakes make driving safer?

20)* A crazy dog drags a big branch 12 m over the next-door neighbour's front lawn, pulling with a force of 535 N. How much work was done?

21)* Calculate the increase in gravitational potential energy when a box of mass 12 kg is raised by 4.5 m. ($g = 10$ N/kg.)

22)* Find the kinetic energy of a 78 kg sheep moving at 23 m/s.

23) How does the kinetic energy formula explain the effect of speed on the stopping distance of a car?

24)* At the top of a roller coaster ride a carriage has 150 kJ of G.P.E. Ignoring friction, how much K.E. will the carriage have at the bottom (where G.P.E. = 0)?

25)* Calculate the speed of a 78 kg sheep just as it hits the floor after falling 20 m. Ignore air resistance.

26)* An electric motor uses 540 kJ of electrical energy in 4.5 minutes. What is its power consumption?

27)* Calculate the power output of a sheep running at 20 m/s exerting a force of 500 N.

28) Describe the relationship between the power of a car's engine and its fuel consumption.

29) Give three factors that affect the fuel consumption of a car.

30) Electric vehicles don't give out polluting gases directly, but they still cause pollution. Explain why.

* Answers on pages 123-124.

Static Electricity

Static electricity is all about charges which are NOT free to move. This causes them to build up in one place, and it often ends with a spark or a shock when they do finally move.

1) Build-up of Static is Caused by Friction

1) Electrons have a negative charge.
2) When two insulating materials are rubbed together, electrons will be scraped off one and dumped on the other.
3) This leaves a positive static charge on one due to a lack of electrons — it lost electrons (–), so this leaves it positively (+) charged.
4) And it leaves a negative static charge on the other due to an excess of electrons — it gained electrons (–).
5) Which way the electrons are transferred depends on the two materials involved.
6) Electrically charged objects attract small neutral objects placed near them. (Try this: rub a balloon on a woolly pullover — then put it near tiddly bits of paper and watch them jump.)
7) The classic examples are polythene and acetate rods being rubbed with a cloth duster, as shown in the diagrams.

With the polythene rod, electrons move from the duster to the rod.

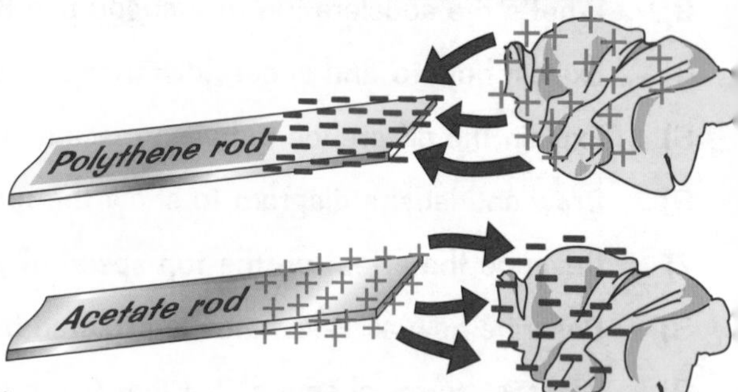

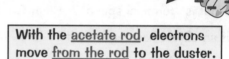

With the acetate rod, electrons move from the rod to the duster.

2) Only Electrons Move — Never the Positive Charges

1) Watch out for this in exams. Both +ve and –ve electrostatic charges are only ever produced by the movement of electrons.
2) The positive charges definitely do not move. A positive static charge is always caused by electrons moving away elsewhere, as shown above. Don't forget!
3) If enough static charge builds up, it can suddenly move which can cause sparks or shocks that can be dangerous (see next page).
4) A charged conductor can be discharged safely by connecting it to earth with a metal strap. This is called earthing (see next page).
5) The electrons flow down the strap to the ground if the charge is negative and flow up the strap from the ground if the charge is positive.

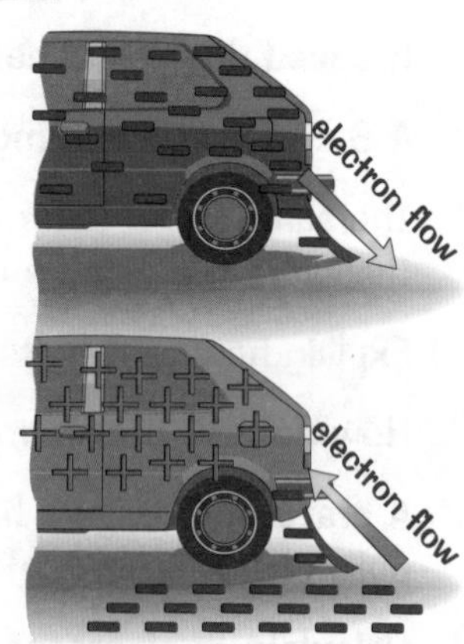

3) Like Charges Repel, Opposite Charges Attract

Hopefully this is kind of obvious.

1) Two things with opposite electric charges are attracted to each other.
2) Two things with the same electric charge will repel each other.
3) These forces get weaker the further apart the two things are.
4) Atoms or molecules that become charged are known as ions.

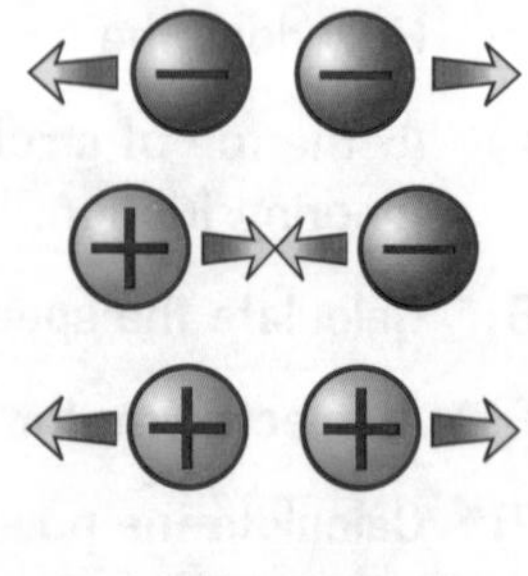

Come on, be +ve — this module's more interesting than the last one...

Static electricity's great fun. You must have tried it — rubbing a balloon against your clothes and trying to get it to stick to the ceiling. It really works... well, sometimes. And it's all due to the build-up of static. Bad hair days are also caused by static — it builds up on your hair, so your strands of hair repel each other. Conditioners try to decrease this, but they don't always work — so not as much fun as the jumper trick...

More on Static Electricity

They like asking you to give quite detailed examples in exams. Make sure you learn all these details.

Static Electricity Being a Nuisance:

1) Attracting Dust

Dust particles are charged and will be attracted to anything with the opposite charge. Unfortunately, many objects around the house are made out of insulators (e.g. TV screen, wood, plastic containers etc.) that get easily charged and attract the dust particles — this makes cleaning a nightmare.

2) Clothing Clings and Crackles

When synthetic clothes are dragged over each other (like in a tumble drier) or over your head, electrons get scraped off, leaving static charges on both parts, and that leads to the inevitable — attraction (they stick together and cling to you) and little sparks or shocks as the charges rearrange themselves.

3) Shocks From Door Handles

If you walk on a nylon carpet wearing shoes with insulating soles, charge builds up on your body. Then if you touch a metal door handle or water pipe, the charge flows via the conductor and you get a little shock.

Static Electricity Can be Dangerous:

1) A Lot of Charge Can Build Up on Clothes

1) A large amount of static charge can build up on clothes made out of synthetic materials if they rub against other synthetic fabrics (see above).
2) Eventually, this charge can become large enough to make a spark — which is really bad news if it happens near any inflammable gases or fuel fumes... KABOOM!

2) Grain Chutes, Paper Rollers and the Fuel Filling Nightmare

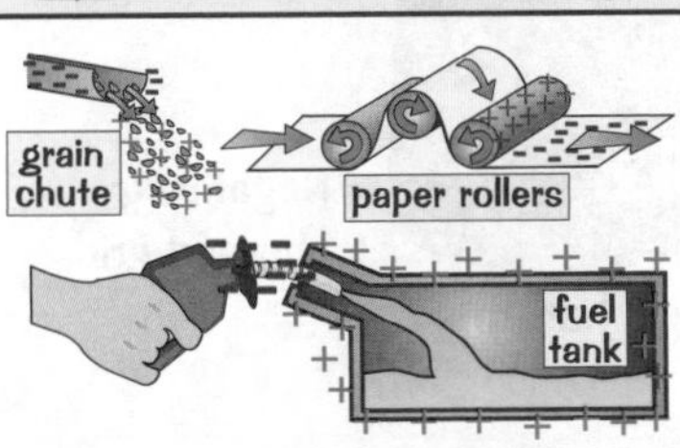

1) As fuel flows out of a filler pipe, or paper drags over rollers, or grain shoots out of pipes, then static can build up.
2) This can easily lead to a spark and might cause an explosion in dusty or fumey places — like when filling up a car with fuel at a petrol station.
3) All these problems with sparks can be solved by earthing charged objects.

Objects Can be Earthed or Insulated to Prevent Sparks

1) Dangerous sparks can be prevented by connecting a charged object to the ground using a conductor (e.g. a copper wire) — this is called earthing and it provides an easy route for the static charges to travel into the ground. This means no charge can build up to give you a shock or make a spark.
2) Static charges are a big problem in places where sparks could ignite inflammable gases, or where there are high concentrations of oxygen (e.g. in a hospital operating theatre).
3) Fuel tankers must be earthed to prevent any sparks that might cause the fuel to explode — refuelling aircraft are bonded to their fuel tankers using an earthing cable to prevent sparks.
4) Anti-static sprays and liquids work by making the surface of a charged object conductive — this provides an easy path for the charges to move away and not cause a problem.
5) Anti-static cloths are conductive, so they can carry charge away from objects they're used to wipe.
6) Insulating mats and shoes with insulating soles prevent static electricity from moving through them, so they stop you from getting a shock.

Static electricity — it's really shocking stuff...

Lightning is an extreme case of a static electricity spark. It always chooses the easiest path between the sky and the ground — that's the nearest, tallest thing. That's why it's never a good idea to fly a kite in a thunderstorm...

Uses of Static Electricity

Static electricity isn't always a nuisance. It's got loads of applications in medicine and industry, and now's your chance to learn all about them, you lucky thing...

1) Paint Sprayers — Getting an Even Coat

The spray gun can be charged either positive or negative. You've just got to remember to charge the object you're painting the opposite charge.

1) Bikes and cars are painted using electrostatic paint sprayers.
2) The spray gun is charged, which charges up the small drops of paint.
3) Each paint drop repels all the others, since they've all got the same charge, so you get a very fine spray.

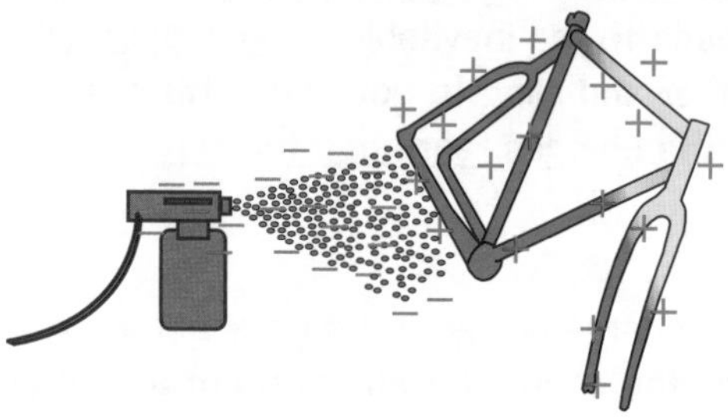

4) The object to be painted is given an opposite charge to the gun. This attracts the fine spray of paint.
5) This method gives an even coat and hardly any paint is wasted. Parts of the bicycle or car pointing away from the spray gun still receive paint too — there are no paint shadows.
6) In the diagram, the paint is negatively charged so it's gained electrons, and the bike is positively charged so it's lost electrons.

2) Dust Precipitators — Cleaning Up Emissions

Factories and power stations produce loads of smoke, which is made up of tiny particles. Fortunately, the smoke can be removed with a precipitator — here's a very simple one:

1) As smoke particles reach the bottom of the chimney, they meet a wire grid or rods with a high voltage and negative charge.
2) The dust particles gain electrons and become negatively charged.
3) The dust particles then induce a charge on the earthed metal plates (the negatively charged dust particles repel electrons on the plates, so that the plates become positively charged).
4) The dust particles are attracted to the metal plates, where they stick together to form larger particles.
5) When heavy enough, the particles fall off the plates or are knocked off by a hammer.
6) The dust falls to the bottom of the chimney and can be removed.
7) So the gases coming out of the chimney have very few smoke particles in them.

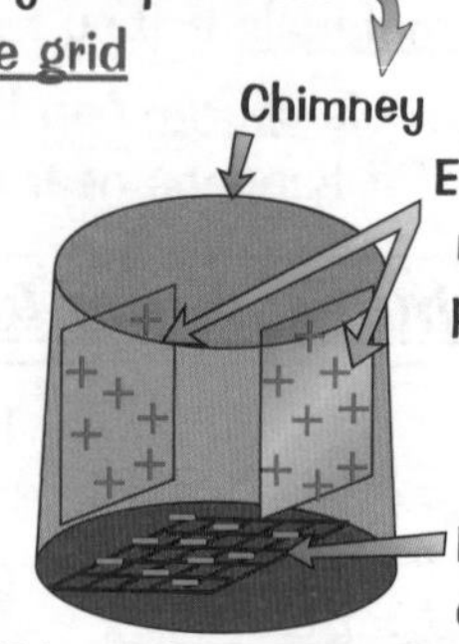

3) Defibrillators — Restarting a Heart

1) The beating of your heart is controlled by tiny little electrical pulses inside your body. So an electric shock to a stopped heart can make it start beating again.
2) Hospitals and ambulances have machines called defibrillators which can be used to shock a stopped heart back into operation.
3) The defibrillator consists of two paddles connected to a power supply.
4) The paddles of the defibrillator are placed firmly on the patient's chest to get a good electrical contact and then the defibrillator is charged up.
5) Everyone moves away from the patient except for the defibrillator operator who holds insulated handles — so only the patient gets a shock.
6) The charge passes through the paddles to the patient to make the heart contract.

If this doesn't get your heart going — nothing will...

You can get your very own special defibrillator now. One to carry around in your handbag, just in case. No, really, you can (okay, maybe it wouldn't fit in your handbag unless you're Mary Poppins, but it's still handy).

Charge in Circuits

If you've got a complete loop (a circuit) of conducting stuff (e.g. metal) connected to an electric power source (like a battery), electricity flows round it. Isn't electricity great.

Charge Flows Around a Circuit

1) **CURRENT** is the flow of electrical charge around a circuit — basically the flow of electrons. It's measured in amps, A. More charge passes around a circuit when a higher current flows. Current will only flow through a component if there is a voltage across that component (unless the component is a superconductor).

2) **VOLTAGE** is the driving force that pushes the current round — kind of like "electrical pressure". Voltage is measured in volts, V.

3) **RESISTANCE** is anything in the circuit which slows the flow down. Resistance is measured in ohms, Ω.

4) **THERE'S A BALANCE:** the voltage is trying to push the current round the circuit, and the resistance is opposing it — the relative sizes of the voltage and resistance decide how big the current will be:

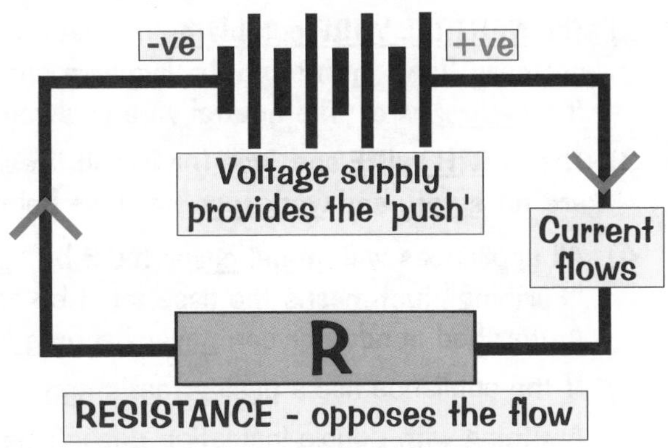

If you increase the VOLTAGE — then MORE CURRENT will flow.
If you increase the RESISTANCE — then LESS CURRENT will flow
(or MORE VOLTAGE will be needed to keep the SAME CURRENT flowing).

It's Just Like the Flow of Water Around a Set of Pipes

1) The current is simply like the flow of water.
2) The voltage is like the force provided by a pump which pushes the stuff round.
3) Resistance is any sort of constriction in the flow, which is what the pressure has to work against.
4) If you turn up the pump and provide more force (or "voltage"), the flow will increase.
5) If you put in more constrictions ("resistance"), the flow (current) will decrease.

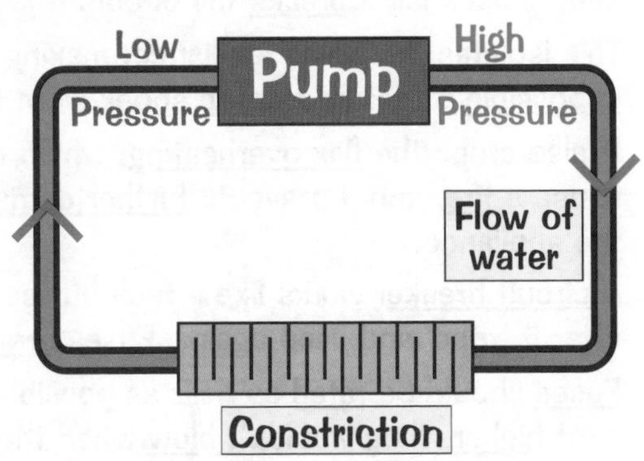

If You Break the Circuit, the Current Stops Flowing

1) Current only flows in a circuit as long as there's a complete loop for it to flow around. Break the circuit and the current stops.
2) Wire fuses and circuit breakers (resettable fuses) are safety features that break a circuit if there's a fault (see p. 74).

Teachers — the driving force of revision...

The funny thing is — the electrons in circuits actually move from –ve to +ve... but scientists always think of current as flowing from +ve to –ve. Basically it's just because that's how the early physicists thought of it (before they found out about the electrons), and now it's become convention.

Plugs and Fuses

Now then, did you know... electricity is dangerous. It can kill you. Well just watch out for it, that's all.

All the Wires in a Plug are Colour Coded

In plugs, the correct coloured wire is connected to each pin, and firmly screwed in place so no bare wires show.
You need to learn what each of the wires is there for:

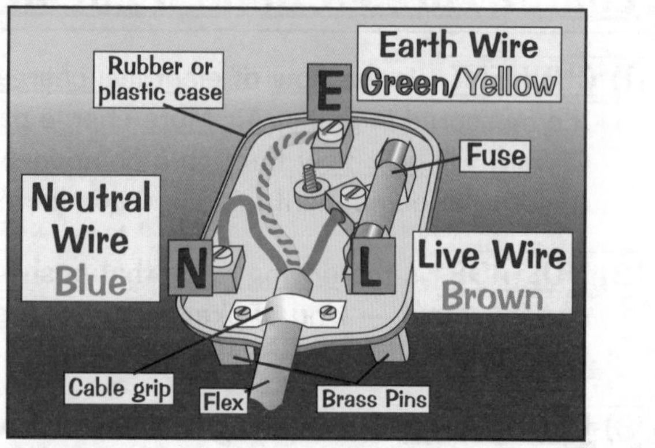

1) The LIVE WIRE carries the voltage. It alternates between a high +ve and −ve voltage of about 230 V.
2) The NEUTRAL WIRE completes the circuit — electricity normally flows in through the live wire and out through the neutral wire. The neutral wire is always at 0 V.
3) The EARTH WIRE and fuse (or circuit breaker) are for safety and work together (see below).
4) All appliances with metal cases must be "earthed" to reduce the danger of electric shock. "Earthing" just means the case must be attached to an earth wire. An earthed conductor can never become live — the earth wire stops appliances becoming live.
5) If the appliance has a casing that's non-conductive (e.g. plastic) then it's said to be double insulated.
6) Anything with double insulation doesn't need an earth wire as it can't become live.

Earthing and Fuses Prevent Fires and Shocks

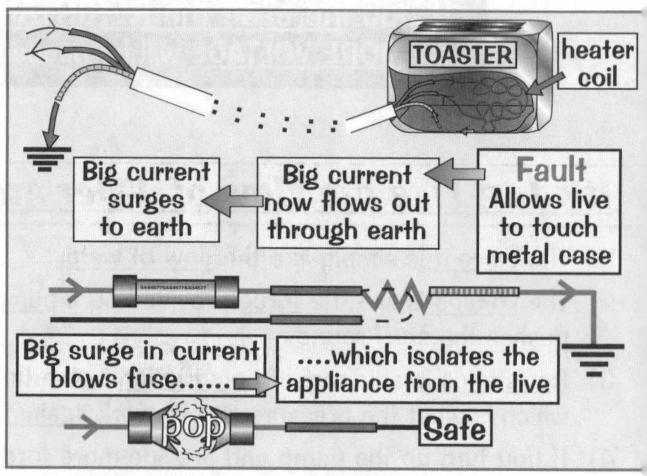

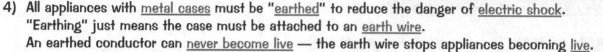

1) If a fault develops in which the live wire somehow touches the metal case, then because the case is earthed, a big current flows in through the live wire, through the case and out down the earth wire.
2) The surge in current 'blows' the fuse and causes the wire inside it to melt. This cuts off the live supply because it breaks the circuit.
3) This isolates the whole appliance, making it impossible to get an electric shock from the case.
4) It also stops the flex overheating, which could cause a fire, and it prevents further damage to the appliance.
5) A circuit breaker works like a fuse but can be reset after it 'trips' and used again. Fuses break when they 'blow' and have to be replaced.
6) Fuses should be rated as near as possible but just higher than the normal operating current. If they were a lot higher, they wouldn't blow when the live wire touched the case or when a fault developed.

Electrical Power and Fuse Ratings

1) The formula for electrical power is: **POWER = VOLTAGE × CURRENT** ($P = V \times I$)
2) Most electrical goods show their power rating and voltage rating.
3) To work out the fuse needed, you need to work out the current that the item will use.
4) The fuse used should be rated just a little higher than the current.
5) Fuses come with fixed ratings, e.g. 3 A, 5 A and 13 A.
Choose the first one that's just higher than the current the appliance uses.

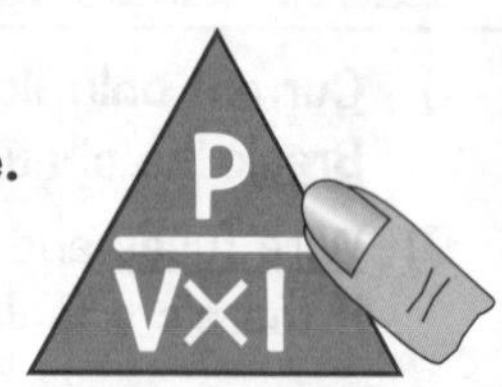

CGP books are ACE — well, I had to get a plug in somewhere...

Have you ever noticed how if anything doesn't work in the house, it's always due to the fuse. But it does make everything a whole load safer. Now have a go at this question: A kettle comes with a power rating of 1200 W and a voltage rating of 230 V. What current will the kettle use and what fuse is needed — 5 A, 7 A or 13 A?*

* Answer on page 124

Resistance

A resistor is a component that reduces the current flowing in a circuit. The higher the resistance, the harder it is for the electricity to flow, and so the lower the current. If you get an electric shock, it's the current that does the damage, not the voltage. So the higher the resistance in a circuit, the smaller the risk of injury.

Variable Resistors

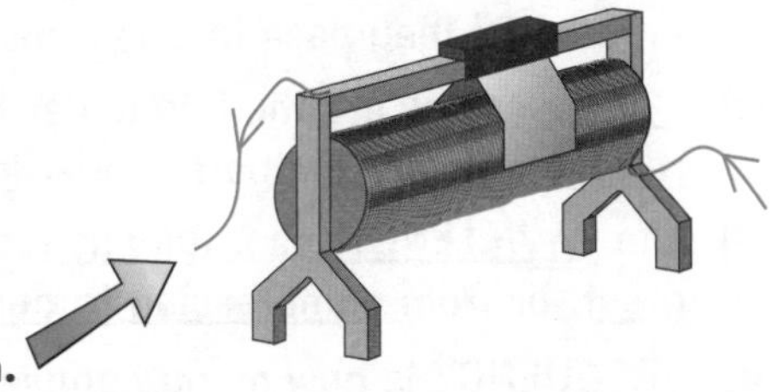

1) A variable resistor (or rheostat) is a resistor whose resistance can be changed by twiddling a knob or something.
2) They're great for altering the current flowing through a circuit. Turn the resistance up, the current drops. Turn the resistance down, the current goes up.
3) The old-fashioned ones are huge coils of wire with a slider on them.
4) As you move the slider, the length of wire that has current flowing through it changes.
5) Longer wires have more resistance, so have less current flowing through them. This is because the longer the wire, the more material electric charge has to flow through, which increases the resistance.
6) The thickness of a wire also matters — thinner wires have more resistance and so less current can flow.
7) The thinner the wire, the less space electric charge has to move through, which increases the resistance. It's like being on the motorway when only one lane's open — fewer cars make it down the road.

Calculating Resistance: R = V/I

1) The resistance of a (non-variable) resistor is steady (at constant temperature).
2) If you increase the voltage across a resistor, the current increases as well.
3) For the same voltage, current increases as resistance decreases.
4) You can calculate the resistance of a resistor using the formula:

$$\text{Resistance} = \frac{\text{Voltage}}{\text{Current}}$$

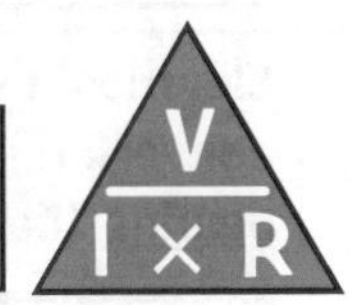

Use a Test Circuit to Measure Resistance

This is standard test circuit:

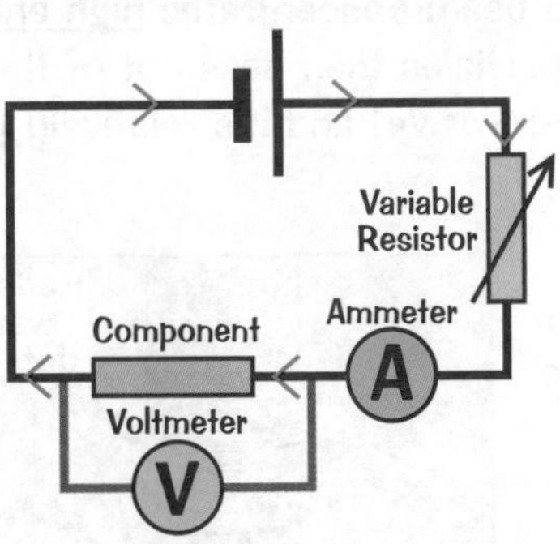

1) As you vary the variable resistor it alters the current flowing through the circuit.
2) This allows you to take several pairs of readings from the ammeter and voltmeter.
3) The ammeter measures the current (in amps) through the component. It's placed in series (in line) with the other components.
4) The voltmeter measures the voltage (in volts) across the component. It's placed in parallel around the component being tested.
5) The proper name for voltage is potential difference, pd .

Calculating Resistance — An Example

EXAMPLE. Voltmeter V reads 6 V and resistor R is 4 Ω. What is the current through ammeter A?

ANSWER. Rearrange the resistance formula to give: I = V/R.

Then put in the values: I = 6/4 which is 1.5 A.

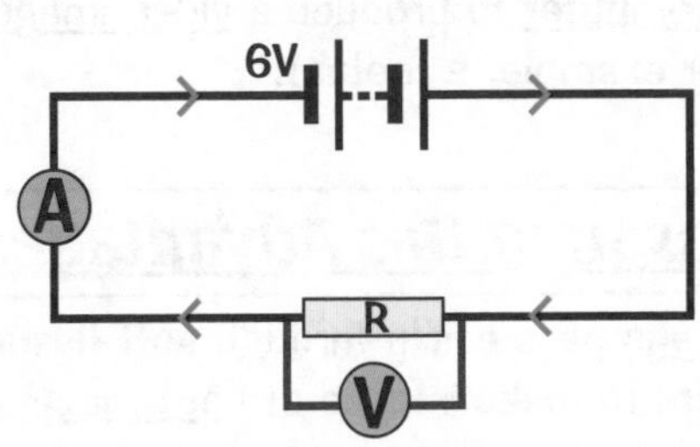

You have to learn this — resistance is futile...

Sometimes you can get funny light switches which fade the light in and out. Some of them work by resistance, and are perfect for getting that nice romantic atmosphere you want for your dinner for two. Handy.
Some questions to try: 1) Calculate the resistance of a resistor which draws 3 A of current from a 9 V battery.*
2) A resistor with a resistance of 2.5 Ω draws 6.4 A of current. What's the voltage of the power supply?*

* Answer on page 124.

Ultrasound Treatments and Scans

Ultrasound — it's used for more than looking at babies, you know. Learn all about it, right here...

Sound is a Longitudinal Wave

You need to know the features of longitudinal waves:

1) Sound waves squash up and stretch out the arrangement of particles in material they pass through, making compressions and rarefactions.
2) Compressions are the bits under high pressure (lots of particles) and rarefactions are the parts under low pressure (fewer particles).
3) The WAVELENGTH is a full cycle of the wave, e.g. from crest to crest, or from compression to compression.

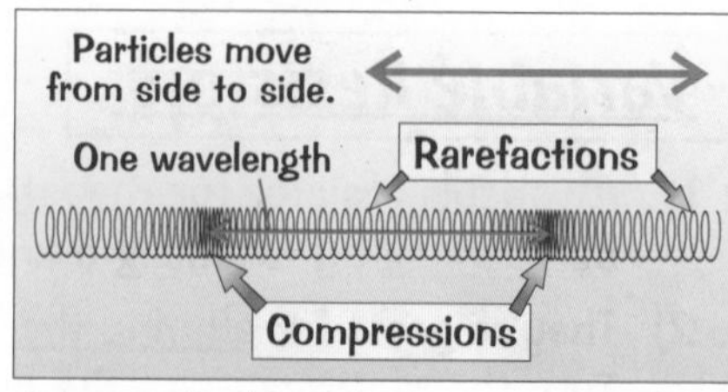

A longitudinal wave in a spring (in spring).

4) FREQUENCY is how many complete waves there are per second (passing a certain point). Frequency is measured in hertz. 1 Hz is 1 complete wave per second. For sound, high frequency = high pitch.

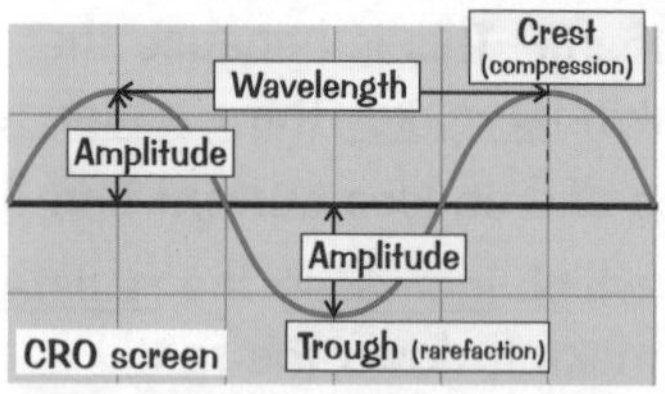

5) The AMPLITUDE tells you how much energy the wave is carrying, or how loud the sound is. You can see the amplitude of a sound on a CRO (oscilloscope). CRO displays show sounds as transverse waves so you can see what's going on. You measure the amplitude from the middle line to the crest, NOT from a trough to a crest.

In LONGITUDINAL waves the vibrations are along the SAME DIRECTION as the wave is travelling.	In TRANSVERSE waves the vibrations are at 90° to the DIRECTION OF TRAVEL of the wave.

Ultrasound is Sound with a Higher Frequency Than We Can Hear

Electrical devices can be made which produce electrical oscillations of any frequency. These can easily be converted into mechanical vibrations to produce longitudinal (sound) waves beyond the range of human hearing (i.e. frequencies above 20 000 Hz). This is called ultrasound and it has loads of uses in hospitals:

1) Breaking Down Accumulations in the Body — Getting Rid of Kidney Stones

An important example is the removal of kidney stones... An ultrasound beam concentrates high energy waves at the kidney stone and turns it into sand-like particles. These particles then pass out of the body in urine. It's useful because the patient doesn't need surgery (it's non-invasive) and it's relatively painless.

2) For Body Scanning

Ultrasound waves can pass through the body, but whenever they reach a boundary between two different media (like fluid in the womb and the skin of the foetus) some of the wave is reflected back and detected, returning back from different depths at different times.

The exact timing and distribution of these echoes are processed by a computer to produce a video image of whatever is being scanned (for example, a foetus).

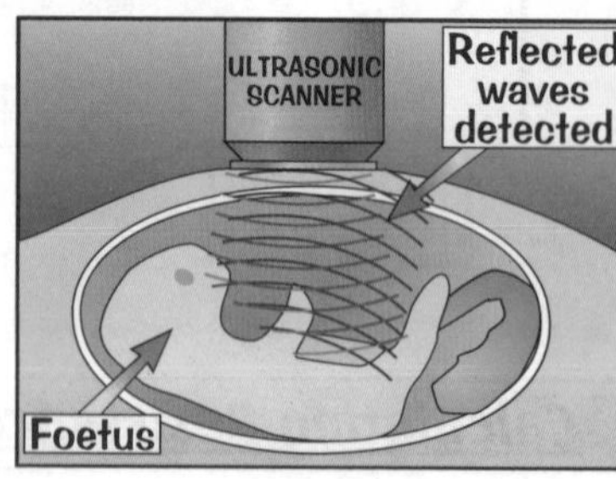

Ultrasound Has Advantages over X-Rays

1) X-rays pass easily through soft tissues like muscle and skin, so you can usually only use them to make images of hard things like bone. Ultrasound is great for imaging soft tissue.
2) The other advantage is that ultrasound is, we're pretty sure, safe — it doesn't damage living cells. X-rays are ionising radiation. They can damage living cells and cause cancer if you're exposed to too high a dose.

Looking at things with sound — weird if you ask me...

Pity that you can't see into peoples minds when they have headphones on... Well, you win some, you lose some.

Radioactive Decay

Phew. Now all that electricity and sound stuff is out of the way we can get onto more exciting stuff. Ooooh.

Radioactivity Comes From an Unstable Nucleus

1) Radioactive materials are made up of atoms with unstable nuclei that naturally decay at random.
2) As they decay, they can give out three forms of radiation — alpha (α), beta (β) and gamma (γ). During the decay, the nucleus will often change into a new element.
3) Gamma radiation happens after α and β emission if the nucleus has some extra energy to get rid of.
It emits a γ-ray that has no mass or charge.
This means the atomic and mass numbers don't change.

All elements in the periodic table have two numbers:
Relative atomic mass number (mass number) = number of protons and neutrons.
Atomic number = number of protons.
$^{23}_{11}\mathrm{Na}$
Atoms of the same element have the same number of protons, atoms of different elements have different numbers of protons. Isotopes are atoms with the same atomic number, but different mass numbers.

Alpha Radiation is a Helium Nucleus

1) An α-particle is a helium nucleus, mass 4 and charge of +2, made up of two protons and two neutrons.
2) So, when a nucleus emits an alpha particle:
   - The mass number decreases by 4 — because it loses two protons and two neutrons.
   - The atomic number decreases by 2 — because it has two less protons.
   - It forms a new element — because the number of protons has changed.
3) A typical alpha emission:

You need to remember the mass and atomic numbers for alpha and beta particles.

Beta Radiation is a Fast-Moving Electron

Beta particles can be written as $^{0}_{-1}e$ too.

1) A β-particle is a fast-moving electron, with virtually no mass and a charge of −1.
2) So, when a nucleus emits a beta particle:
   - The mass number doesn't change — because it has lost a neutron but gained a proton.
   - The atomic number increases by 1 — because it has one more proton.
   - It forms a new element — because the number of protons has changed.
3) A typical beta emission:

A neutron turns into a proton and a β particle (electron) is emitted.

Nuclear Equations — Not Half as Bad as They Sound

The mass numbers and atomic numbers should balance on both sides.

You can check a periodic table to find out the mass and atomic numbers, or the new element.

ALPHA EMISSION An α-particle has a mass of 4 and charge of +2: $^{4}_{2}\alpha$

A typical alpha emission: $^{226}_{88}\mathrm{Ra} \longrightarrow \, ^{222}_{86}\mathrm{Rn} + \, ^{4}_{2}\alpha$

mass number	226	$\longrightarrow$ 222 + 4 = 226
atomic number	88	$\longrightarrow$ 86 + 2 = 88

BETA EMISSION A β-particle has (virtually) no mass and a charge of −1: $^{0}_{-1}\beta$

A typical beta emission: $^{14}_{6}\mathrm{C} \longrightarrow \, ^{14}_{7}\mathrm{N} + \, ^{0}_{-1}\beta$

mass number	14	$\longrightarrow$ 14 + 0 = 14
atomic number	6	$\longrightarrow$ 7 + (− 1) = 6

Sorry, no clear equations on this page...

he most important thing to remember is the symbol for each type of particle with its atomic number and nass number. As long as you know those, you should be able to write down an equation for alpha or beta decay.

Radioactivity and Half-Life

Radioactivity is measured in becquerels (Bq) or counts per minute (cpm). 1 Bq is 1 decay emitted per second

The Radioactivity of a Sample Always Decreases Over Time

1) Each time an unstable nucleus decays and emits radiation, that means one more radioactive nucleus isn't there to decay later.
2) As more unstable nuclei decay, the radioactivity of the source as a whole decreases — so the older a radioactive source is, the less radiation it emits.
3) How quickly the activity decreases varies a lot. For some isotopes it takes just a few hours before nearly all the unstable nuclei have decayed. For others it can take millions of years.
4) The problem with trying to measure this is that the activity never reaches zero, which is why we have to use the idea of half-life to measure how quickly the activity decreases.
5) Learn this important definition of half-life:

HALF-LIFE is the TIME TAKEN for HALF of the radioactive nuclei now present to DECAY.

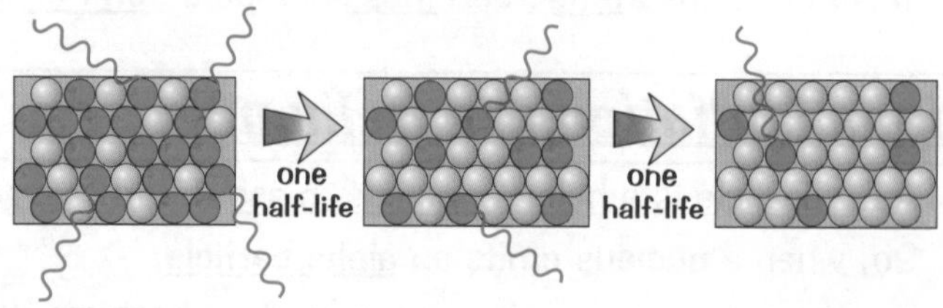

6) A short half-life means the activity falls quickly, because lots of the nuclei decay in a short time.
7) A long half-life means the activity falls more slowly because most of the nuclei don't decay for a long time — they just sit there, basically unstable, but kind of biding their time.

Do Half-Life Questions Step by Step

Half-life can be confusing, but exam calculations are straightforward so long as you do them STEP BY STEP:

A Very Simple Example:

The activity of a radioactive sample is 640 Bq. Two hours later it has fallen to 40 Bq. Find its half-life.

ANSWER: Go through it in short simple steps like this:

INITIAL count:		after ONE half-life:		after TWO half-lives:		after THREE half-lives:		after FOUR half-lives:
640	(÷2) →	320	(÷2) →	160	(÷2) →	80	(÷2) →	40

This careful step-by-step method shows that it takes four half-lives for the activity to fall from 640 to 40. So two hours represents four half-lives — so the half-life is 2 hours ÷ 4 = 30 MINUTES.

You also need to be able to find the half-life of a sample from a graph. Relax, this is (almost) fun.

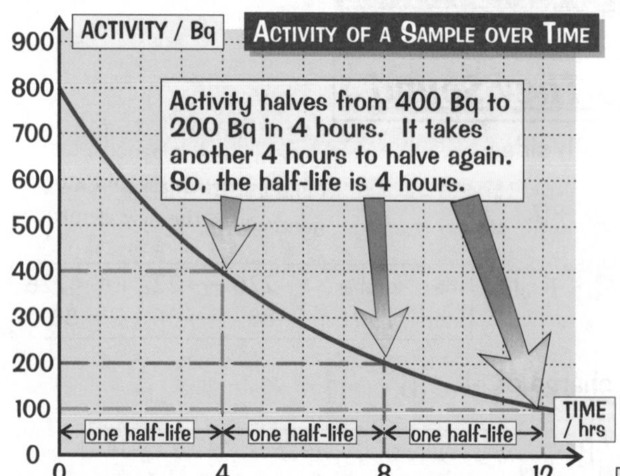

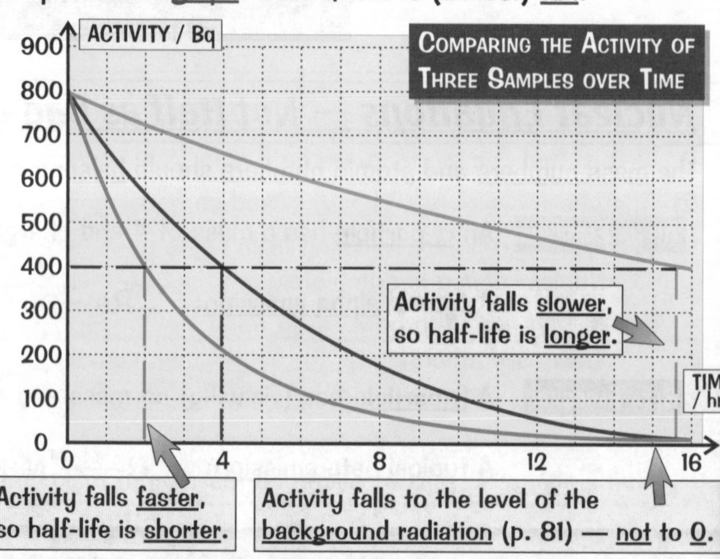

Half-life of a box of chocolates — about five minutes...

To measure half-life, you time how long it takes for the number of decays per second to halve. Simples.

Ionising Radiation

Nuclear radiation (alpha, beta and gamma) and X-rays are ionising radiation — they can damage living cells.

Ionising Radiation Harms Living Cells

1) Nuclear radiation (alpha α, beta β, gamma γ) and X-rays are ionising radiation.
2) Some materials absorb ionising radiation — it can enter living cells and interact with molecules.
3) These interactions cause ionisation — they produce charged particles called ions.
4) Ionisation occurs because the particle gains or loses electrons.
5) X-rays and gamma rays can transfer energy to electrons. The electrons then have enough energy to escape from the atom, ionising it and leaving it positively charged.
6) Beta particles can remove electrons from atoms or molecules they collide with, leaving them positively charged. A beta particle (an electron) can also stick to an atom, ionising it and making it negatively charged.
7) Alpha particles can remove electrons from atoms and molecules they pass by or hit, making them positive.
8) Alpha particles are good ionisers for two reasons:

- They're relatively large — so it's easy for them to collide with atoms or molecules.
- They're highly charged — so they can easily remove electrons from the atoms they pass or collide with.

8) Lower doses of ionising radiation tend to cause minor damage without killing the cell. This can give rise to mutant cells which divide uncontrollably. This is cancer.
9) Higher doses tend to kill cells completely, which causes radiation sickness if a lot of cells all get blasted at once.

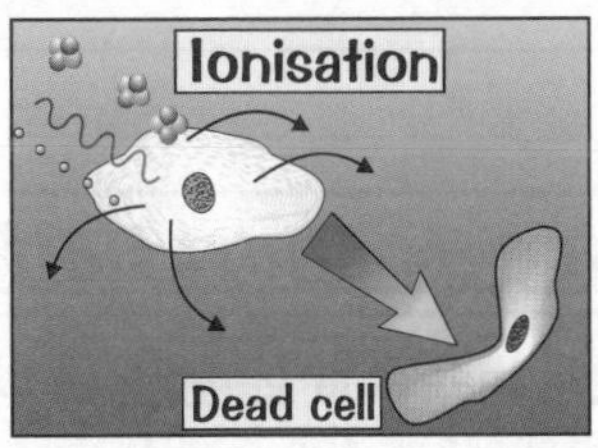

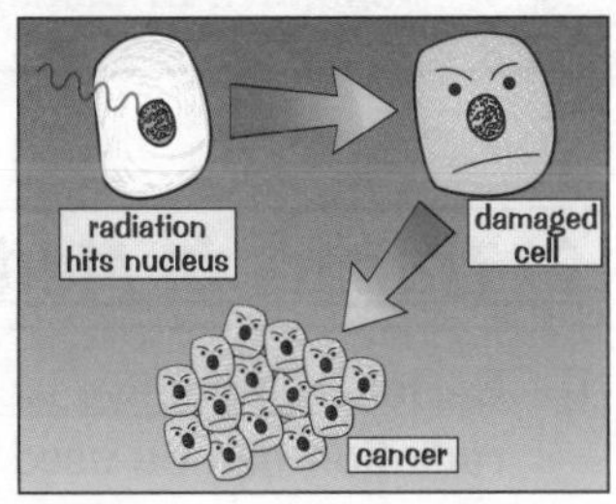

Which Radiation is the Most Dangerous Depends on Where it is

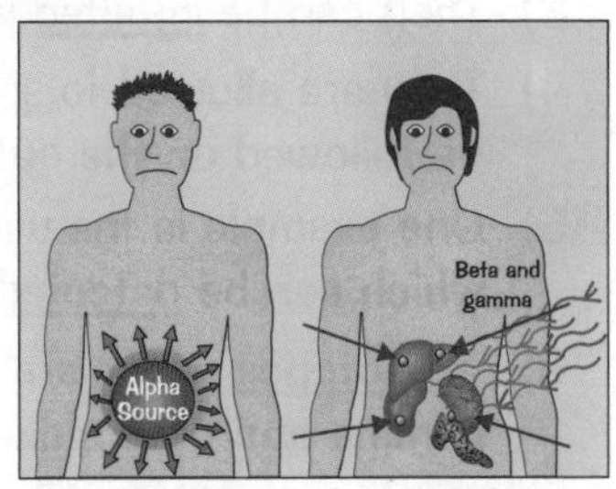

1) OUTSIDE the body, beta and gamma sources are the most dangerous.
2) This is because beta and gamma can still get inside to the delicate organs — they can pass through the skin.
3) Alpha is much less dangerous because it can't penetrate the skin.
4) INSIDE the body, an alpha source is the most dangerous because they do all their damage in a very localised area.
5) Beta and gamma sources on the other hand are less dangerous inside the body because they are less ionising, and mostly pass straight out without doing much damage.

X-rays and Gamma Rays are Electromagnetic Waves

You learnt about electromagnetic waves in P1 — see page 20.

1) X-rays and gamma rays are both high frequency, short wavelength electromagnetic waves.
2) They have similar wavelengths, and so have similar properties, but are made in different ways:
   - Gamma rays are released from some unstable atomic nuclei when they decay (see p. 77). Nuclear decay is completely random, so there's no way to control when they're released.
   - X-rays can be produced by firing high-speed electrons at a heavy metal like tungsten. These are much easier to control than gamma rays.
3) X-rays pass easily through flesh but not so easily through thicker and denser materials like bones or metal.
4) The thicker or denser the material, the more x-ray that's absorbed. So it's the varying amount of radiation that's absorbed (or not absorbed really) that makes an x-ray image.

Radiation — easy as α, β, γ...

Well actually this stuff is pretty darn difficult to get your head around. But I'm afraid you're just gonna have to pull those socks up and get down to it. There's no other way — cover, scribble, check. Do it now.

Medical Uses of Radiation

Ionising radiation has loads of uses in hospitals, and you have to know all about them. Whoop-ti-do.

1) Radiotherapy — the Treatment of Cancer Using Gamma Rays

1) Since high doses of gamma rays will kill all living cells, they can be used to treat cancers.
2) The gamma rays have to be directed carefully and at just the right dosage, so as to kill the cancer cells without damaging too many normal cells.
3) However, a fair bit of damage is inevitably done to normal cells, which makes the patient feel very ill. But if the cancer is successfully killed off in the end, then it's worth it.

TO TREAT CANCER:

1) The gamma rays are focused on the tumour using a wide beam.
2) This beam is rotated round the patient with the tumour at the centre.
3) This minimises the exposure of normal cells to radiation, and so reduces the chances of damaging the rest of the body.

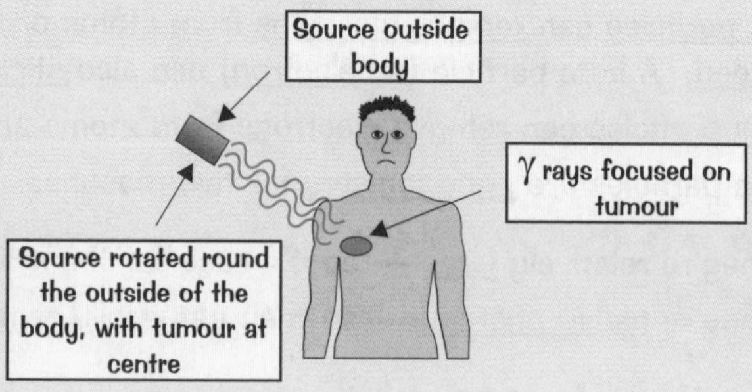

2) Tracers in Medicine — Short Half-life Gamma and Beta Emitters

1) Certain radioactive isotopes that emit gamma (and sometimes beta) radiation can be used as tracers in the body.
2) They should have a short half-life — around a few hours, so that the radioactivity inside the patient quickly disappears.
3) They can be injected inside the body, drunk or eaten or ingested.
4) They are allowed to spread through the body and their progress can be followed on the outside using a radiation detector.

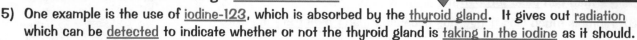

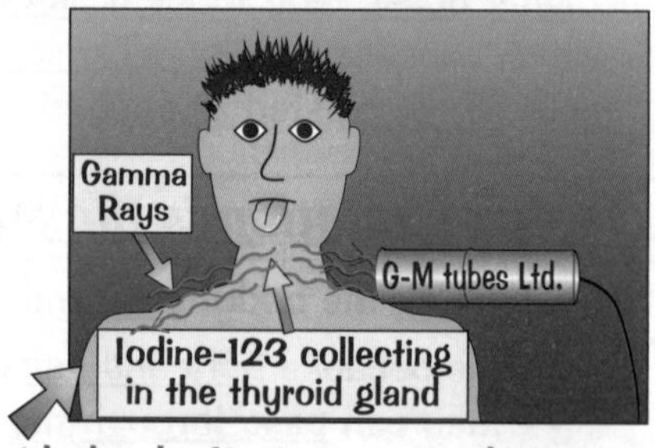

5) One example is the use of iodine-123, which is absorbed by the thyroid gland. It gives out radiation which can be detected to indicate whether or not the thyroid gland is taking in the iodine as it should.
6) All isotopes which are taken into the body must be GAMMA or BETA (never alpha). This is because gamma and beta radiation can penetrate tissue and so are able to pass out of the body and be detected.
7) Alpha radiation can't penetrate tissue, so you couldn't detect the radiation on the outside of the body. Also alpha is more dangerous inside the body (see previous page).

3) Sterilisation of Surgical Instruments Using Gamma Rays

1) Medical instruments can be sterilised by exposing them to a high dose of gamma rays, which will kill all microbes.
2) The great advantage of using radiation instead of boiling is that it doesn't involve high temperatures, so heat-sensitive things like thermometers and plastic instruments can be totally sterilised without damaging them.

Ionising radiation — just what the doctor ordered...

See — radiation isn't all bad. It also kills bad things, like disease-causing bacteria. Radiotherapy and chemotherapy (which uses chemicals instead of gamma rays) are commonly used to treat cancer. They both work in the same way — by killing lots and lots of cells, and trying to target the cancerous ones...

Uses of Radiation and Background Radiation

Radioactive materials aren't just used in hospitals (p. 80) — you've got to know these uses too.

Tracers in Industry — For Finding Leaks

This is much the same technique as the medical tracers.

1) Radioactive isotopes can be used to track the movement of waste materials, find the route of underground pipe systems or detect leaks or blockages in pipes.
2) To check a pipe, you just squirt the radioactive isotope in, then go along the outside with a detector. If the radioactivity reduces or stops after a certain point, there must be a leak or blockage there. This is really useful for concealed or underground pipes — no need to dig up the road to find the leak.

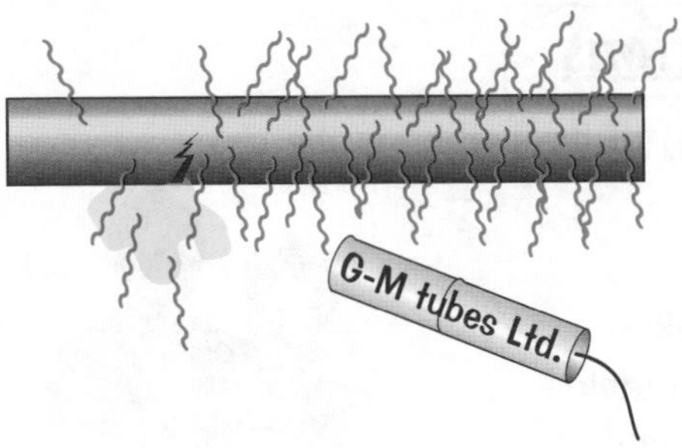

3) The isotope used must be a gamma emitter, so that the radiation can be detected even through metal or earth which may be surrounding the pipe. Alpha and beta radiation wouldn't be much use because they are easily blocked by any surrounding material.
4) It should also have a short half-life so as not to cause a hazard if it collects somewhere.

Smoke Detectors — Alpha Radiation

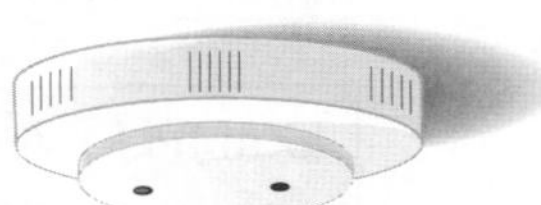

1) A weak alpha radioactive source is placed in the detector, close to two electrodes.
2) The source causes ionisation of the air particles which allows a current to flow.
3) If there is a fire, then smoke particles are hit by the alpha particles instead.
4) This causes less ionisation of the air particles — so the current is reduced causing the alarm to sound.

Background Radiation Comes from Many Sources

The background radiation we receive comes from:

1) Radioactivity of naturally occurring unstable isotopes which are all around us — in the air, in food, in building materials and in the rocks under our feet. A large proportion of background radiation comes from these natural sources.
2) Radiation from space, which is known as cosmic rays. These come mostly from the Sun.
3) Radiation due to human activity, e.g. fallout from nuclear explosions, or waste from industry and hospitals. But this represents a small proportion of the total.
4) The amount of background radiation can vary depending on where you are and your job. For example, what type of rock your house is built on (some rocks are more radioactive than others), or if you're in an aeroplane (because you're exposed to more cosmic rays), or if you work in an industry that uses radiation (nuclear power or medical related).

The RELATIVE PROPORTIONS of background radiation:

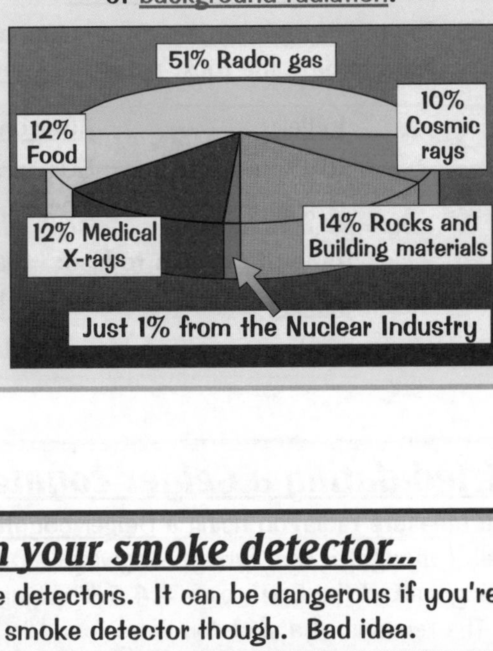

No need to be alarmed, but there's radiation in your smoke detector...

Nuclear radiation is used for loads more things than tracers and smoke detectors. It can be dangerous if you're not careful with it, but mostly it's really handy. Please don't eat your smoke detector though. Bad idea.

Radioactive Dating

Yet another use of radiation is radioactive dating. Some of the naturally occurring radiation on earth can be useful for dating things — like rocks and fossils and stuff. It's pretty cool, if you're into that kind of thing.

Radioactive Dating of Rocks and Archaeological Specimens

1) The discovery of radioactivity and the idea of half-life gave scientists their first opportunity to accurately work out the age of some rocks and archaeological specimens.
2) By measuring the amount of a radioactive isotope left in a sample, and knowing its half-life, you can work out how long the thing has been around.

Radiocarbon Dating — Carbon-14 Calculations

1) Carbon-14 makes up about 1/10 000 000 (one ten-millionth) of the carbon in the air.
2) The level stays fairly constant in the atmosphere — it hasn't changed for thousands of years.
3) The same proportion of carbon-14 is also found in living things.
4) But when they die, they stop exchanging gases with the air outside and the carbon-14 is trapped inside, and it gradually decays with a half-life of 5730 years.
5) By measuring the proportion of carbon-14 found in some old axe handle, burial shroud, etc. you can calculate how long ago the item was living material using the known half-life.

Phil took radioactive dating a bit too far.

EXAMPLE: An axe handle was found to contain 1 part in 40 000 000 carbon-14. How old is the axe?

ANSWER: The carbon-14 was originally 1 part in 10 000 000.
After one half-life it would be down to 1 part in 20 000 000.
After two half-lives it would be down to 1 part in 40 000 000.
Hence the axe handle is two carbon-14 half-lives old, i.e. $2 \times 5730 = 11\,460$ years old.

You can use the same old stepwise method from page 78, going down one half-life at a time.

Dating Rocks — Relative Proportions Calculations

1) Uranium isotopes have very long half-lives and decay via a series of short-lived particles to produce stable isotopes of lead.
2) The relative proportions of uranium and lead isotopes in a sample of rock can therefore be used to date the rock, using the known half-life of the uranium. It's as simple as this:

Initially	After one half-life	After two half-lives
100% uranium	50% uranium	25% uranium
0% lead	50% lead	75% lead

Ratio of uranium to lead: (half-life of uranium-238 = 4.5 billion years)

Initially	After one half-life	After two half-lives
1:0	1:1	1:3

I tried dating a Geiger counter once, but we didn't click...

You measure radiation using a Geiger counter. You know, the more it clicks the more radiation you've found. Well, I thought it was funny. Anyway... Did you know that the oldest human ancestor dated by radioactive dating walked the Earth over 4.4 million years ago. Crazy times. Now give this question a try:

1) The remains of a skeleton were found to contain 1 part in 160 000 000 carbon-14. How old is the skeleton?*

* Answer on page 124.

Nuclear Power

One more use for radioactive materials — nuclear power. Keep going, you're nearly at the end of the module.

Nuclear Fission — The Splitting Up of Uranium Atoms

1) Nuclear power stations are powered by nuclear reactors.
2) In a nuclear reactor, a controlled chain reaction takes place in which uranium or plutonium atoms split up and release energy in the form of heat — this is nuclear fission.
3) This heat is then used to heat water to produce steam.
4) The steam turns a turbine which drives a generator that produces electricity.

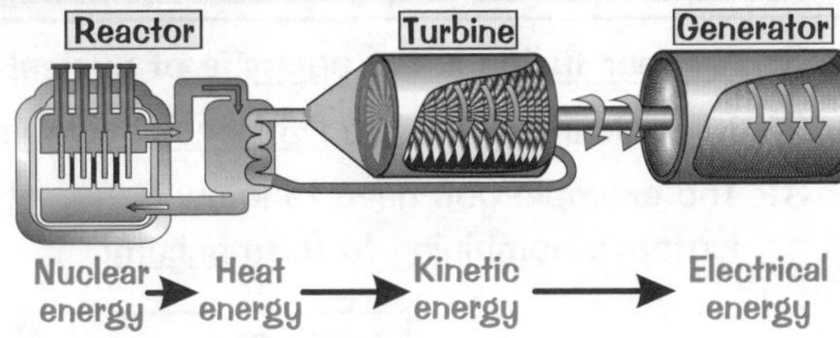

The Splitting of Uranium-235 Needs Neutrons

Uranium-235 (i.e. a uranium atom with an atomic mass of 235) is used in some nuclear reactors and bombs.

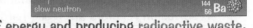

1) Uranium-235 (U-235) is actually quite stable, so it needs to be made unstable before it'll split.
2) Materials can become radioactive when they absorb extra neutrons — so slow-moving neutrons are fired at the U-235 atom.
3) A neutron joins the nucleus to create U-236, which is unstable.
4) The U-236 then splits into two smaller nuclei, releasing loads of energy and producing radioactive waste.
5) The split nucleus also releases 2 or 3 fast-moving neutrons which go onto produce a chain reaction...

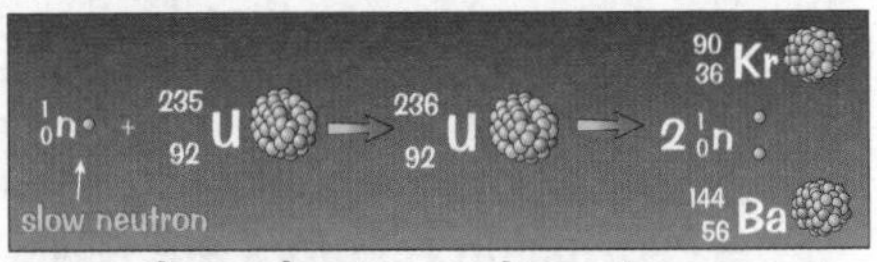

You Can Split More than One Atom — Chain Reactions

1) To get a useful amount of energy, loads of U-235 atoms have to be split. So neutrons released from previous fissions are used to hit other U-235 atoms.
2) Each split uranium nucleus releases more than one neutron.
3) These neutrons cause further nuclei to split, releasing more neutrons, which cause more nuclei to split and release more neutrons... and so on and so on. This process is called a chain reaction.
4) Nuclear bombs are chain reactions that are out of control.
5) But in nuclear reactors the chain reaction is controlled using control rods...

Control Rods Control the Chain Reaction

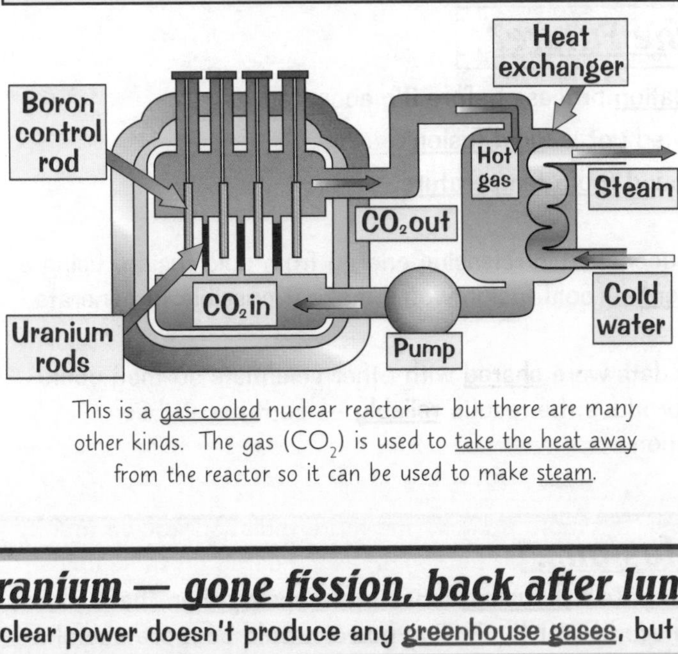

This is a gas-cooled nuclear reactor — but there are many other kinds. The gas (CO_2) is used to take the heat away from the reactor so it can be used to make steam.

1) Free neutrons in the reactor "kick-start" the fission process.
2) Neutrons collide with surrounding uranium atoms, causing them to split and the temperature in the reactor to rise.
3) Control rods, often made of boron, limit the rate of fission by absorbing excess neutrons.
4) This stops the reaction going out of control but allows enough neutrons to hang around to keep the process going.

Uranium — gone fission, back after lunch...

Nuclear power doesn't produce any greenhouse gases, but it leaves behind radioactive waste instead. Hmm...

Nuclear Fusion

Loads of energy's released either when you break apart really big nuclei or join together really small nuclei. You can't do much with the ones in the middle, I'm afraid. (Don't ask, you don't want to know.)

Nuclear Fusion — The Joining of Small Atomic Nuclei

1) Nuclear fusion is the opposite of nuclear fission.
2) In nuclear fusion, two light nuclei combine to create a larger nucleus.
3) The example you need to know is two atoms of different hydrogen isotopes combining to form helium:

$$^{1}_{1}H + ^{2}_{1}H \rightarrow ^{3}_{2}He$$

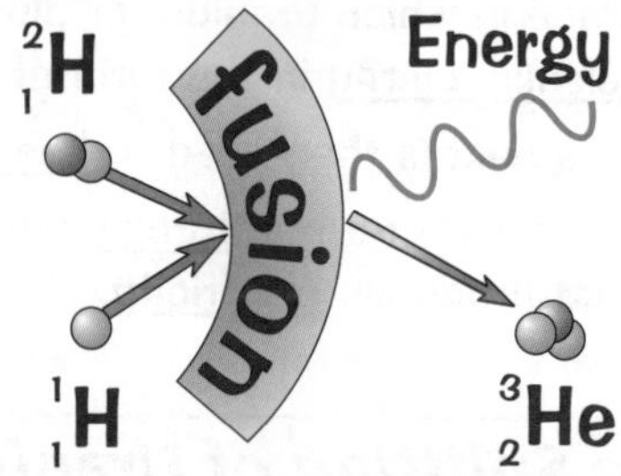

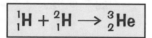

4) Fusion releases a lot of energy (more than fission for a given mass) — all the energy released in stars comes from fusion at extremely high temperatures and pressures. So people are trying to develop fusion reactors to make electricity.
5) Fusion doesn't leave behind much radioactive waste and there's plenty of hydrogen about to use as fuel.
6) The big problem is that fusion only happens at really high pressures and temperatures (about 10 000 000 °C).
7) No material can physically withstand that kind of temperature and pressure — so fusion reactors are really hard to build.
8) It's also hard to safely control the high temperatures and pressures.
9) There are a few experimental reactors around at the moment, the biggest one being JET (Joint European Torus), but none of them are generating electricity yet. It takes more power to get up to temperature than the reactor can produce.
10) Research into fusion power production is carried out by international groups to share the costs, expertise, experience and the benefits (when they eventually get it to work reliably).

FUSION BOMBS

- Fusion reactions also happen in fusion bombs.
- You might have heard of them as hydrogen, or H bombs.
- In fusion bombs, a fission reaction is used first to create the really high temperatures needed for fusion.

Cold Fusion — Hoax or Energy of the Future?

1) A new scientific theory has to go through a validation process before it's accepted.
2) An example of a theory which hasn't been accepted yet is 'cold fusion'.
3) Cold fusion is nuclear fusion which occurs at around room temperature, rather than at millions of degrees Celsius.
4) In 1989, two scientists reported that they had succeeded in releasing energy from cold fusion, using a simple experiment. This caused a lot of excitement — cold fusion would make it possible to generate lots of electricity, easily and cheaply.
5) After the press conference, the experiments and data were shared with other scientists so they could repeat the experiments. But few managed to reproduce the results reliably — so it hasn't been accepted as a realistic method of energy production.

Pity they can't release energy by confusion...*

Fusion bombs are incredibly powerful — they can release a few thousand times more energy than the nuclear fission bombs that destroyed Hiroshima and Nagasaki in World War II. Fusion power would be more useful...

*There'd be plenty of physics books to use as fuel.

Revision Summary for Module P4

Some of this stuff can be just learnt and regurgitated — other parts actually need thinking about. All the information's there, you've just got to sit down and put the effort in. The best thing to do is take it a page at a time, break it down and make sure you've learnt every little thing. If you can answer these questions, you should have no problem with anything the examiners throw at you. You'd better get going.

1) What causes static charge to build up?
2) Which particles move when static charge builds up?
3) Give two examples each of static electricity being: a) a nuisance, b) dangerous.
4) Explain how you can reduce the danger of getting a static electric shock.
5) Give three examples of how static electricity can be helpful. Write all the details.
6) Explain what current, voltage and resistance are in an electric circuit.
7) Describe what earthing and double insulation are. Why are they useful?
8)* A computer has a power rating of 400 W and uses a 230 V mains supply.
What rating of fuse should by used in the plug — 1 A, 3 A, 5 A or 13 A?
9) What happens to the current flowing through a circuit if the resistance of a variable resistor is increased?
10) Explain how you could work out the resistance of a resistor in a circuit.
11) Define the frequency, wavelength and amplitude of a wave.
12) Explain why ultrasound rather than X-rays are used to take images of a foetus.
13)* Write down the nuclear equation for the alpha decay of: a) $^{234}_{92}U$, b) $^{230}_{90}Th$, c) $^{241}_{95}Am$.
14)* Write down the nuclear equation for the beta decay of: a) $^{234}_{90}Th$, b) $^{90}_{38}Sr$, c) $^{131}_{53}I$.
15) Give a proper definition of half-life.
16) Briefly describe what nuclear radiation does to living cells.
17) Why are alpha particles so good at ionising atoms?
18) What is the main difference between X-rays and gamma rays?
19) Describe in detail how radioactive sources are used in each of the following:
a) treating cancer, b) tracers in medicine.
20) Describe in detail how radioactive sources are used in each of the following:
a) tracers in industry, b) smoke alarms.
21)* An old bit of cloth was found to contain 1 part in 80 000 000 carbon-14.
If carbon-14 decays with a half-life of 5730 years, find the age of the cloth.
22) What type of particle is uranium-235 bombarded with in a nuclear reactor to make it split?
23) Explain how a chain reaction is created in a nuclear reactor.
24) What is the difference between nuclear fission and nuclear fusion?
25) Briefly explain why cold fusion isn't accepted as a realistic method of energy production.

* Answers on page 124.

Speed and Velocity

When you're talking about the motion of a car, it's not enough just to talk about its speed. Sure, I'm driving at 30 mph, but which way am I going? Am I heading towards that tree over there or not? And that lorry over there is also going at 30 mph — but is it heading towards me? And am I getting paranoid? Yes.

Speed is Just a Number, but Velocity Has Direction Too

1) To measure the speed of an object, you only need to measure how fast it's going — the direction is not important.
E.g. speed = 30 mph.
2) Velocity is a more useful measure of motion, because it describes both the speed and direction.
E.g. velocity = 30 mph due north.

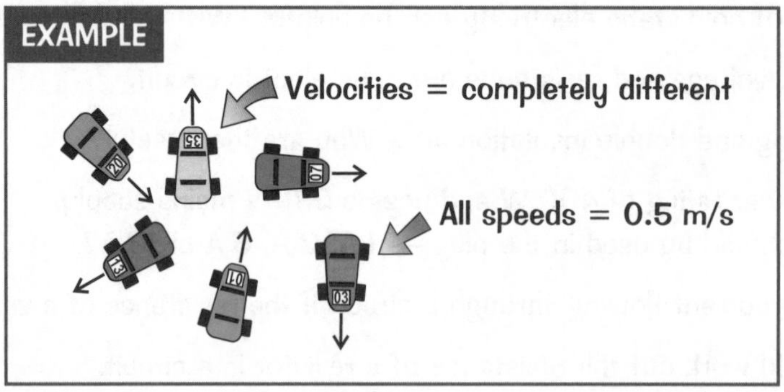

3) A quantity like speed, that has only a number, is called a scalar quantity.

Scalar quantities:
speed, mass, temperature, time, length, etc.

4) A quantity like velocity, that has a direction as well, is a vector quantity.

Vector quantities:
velocity, force, displacement, acceleration, momentum, etc.

Relative Speed Compares the Speeds of Two Different Objects

1) When you look out of a car window, a car that's overtaking you looks like it's not moving very fast.
2) Whereas a car on the opposite side of the motorway seems to whizz past at 100 miles an hour.
3) It's all to do with relative speed — how fast something's going relative to something else.
4) The easiest way to think of it is to imagine yourself in a moving car, watching another vehicle from the window.

A car going the same way as you will only have a small speed relative to your car...

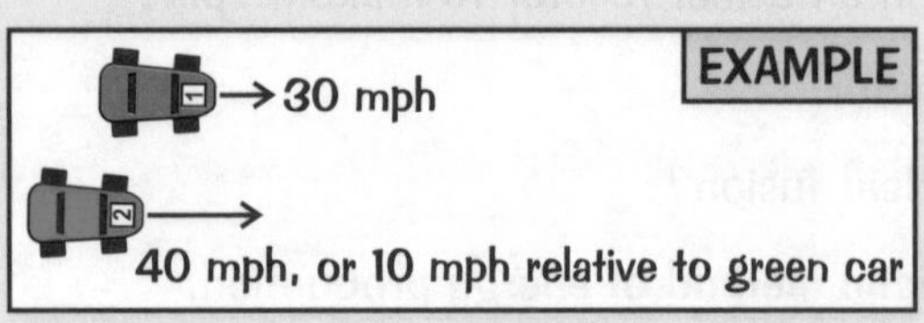

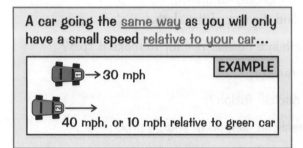

...whereas a car going the opposite way will have a much bigger speed relative to you.

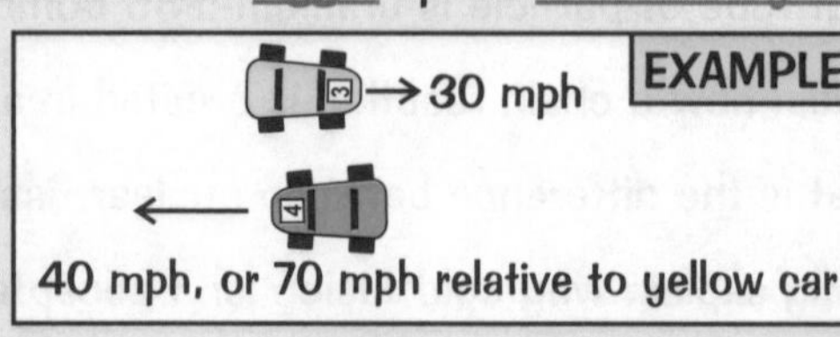

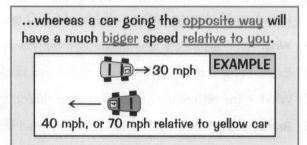

My speed relative to Lewis Hamilton is — well, slower...

You could do an experiment in the lab to find relative speeds. Put a ticker tape machine on a trolley, and attach the ticker tape to a toy car. Depending on whether the car and trolley are moving in the same or opposite directions, you'd get different results. Experiments — good excuse to put the books down for a bit, anyway.

Combining Velocities and Forces

If a parrot has the wind behind it, it flies a bit faster. Likewise, if it's flying into the wind, it'll be slower. To work out the velocity as seen by a "stationary observer" (someone standing still), you have to combine the velocity of the parrot with the velocity of the wind. Get ready for a bit of maths — this is vector stuff...

To Combine Two Vectors, You Add Them End to End

1) With or Against the Current — EASY

It's easy when the plane (or whatever) is flying directly into the wind (or whatever), or with the wind behind it. On the vector diagrams you just need arrows going back and forwards, like this:

EXAMPLE: A light plane is flying east. Its airspeed indicator shows 120 km/h. It is flying into a wind of 20 km/h — i.e. within a stream of air that's moving west at 20 km/h. What is its resultant velocity?

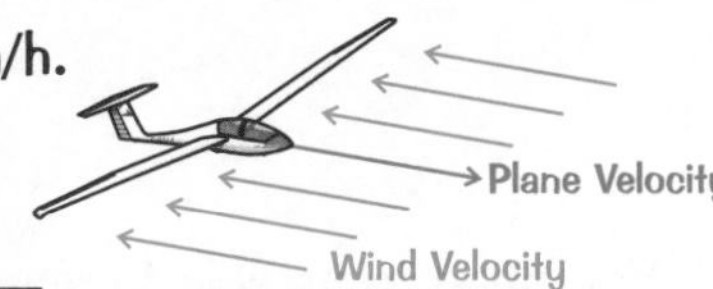

Draw the vectors end to end:

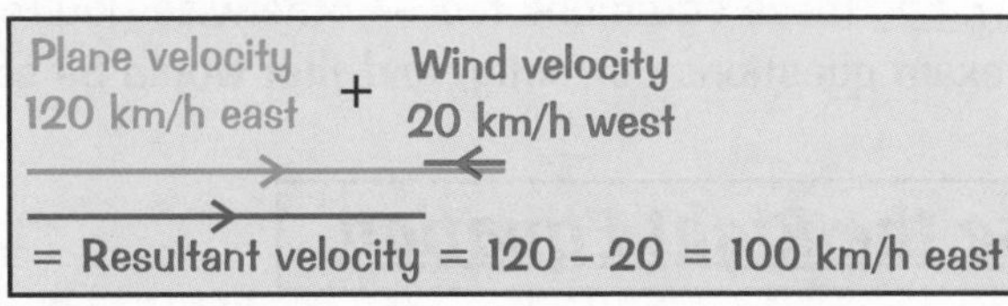

Sometimes these are called vector sums.

So an observer on the ground would see the plane going east at 100 km/h. (If the plane and the wind were in the same direction you'd add the velocities together to get the resultant velocity.)

2) Across the Current — A Bit More Maths

If the plane (or whatever) is flying across the wind (or whatever), it's a bit more tricky.

EXAMPLE: A boat is going west at 14 m/s (according to the speed indicator) in a river with a current running north at 8 m/s. What is its resultant velocity?

Draw the vectors end to end.
It makes a triangle (because the vectors are at right-angles):

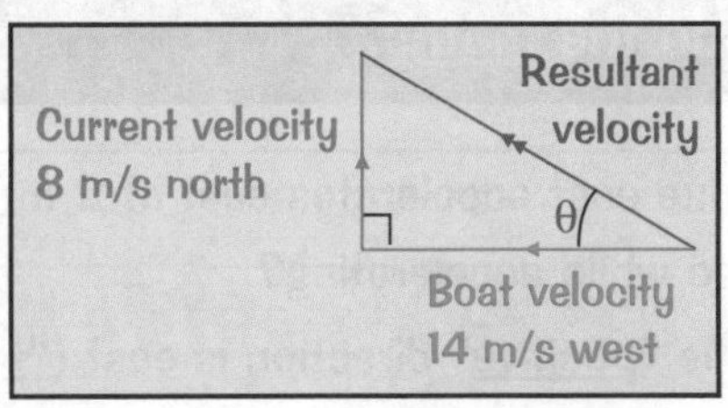

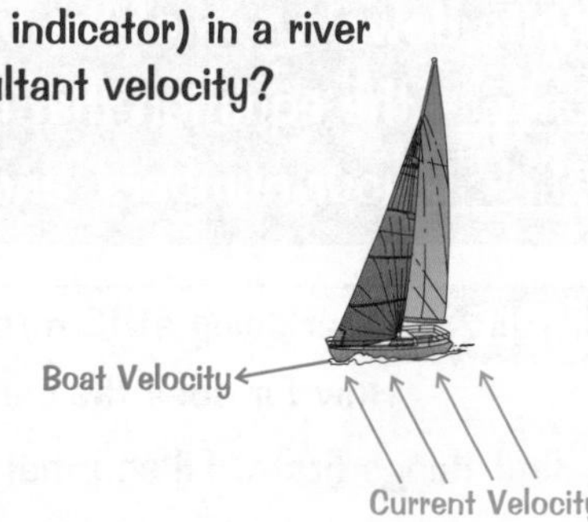

To work out the resultant velocity, you need both speed and direction. It's a right-angled triangle, so:

For speed you need Pythagoras' theorem: speed = $\sqrt{(8^2 + 14^2)}$ = 16.1 m/s

And for direction, it's good old trigonometry: $\tan\theta = 8/14$, so $\theta = \tan^{-1}(8/14) = 29.7°$

It's the Same with Forces and ANY Vectors at Right Angles

EXAMPLE: Two big beasties are pulling a boat along a canal, with forces at right angles to each other. Find the resultant force.

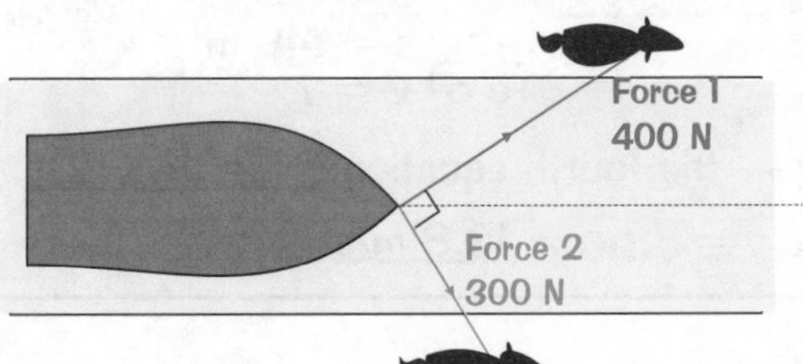

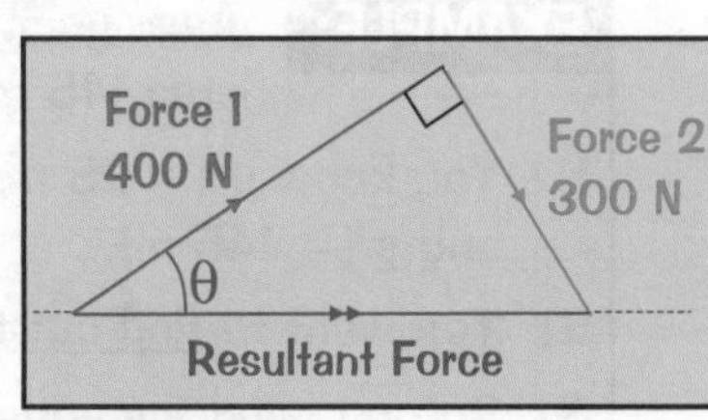

Draw the vectors end to end, to make a right-angled triangle:

And it's Pythagoras again:

Size of Force = $\sqrt{(300^2 + 400^2)}$ = 500 N

Direction = angle of θ to Force 1, which you find by trig:
$\tan\theta = 300/400$, so $\theta = \tan^{-1}(3/4) = 36.9°$

I've got a brand new combine velocity...

You use the same trick to combine any vectors — momentum, displacement, acceleration, anything. Just draw the vectors end to end and, with a bit of maths, you can find the overall (resultant) vector.

Equations of Motion

These <u>equations of motion</u> are dead handy for working out <u>velocity</u>, <u>acceleration</u> and other goodies...

You Need to Know These Four Equations of Motion

Which of these equations you need to use depends on what you <u>know</u>, and what you need to <u>find out</u>. They're <u>easier</u> to use if you know them like the back of your hand.

Altogether, there are <u>5 things</u> involved in these equations:
- u = <u>initial velocity</u> (or speed),
- v = <u>final velocity</u> (or speed),
- s = <u>displacement</u> (or distance),
- t = <u>time</u>,
- a = <u>acceleration</u>.

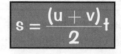

$$s = \frac{(u+v)}{2}t \qquad v = u + at$$

$$s = ut + \frac{1}{2}at^2 \qquad v^2 = u^2 + 2as$$

You need to be able to <u>rearrange</u> these equations too — otherwise you're not going to be able to do the exam questions correctly, and that would be sad.

Make Sure You Use the Right Equation

If you know <u>three things</u>, you can find out <u>either</u> of the <u>other two</u> — if you use the <u>right equation</u>, that is. And if you use this method <u>twice</u>, you can find out <u>both</u> things you don't know.

HOW TO CHOOSE YOUR EQUATION:
1) Write down which <u>three</u> things you <u>already know</u>.
2) Write down <u>which</u> of the other things you want to <u>find out</u>.
3) <u>Choose</u> the equation that involves <u>all</u> the things you've <u>written down</u>.
4) <u>Stick in</u> your numbers, and do the <u>maths</u>.

<u>REMEMBER</u>: <u>Direction's</u> important for <u>velocity</u>, <u>acceleration</u> & <u>displacement</u> — always choose which direction's <u>positive</u>, and <u>stick</u> with it.

EXAMPLE: A car going at 10 m/s due east accelerates east at 2 m/s² for 8 s. How far does the car go while accelerating?

Now, first things first... I'll say that the "<u>positive</u>" direction is east ("<u>to the right</u>").

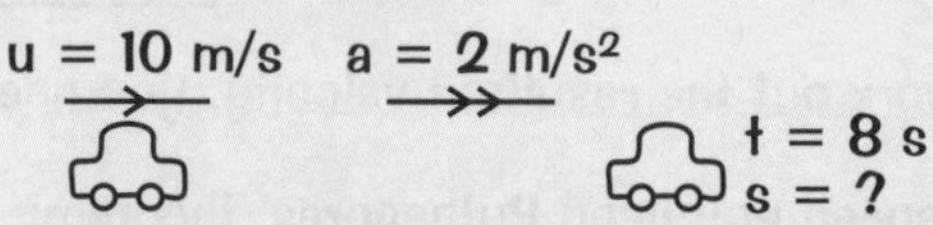

1) You know <u>u</u> (= 10 m/s), <u>a</u> (= 2 m/s²) and <u>t</u> (= 8 s).
2) You want to <u>find out</u> the displacement, <u>s</u>.
3) So you need the equation with <u>all</u> these in: <u>u</u>, <u>a</u>, <u>t</u> and <u>s</u> — the third equation: $s = ut + \frac{1}{2}at^2$.
4) Put the numbers in: $s = (10 \times 8) + ½(2 \times 8^2) = 80 + 64 =$ <u>144 m</u> due east.

EXAMPLE: A car going at 25 m/s decelerates at 1.5 m/s² as it heads towards a built-up area 145 m away. What will its speed be when it reaches the built-up area?

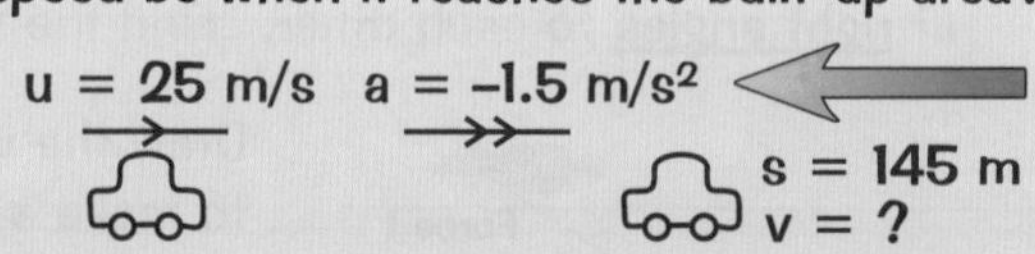

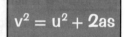

<u>a</u> is –ve, because it's <u>deceleration</u>.

1) You know <u>u</u> (= 25 m/s), <u>a</u> (= –1.5 m/s²) and <u>s</u> (= 145 m).
2) You want to <u>find out</u> the final speed, <u>v</u>.
3) So you need the equation with <u>all</u> these in: <u>u</u>, <u>a</u>, <u>s</u> and <u>v</u> — the fourth equation: <u>$v^2 = u^2 + 2as$</u>.
4) Put the numbers in: $v^2 = 25^2 + 2(-1.5)(145) = 190$ so $v = \sqrt{190} =$ <u>13.8 m/s</u>

Motion problems — eat more figs or follow the method above...

1) <u>LEARN THE EQUATIONS IN THE RED BOXES</u>. It's better to learn them, there's no way round that.
2) <u>LEARN THE METHOD IN THE BLUE BOX</u>. Motion questions can look tricky at first, but that method works for all of them. Practise the examples again — cover up my working and do them yourself.

Projectile Motion

Is it a bird? Is it a plane? No, it's a projectile. Hmm... exciting stuff, this — things flying through the air, where the only force on them is due to gravity.

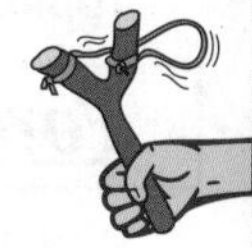

The Path of a Projectile is Always a Parabola

1) A projectile is something that is projected, or dropped, and from then on only has Earth's gravitational field (gravity) acting on it (ignoring air resistance).
2) So things like missiles, golf balls and footballs are all projectiles.
3) The path a projectile takes through the air (called its trajectory) is always parabolic, which is this shape:

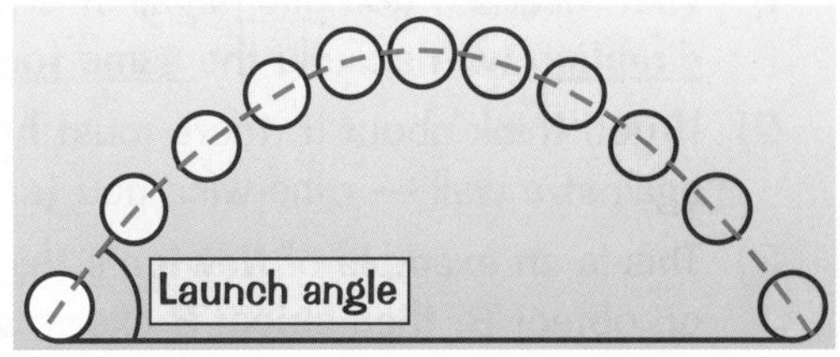

4) How far a ball (or other projectile) travels depends on the angle it's launched at. It will travel furthest if it's launched at 45°.
5) If the angle's less than 45°, then the projectile won't travel as far.
6) An angle greater than 45° means the projectile will take longer to hit the ground but won't travel as far.

Deal with Horizontal and Vertical Motion Separately

1) Motion can be split into two separate bits — the horizontal bit and the vertical bit.
2) These bits are totally separate — one doesn't affect the other.
3) So gravity (which only acts downwards) doesn't affect horizontal motion at all.
4) An object projected horizontally accelerates vertically due to gravity, but has no acceleration horizontally (i.e. its velocity stays the same).

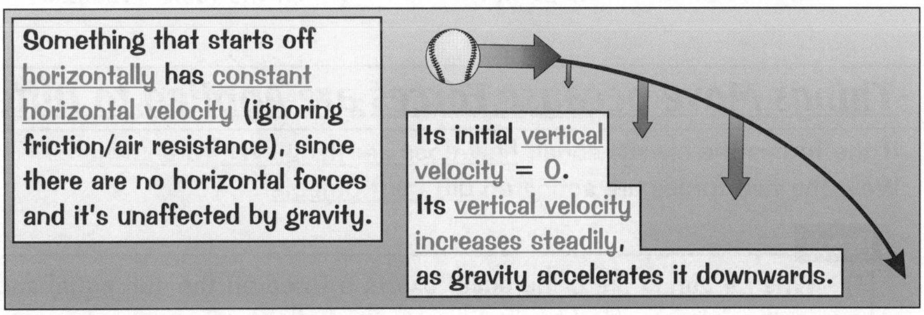

Something that starts off horizontally has constant horizontal velocity (ignoring friction/air resistance), since there are no horizontal forces and it's unaffected by gravity.
Its initial vertical velocity = 0.
Its vertical velocity increases steadily, as gravity accelerates it downwards.

5) An object can also be projected at an angle, and the motion can be split into horizontal and vertical parts. You can apply this to real-life situations, e.g. how far a ball travels depends on the angle it's struck at.
6) Both bits of the motion — the horizontal velocity and the vertical velocity — are vectors. The overall (resultant) velocity of the ball at any point is the vector sum of the separate bits (see p. 87).

Projectile Calculations Use the Equations of Motion

g = acceleration due to gravity

Example: A football is kicked horizontally from a 20 m high wall. How long is it before it lands? Take $g = 10\ \text{m/s}^2$, and ignore air resistance.

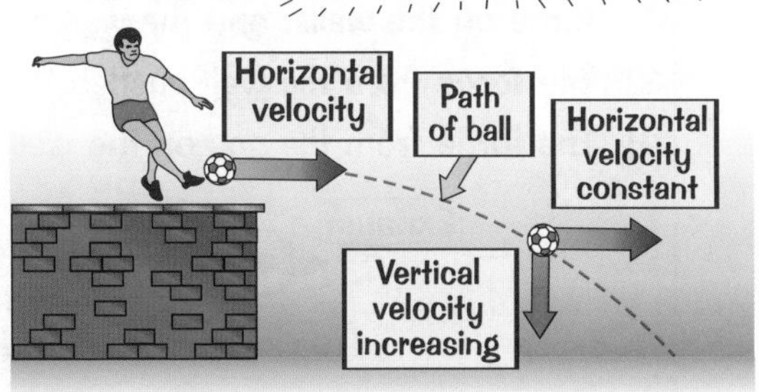

Not to scale (otherwise he'd be a very tall man).

It lands when it's travelled 20 m vertically (height of the wall).
Using $s = ut + \frac{1}{2}at^2$, where $u = 0$, $a = 10\ \text{m/s}^2$, $s = 20$ m:
$20 = (0 \times t) + \frac{1}{2}at^2 = \frac{10t^2}{2}$, i.e. $t = 2$ s when it lands.

If its horizontal velocity is 5 m/s, how far does it travel before it lands?

Using "distance = speed × time", where $v = 5$ m/s and $t = 2$ s: $s = 5 \times 2 = 10$ m.

From above.

See previous page for more equations of motion.

What do mathematicians do if they have motion problems...?

Get a pencil and, er, draw a diagram. Always start projectile questions with a diagram. If it doesn't look like you've much info... DON'T PANIC. Remember — if it starts from rest, you know that initial velocity = 0. You also know that if it's moving under gravity, the acceleration is $10\ \text{m/s}^2$ downwards. And take it from there.

Forces and Newton's Third Law

Typical — you wait ages for a force and then two come along at once. Well, that's physics for you.

Forces Occur When Two Objects Interact

When an object exerts a force on another object it always experiences a force in return.
These two forces are sometimes called an 'interaction pair'.

1) That means if you push against a wall, the wall will push back against you in the opposite direction with exactly the same force and as soon as you stop pushing, so does the wall.
2) If you think about it, there must be an opposing force when you push (or lean) against a wall — otherwise you (and the wall) would fall over.
3) This is an example of Newton's third law of motion — if object A exerts a force on object B, then object B exerts an equal and opposite force on object A.

4) The same is true in a collision — colliding objects exert equal and opposite forces on each other.

Objects Exert a Downward Force Due to Gravity

1) If you put a book on a table, the book pushes down on the table with a force equal to its weight — and the table exerts an equal and opposite force upwards on the book.
2) This upward force is called a reaction force — because it's the table's 'response' to the force exerted by the book. If the book weighs 10 N then the table's reaction force will be 10 N.

Things Move because Forces are Applied to Different Objects

If the forces are always equal, how does anything ever go anywhere?
Well, the two forces are acting on different objects.

Recoil

1) When a gun is fired, the bullet exerts a force on the gun equal and opposite to the force exerted by the gun on the bullet.
2) So, the bullet travels out of the barrel and the gun recoils in the opposite direction.
3) The bullet travels much faster forwards than the gun does backwards because the bullet is much lighter.

Rockets

1) When gas particles collide with things they exert a force on them (see p. 92).
2) In a rocket engine particles of hot gas collide with the walls, exerting a force on the walls, and the wall exerts an equal but opposite force on them.
3) The force from the wall pushes the gas particles out of the exhaust.
4) The force from the gas on the wall pushes the rocket forwards.

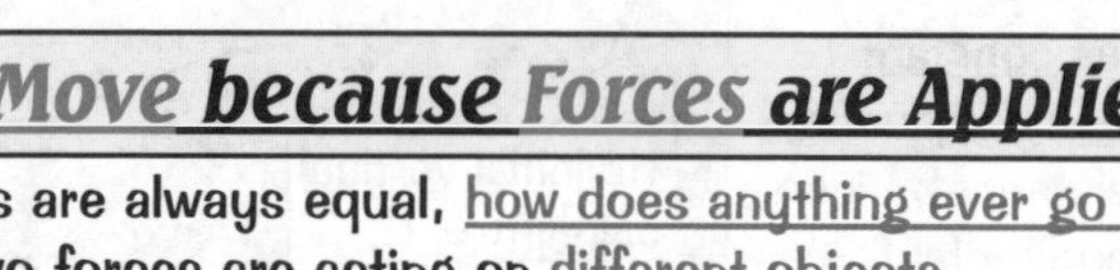

5) The force pushing the rocket upwards must be larger than the force of gravity and air resistance, or it won't take off.
6) So, for large rockets, used to lift satellites into orbit above the Earth, you need a large number of particles moving at high speed to produce enough force to lift the rocket.

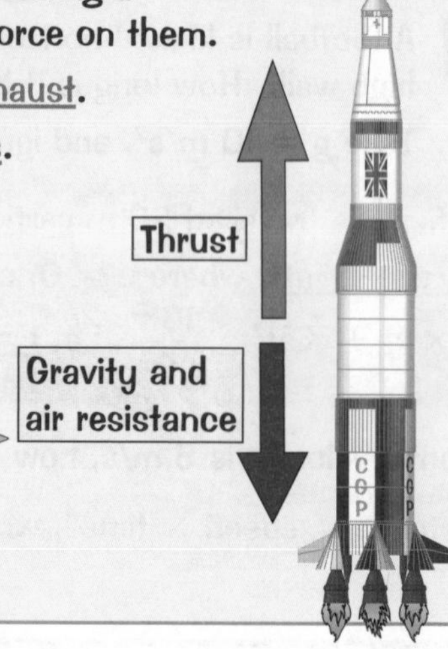

I have a reaction to forces — they bring me out in a rash...

Funnily enough, Newton's fourth law is "more revision equals better exam results". Newton was a smart guy.

Conservation of Momentum

You know that when two objects collide they exert equal but opposite forces on each other. Well now you also get to learn that momentum is conserved (but not in the same way as tigers).

Momentum = Mass × Velocity

Quick reminder (you did this is P3): The greater the mass of an object and the greater its velocity, the more momentum the object has.

Momentum (kg m/s) = Mass (kg) × Velocity (m/s)

Momentum Before = Momentum After

1) In a collision when no other (external) forces act, momentum is conserved — i.e. the total momentum after is the same as it was before.
2) This explains the recoil action of guns too — before a shot is fired the gun and bullet have no velocity, so they have no momentum either. When a shot's fired, the bullet travels forward (with positive momentum) and the gun recoils backward (with negative momentum). The combined momentum of the bullet and the gun will be zero (because they each have the same amount of momentum, but in opposite directions).
3) Conservation of momentum also explains rocket propulsion and explosions:

Momentum of bullet = momentum of gun.

Rockets work in much the same way as guns — they chuck a load of exhaust gases out backwards, and since momentum is conserved, the rocket moves forwards.

Before an explosion, total momentum = 0. When something explodes, particles are thrown out at different speeds and in all directions, so they have different momentums that all add up to 0.

4) If two objects collide and coalesce (join together), then the total momentum of both objects before the collision = momentum of the combined objects after the collision:

$$(m_1 \times u_1) + (m_2 \times u_2) = (m_1 + m_2) \times v$$

Where:
m_1 = mass of first object
u_1 = velocity of first object
m_2 = mass of second object
u_2 = velocity of second object
v = velocity of combined objects

Example 1:

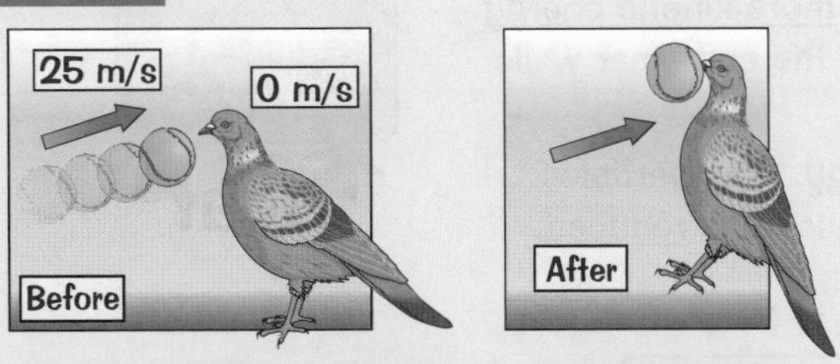

A tennis ball (60 g) collides with a perching pigeon (350 g), as shown, and they move off together. Calculate the momentum after the collision.

1) Convert masses into kg (because momentum is measured in kg m/s):
mass of ball = 60 g ÷ 1000 = 0.06 kg
mass of pigeon = 350 g ÷ 1000 = 0.35 kg
2) Momentum is conserved, so momentum before = momentum after = $(m_1 \times u_1) + (m_2 \times u_2)$
3) Treat the direction the ball is moving as positive, and put the numbers into the equation:
$(0.06 \times 25) + (350 \times 0)$ = 1.5 kg m/s

Example 2:

Two skaters approach each other, collide and move off together as shown. At what velocity do they move after the collision?

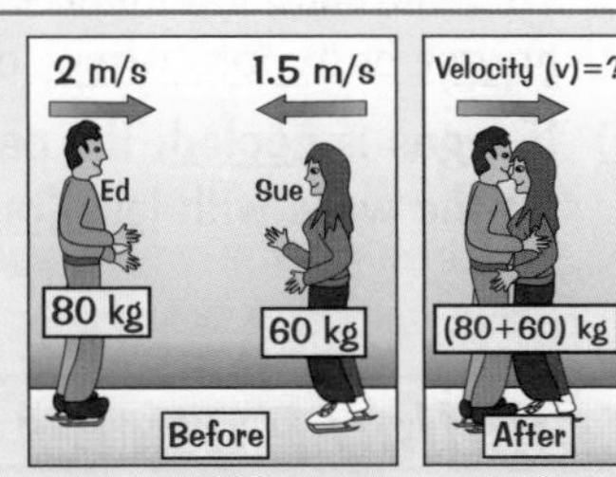

1) Choose which direction is positive. I'll say "positive" means "to the right".
2) Ed and Sue collide and join together, so:
$(m_{Ed} \times u_{Ed}) + (m_{Sue} \times u_{Sue}) = (m_{Ed} + m_{Sue}) \times v$
3) Put in the numbers:
$(80 \times 2) + (60 \times (-1.5)) = (80 + 60) \times v$
so $70 = 140v$
4) Find the velocity:
$v = 70 \div 140$
v = 0.5 m/s to the right

Because it's positive.

Crash test dummies know all too well about momentum...

There are loads of great things that are conserved — momentum, pandas, fruit, energy... I could go on.

Pressure

Gases fly around, bump into things and exert a force on them. This is happening to you right now — the air around you is exerting pressure on you (unless you're somehow reading this in space).

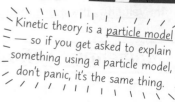

Kinetic Theory Says Gases are Randomly Moving Particles

1) Kinetic theory says that gases consist of very small particles. Which they do — oxygen consists of oxygen molecules, neon consists of neon atoms, etc.
2) These particles are constantly moving in completely random directions.
3) They constantly collide with each other and with the walls of their container. When they collide, they bounce off each other, or off the walls.
4) The particles hardly take up any space. Most of the gas is empty space.

Kinetic theory is a particle model — so if you get asked to explain something using a particle model, don't panic, it's the same thing.

A Decrease in Volume Gives an Increase in Pressure

1) As gas particles move about, they bang into each other and whatever else happens to get in the way.
2) Gas particles have some mass, so when they collide with something, they exert a force on it.
3) In a sealed container, gas particles smash against the container's walls — creating an outward pressure.
4) If you put the same amount of gas in a bigger container (increased volume), the pressure will decrease, cos there'll be fewer collisions between the gas particles and the container's walls.
5) When the volume's reduced, the particles get more squashed up and so they hit the walls more often, hence the pressure increases.

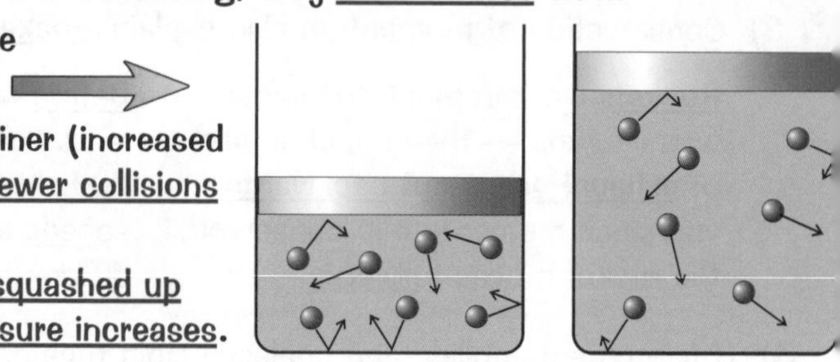

Increasing the Temperature Increases the Pressure

1) The pressure of a gas depends on how fast the particles are moving and how often they hit the walls of the container they're in.
2) If you heat a gas, the particles move faster and have more kinetic energy. This increase in kinetic energy means the particles hit the container walls harder and more often, creating more pressure.
3) If a gas is cooled, the particles have less kinetic energy. The particles hit the walls with less force and less often, so the pressure is reduced.

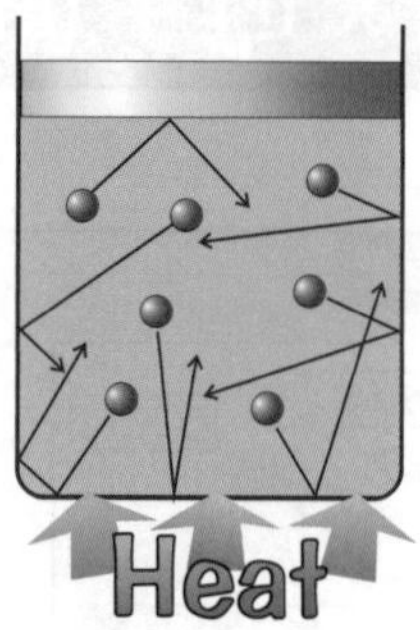

Colliding Particles Change Their Momentum

1) Gas particles are moving and have mass, so they also have momentum — $M = m \times v$.
2) When gas particles collide with the walls of a container their velocity changes.
3) A change in velocity (Δv) also means a change in momentum — $\Delta M = m \times \Delta v$.
4) You know from P3 that force = change in momentum ÷ time taken — $F = \Delta M \div t$.
5) So as particles collide with a container, they experience a change of momentum and exert a force on the walls of the container. This creates pressure.
6) Hotter particles collide more often too, so there are more particles exerting a force on the container and the pressure increases.

Less space, more collisions, more pressure — just like London...

Don't get the volume of a gas confused with the volume of your TV — same word, different thing. Nightmare.

Gravity and Orbits

In case you've forgotten... gravity is the universal force of attraction between masses. It's not really noticeable with normal masses though, only with huge ones like planets, stars and massive biscuits.

Gravity Provides the Centripetal Force That Causes Orbits

1) If an object is travelling in a circle it is constantly changing direction, which means there must be a force acting on it.
2) An orbit is a balance between the forward motion of the object and a force pulling it inwards. This is called a centripetal force (pronounced sen-tree-pee-tal) — it's directed towards the centre of the circle.
3) The planets move around the Sun in almost circular orbits. The centripetal forces that make this happen are provided by the gravitational force (gravity) between each planet and the Sun.
4) Similarly, the Moon orbits the Earth because of the centripetal force produced by the gravitational force between the Earth and the Moon.
5) Artificial satellites (see next page) orbit the Earth. The centripetal force is provided by the Earth's gravity.
6) They keep accelerating towards the Earth but their tangential motion (at a right angle to the acceleration), keeps them in an almost circular orbit.

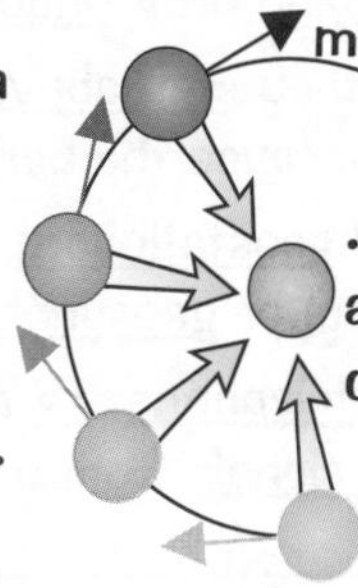
The planet is 'trying' to move in this direction...
... but the force is always towards the centre of the circle.

Gravity Decreases Quickly as You Get Further Away

1) With very large masses like stars and planets, the gravitational force is very big and acts a long way out.
2) The closer you get to a star or a planet, the stronger the force of attraction.
3) Because of this stronger force, planets nearer the Sun move faster and cover their orbit quicker.
4) Moons, artificial satellites and space stations are also held in orbit by gravity. The further out from Earth they orbit, the slower they move (see next page for more on satellites).
5) The size of the gravitational force follows the fairly famous "inverse square" relationship. The main effect of that is that the force decreases very quickly with increasing distance. The formula is $F \propto 1/d^2$, but I reckon it's easier just to remember the basic idea in words:

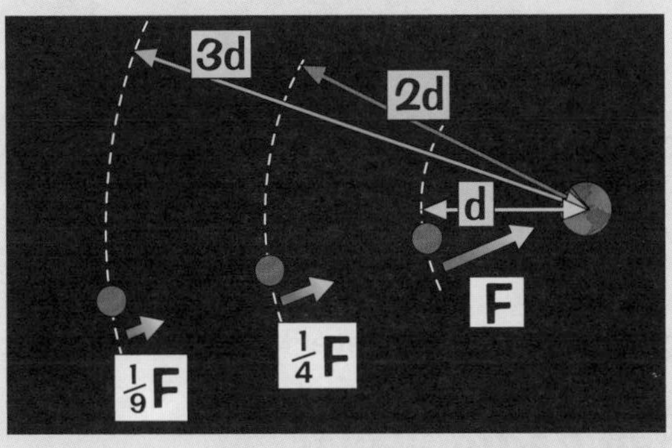
3d
2d
d
F
$\frac{1}{4}$F
$\frac{1}{9}$F

a) If you double the distance from a planet, the size of the gravitational force will decrease by a factor of four (2^2).
b) If you treble the distance, the gravitational force will decrease by a factor of nine (3^2), and so on.
c) On the other hand, if you get twice as close the gravity becomes four times stronger.

Comets Change Speed Because of Gravity

1) Periodic comets orbit the Sun, but have highly elliptical (elongated) orbits.
2) The Sun isn't at the centre of the orbit but near one end, so their orbits take them out a long way from the Sun, then back in close again.
3) The closer the comet is to the Sun the greater the gravitational force of attraction.
4) So, the comet travels much faster when it's nearer the Sun than it does in the more distant parts of its orbit.

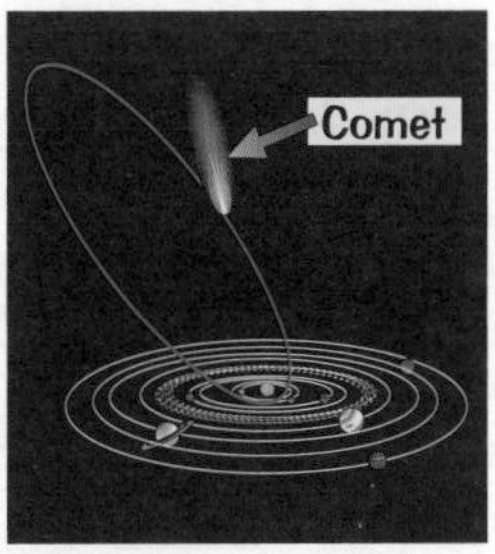
Comet

The gravity of the situation increases as you get closer to the exam...

There are also non-periodic comets, which pass through the Solar System, but don't actually orbit the Sun.

Satellites

A satellite is any object that orbits around a larger object in space. There are natural satellites, like moons, but this page just looks at the artificial ones that we put there ourselves, like for satellite phones and stuff.

Communications Satellites Stay Over the Same Point on Earth

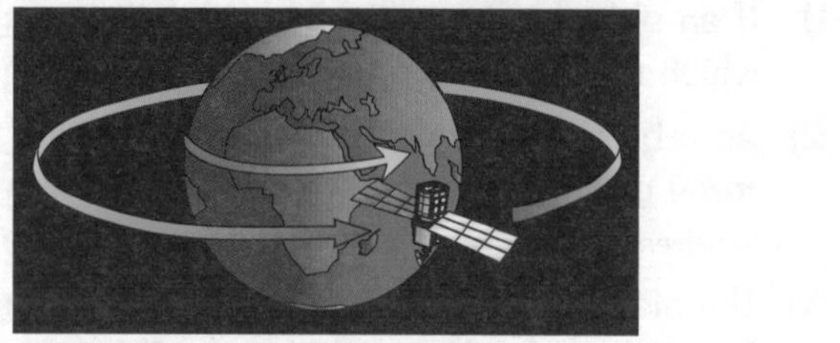

1) Communications satellites are put in quite a high orbit over the equator and orbit once every 24 hours.
2) This means that they stay above the same point on the Earth's surface because the Earth rotates with them.
3) So they're called geostationary artificial satellites (geo(Earth)-stationary) or geosynchronous satellites.
4) They're ideal for telephone, TV and radio because they stay at the same point above the Earth and can transfer signals from one side of the Earth to another in a fraction of a second.

Weather and Spying Satellites Need to be in a Low Orbit

1) Geostationary satellites are too high and too stationary to take good weather or spying photos — you need low polar orbits, which pass over both poles and are nice and low.

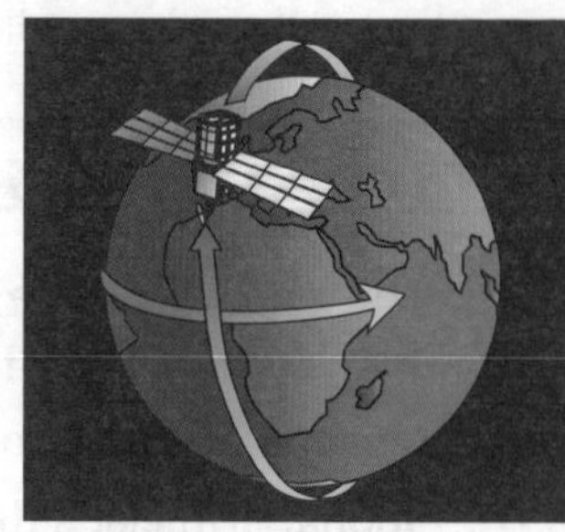

2) In a low polar orbit, the satellite sweeps over both poles whilst the Earth rotates beneath it.
3) They're much closer to the Earth than geostationary satellites, so the pull of gravity is stronger and they move much faster.
4) So they orbit really quickly, often with a period of less than 2 hours.
5) Each time the satellite comes round it can scan the next bit of the globe. This allows the whole surface of the planet to be monitored each day.

Microwaves are Used for Satellite Communication

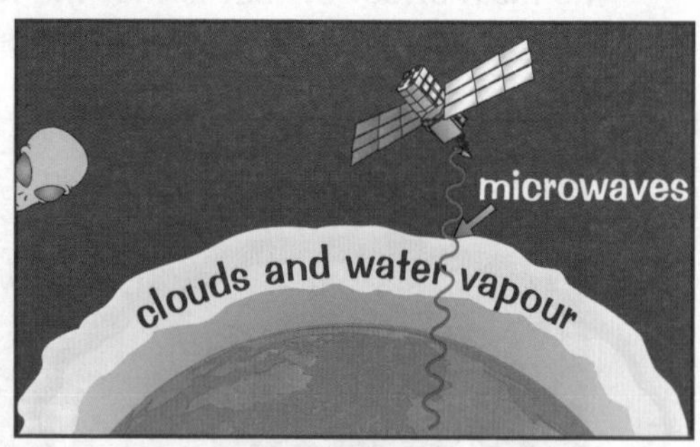

1) Communication to and from satellites (including satellite TV signals and satellite phones) uses microwaves.
2) For satellite TV and phones, the signal from a transmitter is transmitted into space...
3) ... where it's picked up by the satellite's receiver dish orbiting thousands of kilometres above the Earth. The satellite transmits the signal back to Earth in a different direction...
4) ... where it's received by a satellite dish on the ground.
5) Or... satellites receiving the signal then retransmit it to other satellites, and eventually back down to Earth.

Microwaves Have Higher Frequencies than Radio Waves

1) Microwaves have a very high frequency — over 3000 MHz (3 GHz). Radio waves have lower frequencies than this — see next page.
2) Microwaves pass easily through the atmosphere to satellites orbiting the Earth, enabling the signal to reach distant parts of the planet.
3) Satellites in low orbit (closer to the Earth) use lower frequencies than satellites in higher, geostationary orbit (always above the same point on Earth).
4) Satellite signals weaken because they travel long distances (losing intensity and picking up interference).
5) So digital signals are used because they're high quality — they don't suffer as much from interference.

There's more on EM waves and communication on the next page — and you did a bit of it in P1.

So you can thank satellites next time you ring home from Everest...

GPS satellites transmit their position and the time, so you can find out where you are. Pretty clever stuff.

Radio Waves and Microwaves

Microwaves are used for satellite communication and their longer-wavelength cousins, radio waves, are used for (yep, you guessed it) radio communication. I don't communicate with my cousins :-(.

Different Frequency Waves Travel By Different Routes

Electromagnetic (EM) waves with different frequencies are used to transmit different types of communication signal, because they behave differently in the atmosphere:

1) Below 30 MHz — radio waves are reflected off a layer of the atmosphere called the ionosphere. This allows the wave to travel longer distances and deals with the curvature of the Earth.
2) Between 30 MHz and 30 GHz — radio waves and microwaves pass straight through the atmosphere, so transmissions must be by line of sight (because they can't reflect off the atmosphere).
3) Above 30 GHz — rain and dust in the atmosphere absorb and scatter microwaves. This reduces the strength of the signal, so the highest frequency that can be used for satellite transmissions is about 30 GHz.

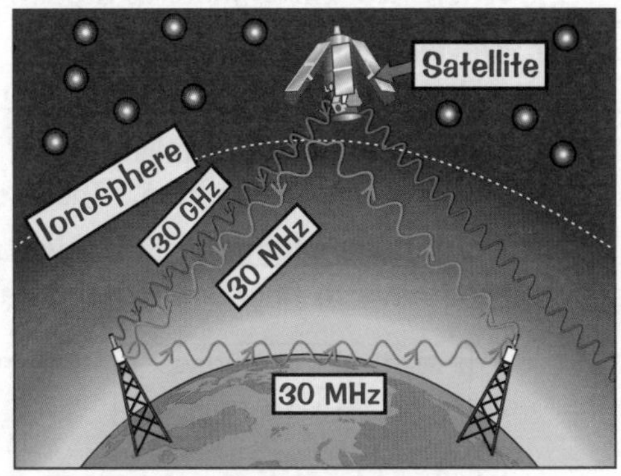

Long Wavelength Radio Waves Diffract

(You did a bit on this in P1 as well.)

1) All waves tend to spread out (diffract) when they pass through a narrow gap or past an object.
2) A "narrow" gap is one which is about the same size as the wavelength.
3) Obviously then, the question of whether a gap is "narrow" or not depends on the wave in question. What may be a narrow gap for a long wavelength radio wave will be a huge gap for a microwave.
4) It should be obvious then that the longer the wavelength of a wave, the more it will diffract. You get maximum diffraction when the size of the gap is equal to the wavelength of the wave.

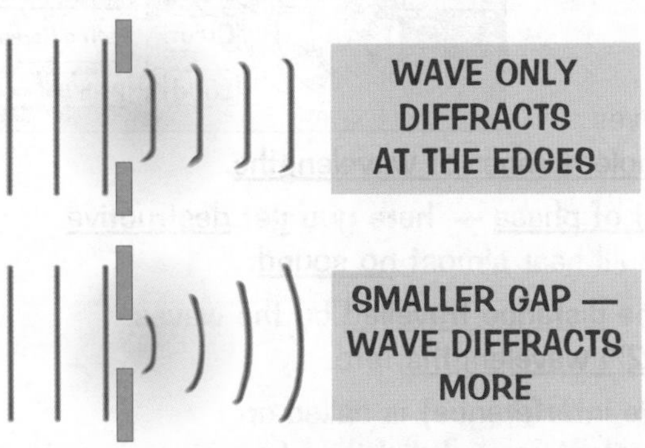

Long Wavelength Radio Waves Diffract Easily over Hills and into Buildings:

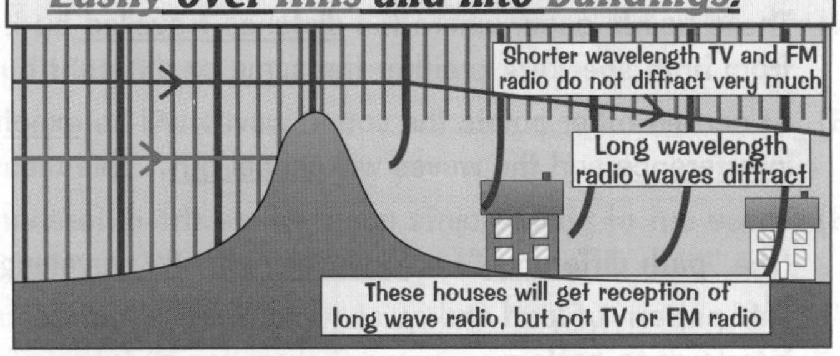

5) So because long wavelength radio waves have a really large wavelength they also have a really long range. They spread out in all directions so are great for broadcasting, and can diffract over hills and through tunnels, and even over the horizon.

Dishes are Used to Receive Microwave Signals

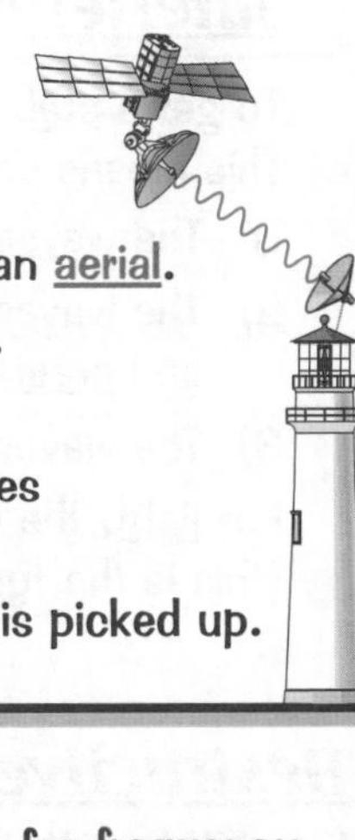

1) Regular (terrestrial) TV and radio signals transmitted using radio waves are received using an aerial.
2) But the wavelength of microwaves is too short for aerials to be effective at receiving them.
3) So satellite TV and radio signals are received and transmitted using a dish.
4) The dishes are many times larger than the wavelength of the microwaves, so the microwaves don't diffract much — this produces a narrow beam that doesn't spread out.
5) This means the transmitting and receiving dishes need to be carefully aligned so the signal is picked up.

Diffraction — it can drive you round the bend...

The first person to transmit and receive radio waves was Heinrich Hertz in 1888. The unit we use for frequency (Hertz, Hz) is named after him. 10 years later, Nikola Tesla managed to build a radio controlled boat. Nifty.

Interference of Waves

Waves can interfere with each other, you know. Uh-huh. They can add to each other or cancel out.

When Waves Meet They Cause a Disturbance

(just like teenagers)

1) All waves cause some kind of disturbance in a medium — water waves disturb water particles, sound waves disturb air particles, electromagnetic waves disturb electric and magnetic fields.
2) When two waves meet at a point they both try to cause their own disturbance.
3) Waves either disturb in the same direction and reinforce each other (constructive interference), or in opposite directions and cancel each other out (destructive interference).
4) Think of a 'pulse' travelling down a slinky spring meeting a pulse travelling in the opposite direction. These diagrams show the possible outcomes:
5) The total amplitude of the waves at a point is the sum of the displacements (you have to take direction into account) of the waves at that point.

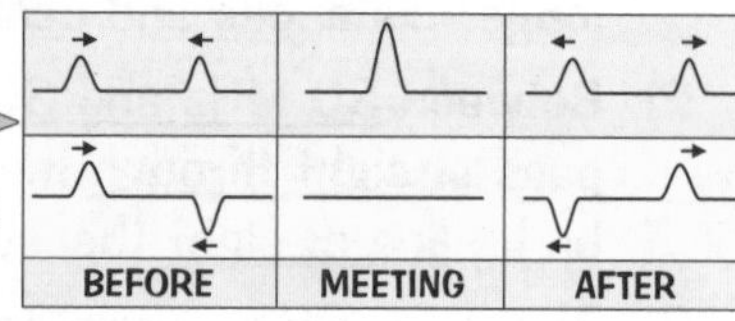

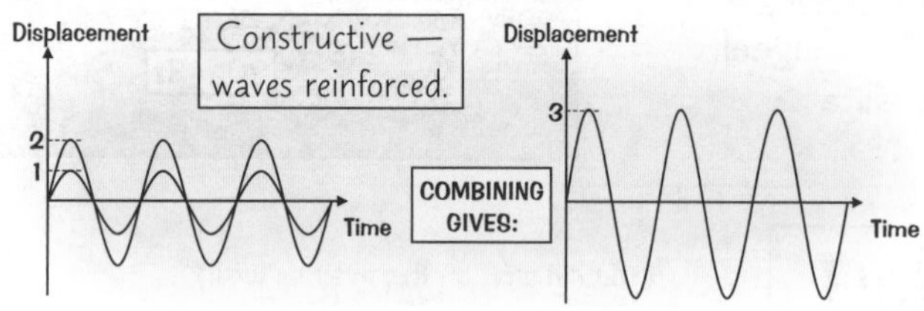

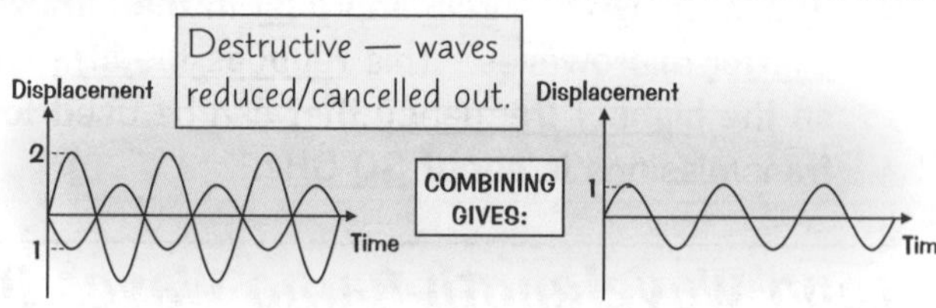

You Get Patterns of 'Loud' and 'Quiet' Bits with Sound

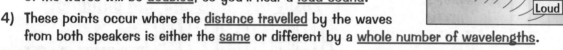

1) Two speakers both play the same note, at exactly the same time.
2) Depending on where you stand in front of them, you'll either hear a loud sound or almost nothing.
3) At certain points, the sound waves will be in phase — here you get constructive interference. The amplitude of the waves will be doubled, so you'll hear a loud sound.
4) These points occur where the distance travelled by the waves from both speakers is either the same or different by a whole number of wavelengths.
5) At certain other points the sound waves will be exactly out of phase — here you get destructive interference and the waves will cancel out. This means you'll hear almost no sound.
6) These out of phase points occur where the difference in the distance travelled by the waves (the "path difference") is ½ wavelength, 1½ wavelengths, 2½ wavelengths, etc.
7) This pattern of loud and quiet (constructive and destructive interference) is called an interference pattern — you get them for all types of waves (e.g. sound, light, water, microwaves).

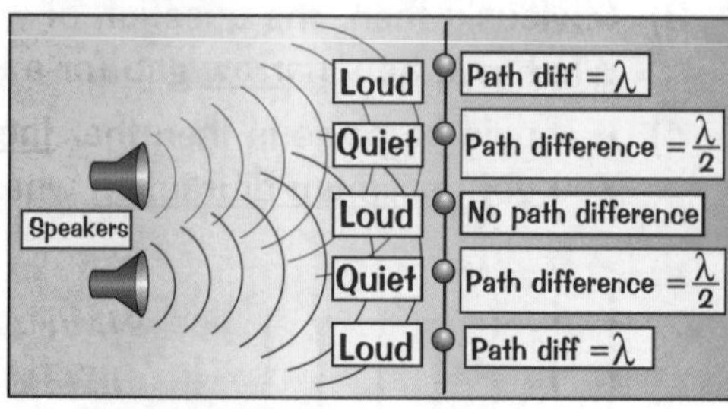

Interference Patterns Need Coherent Wave Sources

To get a stable interference pattern you need to use coherent wave sources. This means sources where:

1) The waves are at the same frequency (and so wavelength).
2) The waves are in phase — the troughs and crests of the waves line up.
3) The waves have the same amplitude.

For light, the coherent sources are monochromatic light (this is the type of light needed to make an interference pattern).

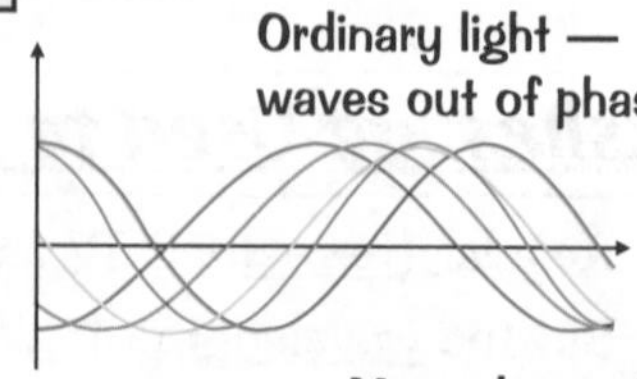

Ordinary light — waves out of phase

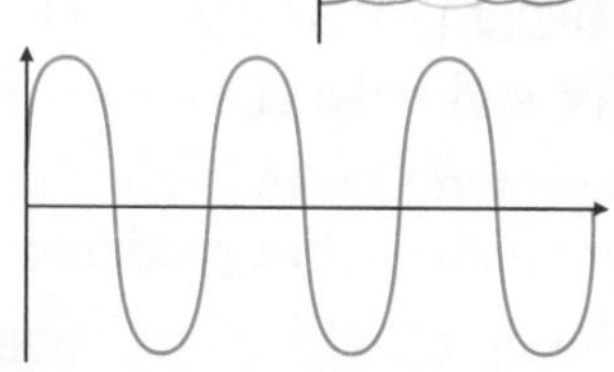

Monochromatic coherent light — waves in phase

Destructive interference — too many cooks spoil the wave...

It's weird, isn't it... I mean, constructive interference makes perfect sense — two waves, bigger sound... it's just destructive interference that gets me. I know WHY it happens... but I still find it weird.

Diffraction Patterns and Polarisation

When light diffracts (spreads out through a gap) it makes an interference pattern.

When Light Diffracts You Get Patterns of Light and Dark

1) You get interference patterns when waves of equal frequency or wavelength overlap.
2) When a wavefront passes through a gap, light from each point along the gap diffracts. It's as if every point along the wavefront is a light source in its own right. Strange but true.
3) The gap must be about the same size as the wavelength of the light, otherwise the light won't be diffracted very much.
4) Diffracted light from each of these points interferes with light diffracted from all the other points. So you get an interference pattern even from just one slit.
5) The pattern has a bright central fringe with alternating dark and bright fringes on either side of it.

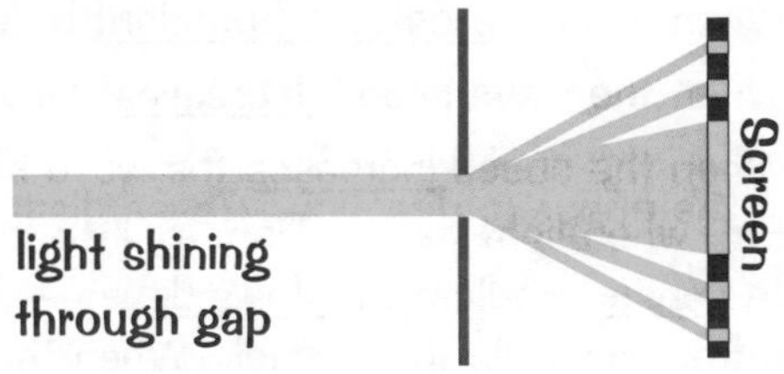

Light Behaves Like a Wave... and a Stream of Particles

1) In the 17th century, there were two theories to explain the nature of light — particle theory (Isaac Newton) and wave theory (Christiaan Huygens).
2) The particle theory of light could explain reflection and refraction, but diffraction and interference are both unique to waves.
3) Thomas Young's double-slit experiment (over 100 years later) showed that light could both diffract (through two narrow slits) and interfere (to form an interference pattern on a screen).
4) In the experiment, a coherent light source (e.g. a laser) is shone through two slits.
5) You get a pattern of light and dark fringes, showing constructive and destructive interference taking place — which shows light also behaves as a wave.
6) So, it's now accepted that light shows properties of a wave (diffraction, interference and polarisation).

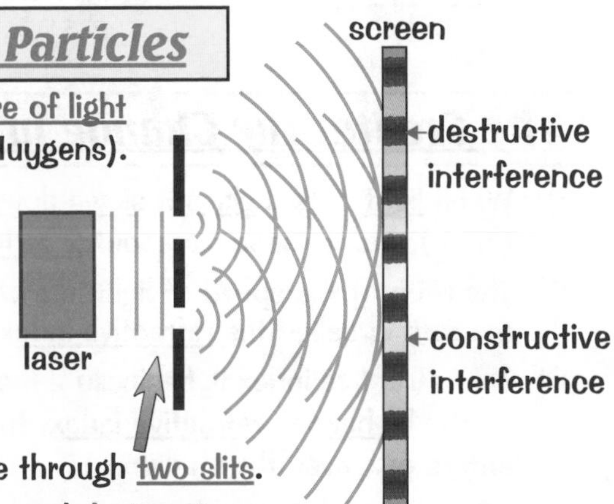

Transverse Waves Can be Plane Polarised

1) Electromagnetic waves are transverse waves — the vibrations are at 90° to the direction of travel of the wave.

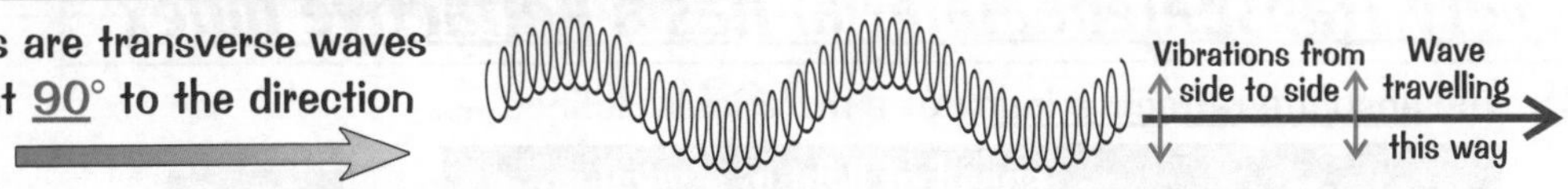

2) You can make a transverse wave by shaking a rope up and down, or side to side, or in a mixture of directions. Whichever plane you're shaking it in, it's still a transverse wave.
3) Now imagine trying to pass a rope that's waving about in all different directions through the slats of a wooden fence.
4) The only vibrations that'll get through the fence are the vertical ones. The fence filters out vibrations in all the other directions. This is called plane polarisation of the wave.

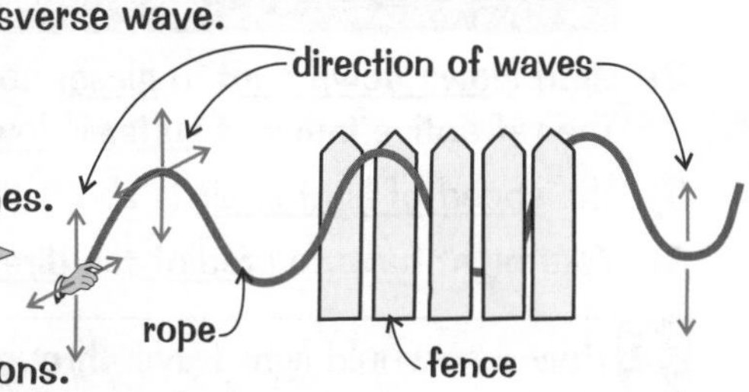

5) Ordinary light waves are a mixture of vibrations in different directions.
6) Passing the light through a polarising filter is like passing the rope through the fence — the filter only transmits (lets through) vibrations in one particular direction.
7) So plane polarised light is made up of vibrations in one direction only.
8) When light is reflected from some surfaces (like water) it is partly plane polarised.
9) Polaroid sunglasses act as polarising filters — they can filter out reflected glare from the sea or the snow.

Plane polarised — a tinted windscreen in your cockpit...

Light can be circularly polarised instead of plane polarised, but this is much more confusing so we'll ignore it.

Refraction

1) Refraction is when waves change direction as they enter a different medium.
2) This is caused entirely by the change in speed of the waves.
3) The speed change also causes the wavelength to change, but remember — the frequency doesn't change.

Refraction — Changing the Speed of a Wave Can Change its Direction

1) Waves (such as light) travel at different speeds in substances which have different densities.
2) When a wave crosses a boundary between two substances (e.g. from glass to air) it changes speed.
3) When the wave speed decreases the wave bends towards the normal.
4) When the speed increases the wave bends away from the normal.
5) E.g. when light passes from air into the glass of a window (a denser medium), it slows down — causing the light to refract towards the normal. When the light reaches the 'glass to air' boundary on the other side of the window, it speeds up and refracts away from the normal.

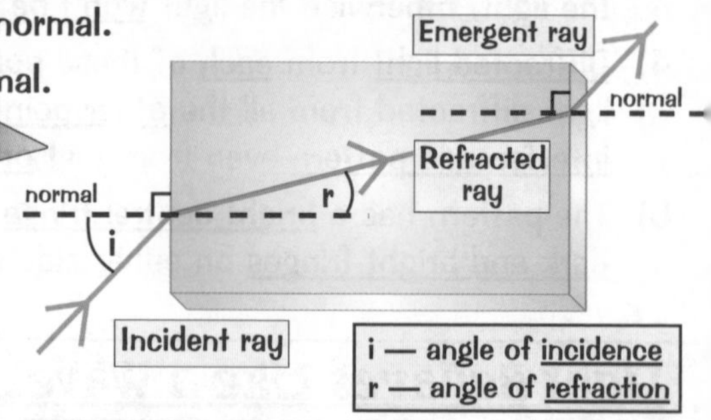

The Greater the Change in Speed the More Waves Bend

1) When light enters glass it slows down to about 2/3 of its normal speed (in air), i.e. its speed is about 2×10^8 m/s rather than 3×10^8 m/s.
2) The ratio of the speed of light in a vacuum to the speed of light in a medium is called the refractive index of the medium (3/2 for glass).
3) The refractive index is basically a measure of the amount of bending — the higher the refractive index, the more the light bends when it enters or leaves the medium.
4) When waves hit a boundary along the normal, i.e. at exactly 90°, then there will be no change in direction. There'll still be a change in speed and wavelength, though.
5) Some light is also reflected when it hits a different medium, such as glass (see next page).

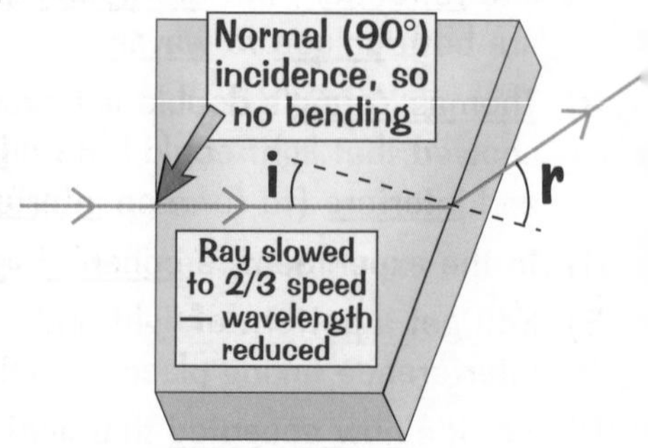

Every Transparent Material Has a Refractive Index

Numbers in standard form are covered back in P1 — p. 17.

1) The absolute refractive index of a material is defined as:

$$\text{refractive index, } n = \frac{\text{speed of light in a vacuum, } c}{\text{speed of light in the medium, } v}$$

$$n = \frac{c}{v} \quad (c = 3 \times 10^8 \text{ m/s})$$

2) Light slows down a lot in glass, so the refractive index of glass is high (around 1.5). The refractive index of water is lower (around 1.33) — so light slows down less in water than in glass.
3) The speed of light in air is about the same as in a vacuum, so the refractive index of air is 1.
4) You might have to predict the direction of refraction when given information on speed or refractive index.

Example

How fast would light travel through a crystal of titanium dioxide (refractive index of 2.5)?
If light passed from air into titanium dioxide at an angle, would it bend towards or away from the normal?
refractive index = speed of light in a vacuum ÷ speed of light in the medium, so speed of light in titanium dioxide = 3×10^8 m/s ÷ 2.5 = 1.2×10^8 m/s. The light slows down, so it would bend towards the normal.

Bending light's alright, but I prefer bendy straws myself...

Answer on p. 124.

Put your refractive index knowledge to the test: Light travels through a sapphire at a speed of 1.7×10^8 m/s. What is the refractive index of sapphire? In what direction would light bend as it passed from a sapphire into air?

Refraction: Two Special Cases

Refractive Index Explains Dispersion

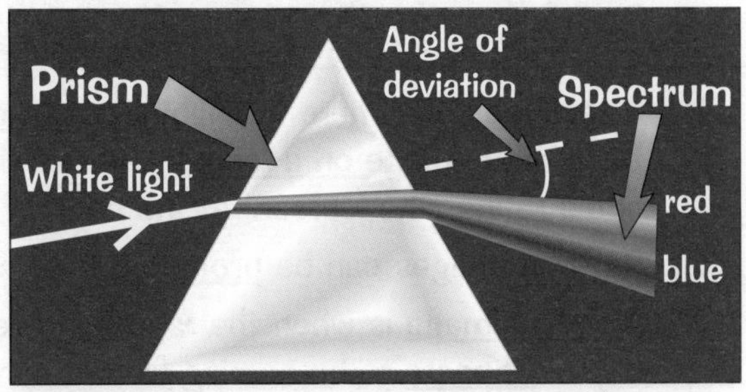

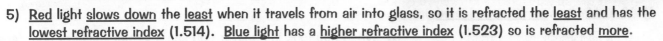

1) Different colours of light are refracted by different amounts.
2) This is because they travel at slightly different speeds in any given medium (but the same speed in a vacuum).
3) The refractive index of a medium is the ratio of speed of light in a vacuum to speed of light in that medium.
4) So any material has a different refractive index for each different speed (colour) of light.
5) Red light slows down the least when it travels from air into glass, so it is refracted the least and has the lowest refractive index (1.514). Blue light has a higher refractive index (1.523) so is refracted more.
6) A prism can be used to make the different colours of white light emerge at different angles.
7) This produces a spectrum showing all the colours of the rainbow. This effect is called DISPERSION.

Total Internal Reflection and the Critical Angle

1) Total internal reflection (TIR) only happens when light travels from a more dense medium with a higher refractive index to a less dense medium with a lower refractive index (e.g. from glass to water).
2) If the angle of incidence is large enough (greater than the critical angle) the ray of light won't come out at all, but will reflect back into the glass (or whatever). This is total internal reflection.
3) You definitely need to learn this set of three diagrams which show the three conditions:

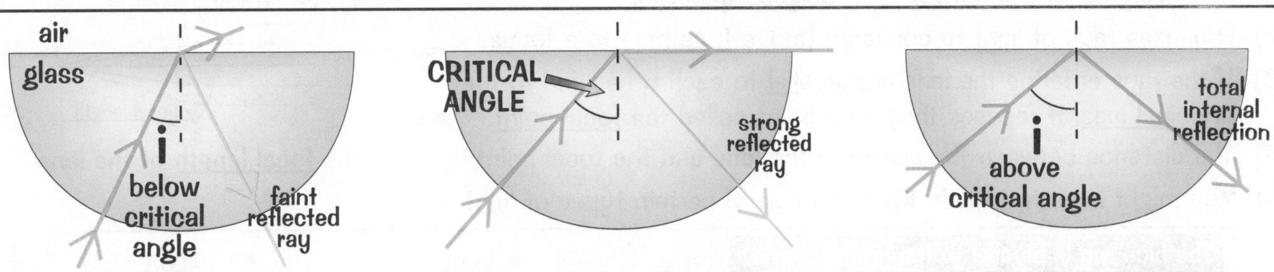

Angle of Incidence LESS than the Critical Angle.
Most of the light passes through into the air but a little bit of it is internally reflected.

Angle of Incidence EQUAL to the Critical Angle.
The emerging ray travels along the surface. There's quite a bit of internal reflection.

Angle of Incidence GREATER than the Critical Angle.
No light comes out.
It's all internally reflected, i.e. total internal reflection.

4) Different media have different critical angles — the higher the refractive index of the medium, the lower the critical angle will be.
5) The critical angle for glass is about 42°. This is handy because it means 45° angles can be used to get TIR, as in optical fibres, prisms in binoculars, reflectors, road signs and cat's eyes on roads.
6) You need to learn the path that light takes through devices that use total internal reflection:

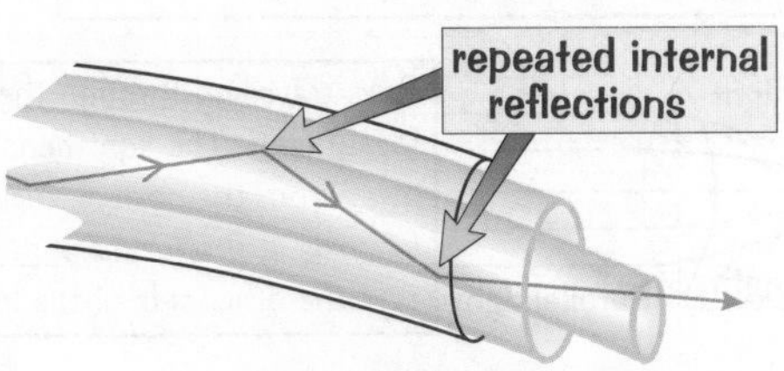

Optical fibres

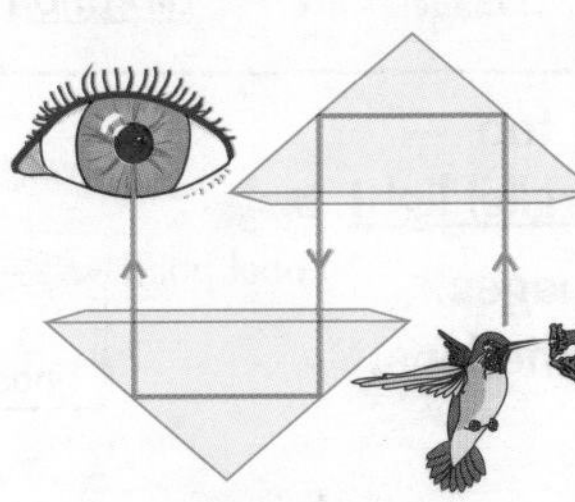

Binoculars

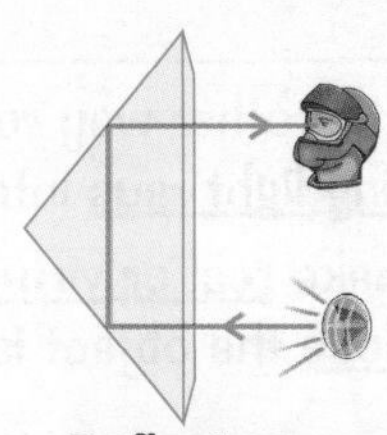

Reflectors and road signs

Road signs are covered in thousands of tiny prisms that reflect light back at drivers.

Yay — rainbows and unicorns (okay, there aren't really any unicorns)...

You're expected to know why dispersion happens, and to remember that red light is refracted less than blue light.

Images and Converging Lenses

Lenses are usually made of glass or plastic. All lenses change the direction of rays of light by refraction.

A Real Image is Actually There — A Virtual Image is Not

1) A real image is where the light from an object comes together to form an image on a 'screen' — like the image formed on an eye's retina (the 'screen' at the back of an eye).
2) So, real images can be projected onto screens.

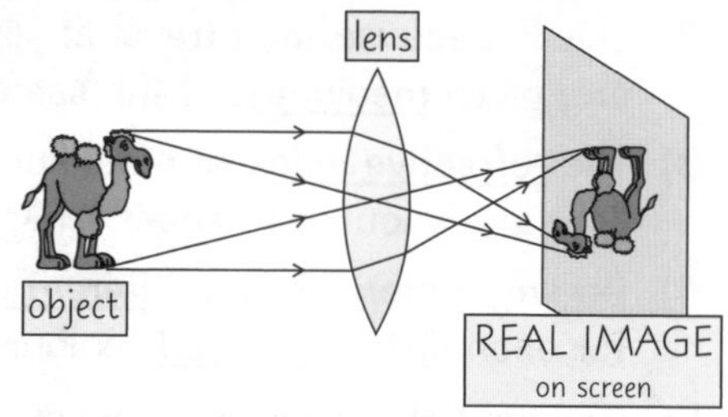

3) A virtual image is when the rays are diverging, so the light from the object appears to be coming from a completely different place.
4) Virtual images can't be projected onto screens.

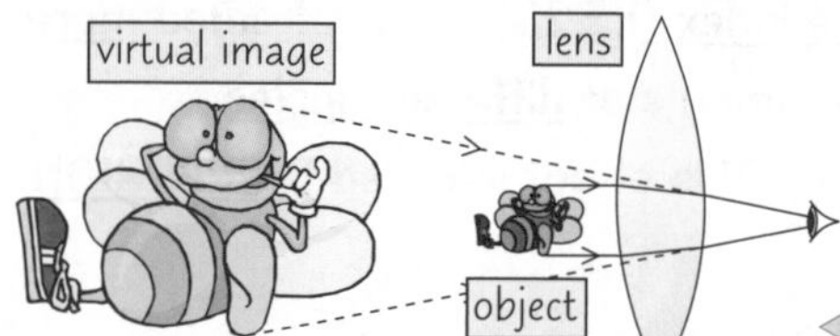

5) When you look in a mirror you see a virtual image of your face — the object (your face) appears to be behind the mirror.
6) You can get a virtual image when looking at an object through a magnifying lens — the virtual image looks bigger and further away than the object actually is.
7) To describe an image properly, you need to say 4 things:
   a) How big it is compared to the object.
   b) Whether it's upright or inverted (upside down).
   c) Whether it's real or virtual.
   d) Where it is (in relation to the lens and the focal points).

Converging (Convex) Lenses Focus Light

1) A converging lens is convex — it bulges outwards.
2) It causes rays of light to converge (move together) to a focus.
3) If the rays entering the lens are parallel to each other and to the principal axis, it focuses them at a point called the focal point.

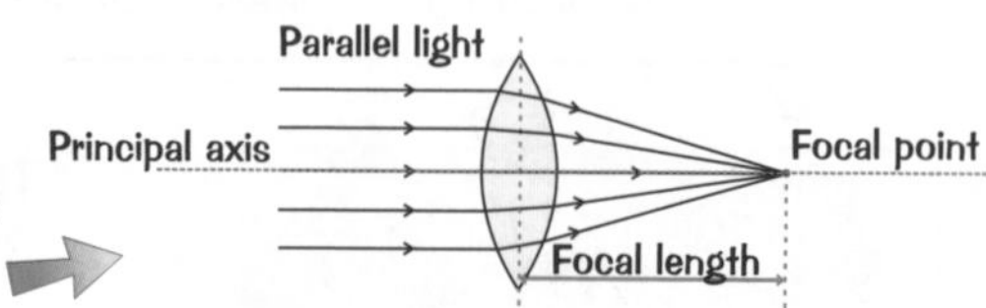

4) The distance between the centre of the lens and the focal point is called the focal length of the lens.
5) You might have to explain the refraction of certain types of light ray:

The blue ray is parallel to the principal axis.

a) A ray travelling parallel to the principal axis slows down as it enters and bends towards the normal.
b) When it hits the 'glass to air' boundary on the other side it speeds up and bends away from the normal.
c) The curvature of the lens means all the parallel rays hitting different parts of the lens are bent towards the same focal point, where an image is formed.

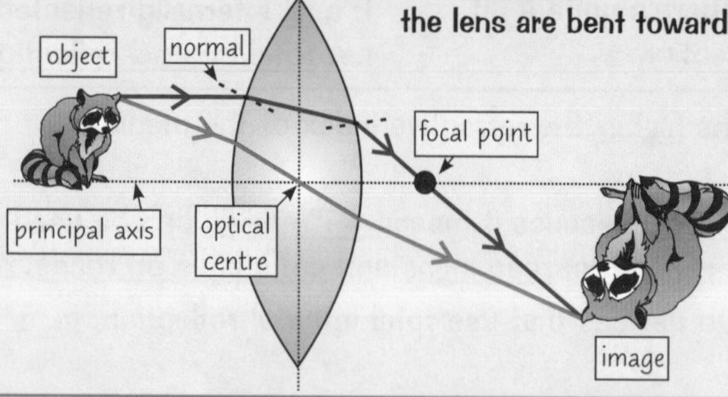

The red ray passes through the optical centre.

a) A ray passing through the optical centre of the lens appears to pass straight through.
b) It exits the lens at the same angle it entered at, but on the opposite side of the principal axis, so it's bent the same amount but in the opposite direction upon entering and exiting the lens.

6) Convex lenses work the other way round too — they can turn diverging light rays into parallel light.
7) Convex lenses can make real or virtual images, depending on how close the object is to the lens.

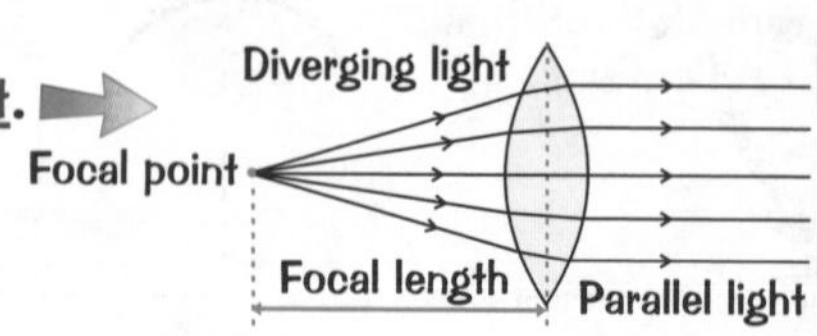

Rays travelling through the focal point: The light bends away from the normal, then towards it, producing parallel rays the other side of the lens.

Important stuff this — come on, focus focus...

So you get an exam question: "Bob looks through a magnifying glass at a beetle one focal length away from the lens. Describe the image he sees." How many things do you need to say about the image in your answer... is it one? Nope. Two? Wrong again. Three? Um, no. Four? Yep, got it. Now you're ready four the exam. Fantastic.

Ray Diagrams

Ray diagrams are those fiddly pictures you draw to work out what the image through a lens looks like. And guess what... you'll probably have to draw one in the exam.

Draw a Ray Diagram to Show the Image From a Convex Lens

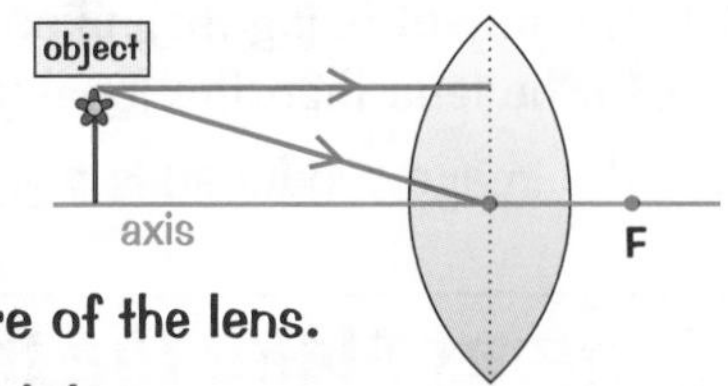

1) Draw in the focal point — e.g. if the focal length is 5 cm, draw the focal point 5 cm along the principal axis from the optical centre of the lens.
2) Pick a point on the top of the object. Draw a ray going from the object to the lens parallel to the principal axis of the lens.
3) Draw another ray from the top of the object going right through the centre of the lens.
4) The incident ray that's parallel to the axis is refracted through the focal point (see previous page). Draw a refracted ray passing through the focal point.
5) A ray passing through the optical centre of the lens doesn't bend (see previous page). In a simple lens this is the in the middle (red dot in the diagram).
6) Mark where the rays meet. That's the top of the image.
7) Repeat the process for a point on the bottom of the object. When the bottom of the object is on the axis, the bottom of the image is also on the axis.

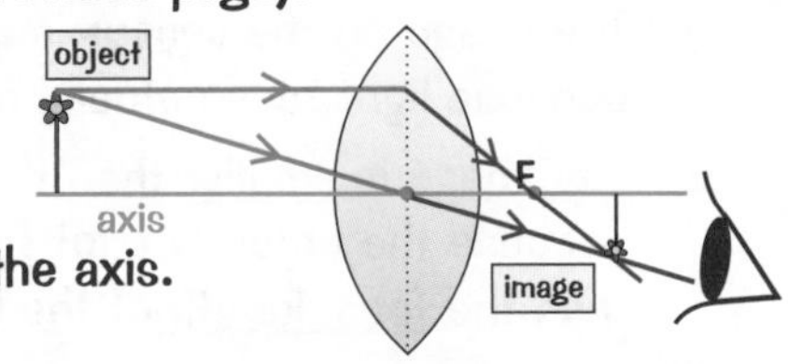

EXAMPLE:

1) and 2) — draw in focal point and incident rays from top of object:

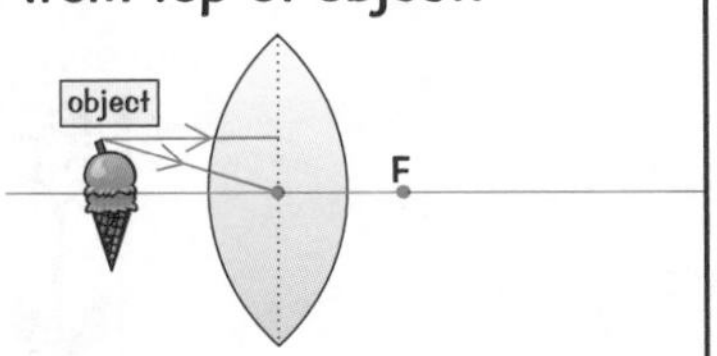

3), 4), 5) — draw refracted rays to find top of image:

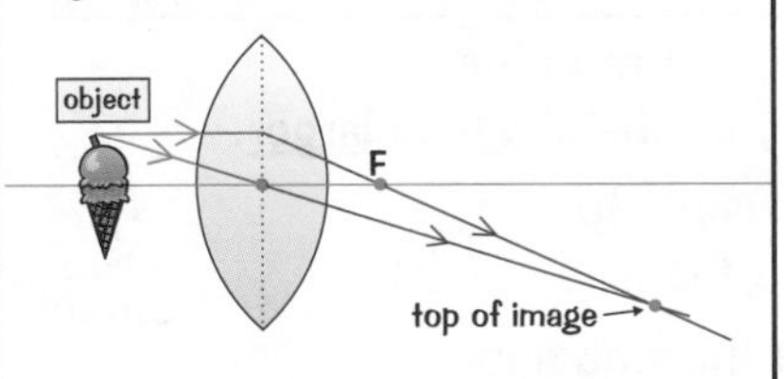

6) — Repeat for bottom of object:

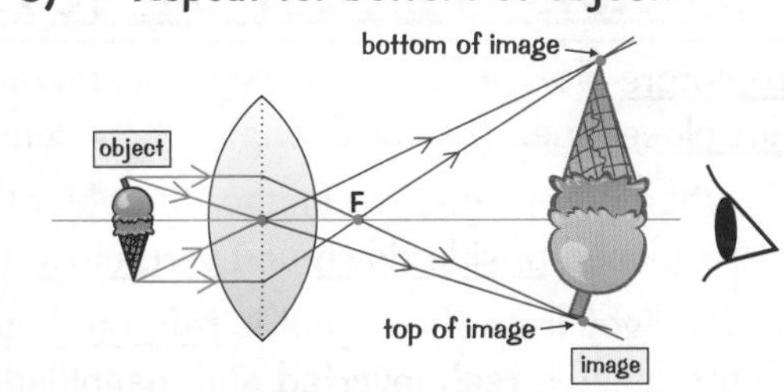

If you really want to be sure, you can draw a third incident ray.
Draw a line from the top of the object, passing through the focal point in front of the lens.
Refract it so that it leaves the lens parallel to the axis.
In the exam you can get away with just two rays, so you only need bother with the third if you want to double-check.

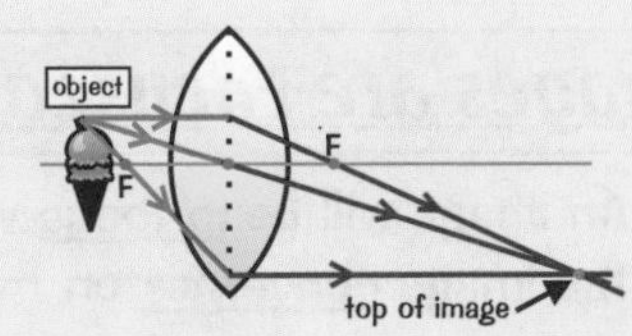

Distance from the Lens Affects the Image

1) An object at 2F will produce a real, upside down image the same size as the object, and at 2F.

2) Between F and 2F it'll make a real, upside down image bigger than the object, and beyond 2F.

3) An object nearer than F will make a virtual image the right way up, bigger than the object and on the same side of the lens.

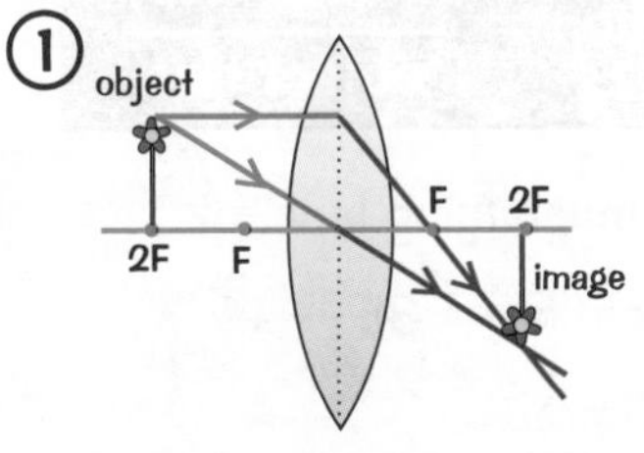

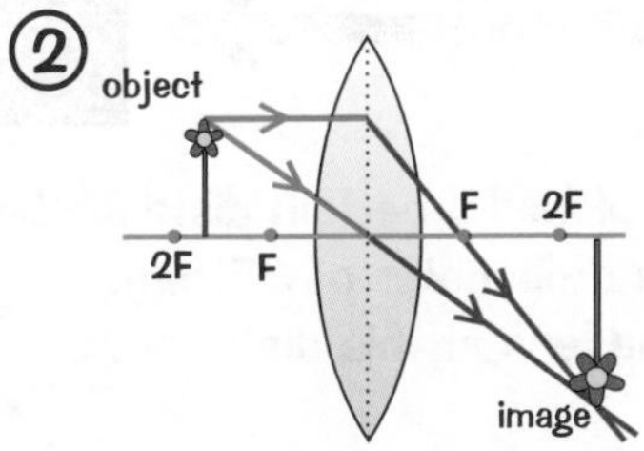

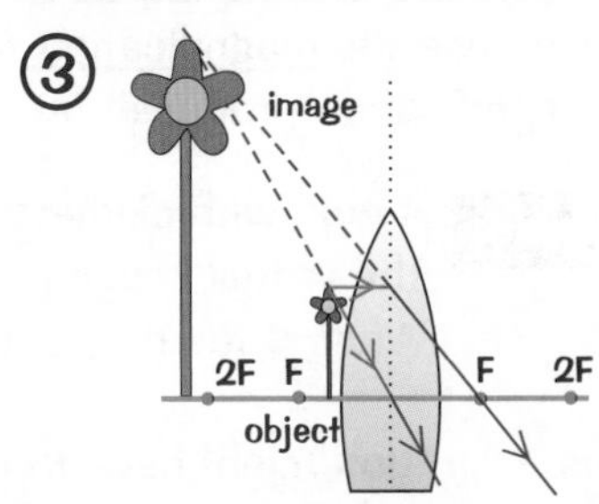

Ray...

Ray diagrams. Hmm, not the easiest things in the world. But to be frank, the method's pretty simple — it's just drawing them accurately that people fall down on — one little mistake can ruin the whole thing. No excuses.

Magnification, Cameras and Projectors

Convex lenses are used in magnifying glasses, cameras and projectors.

Convex Lenses Create Magnified Images

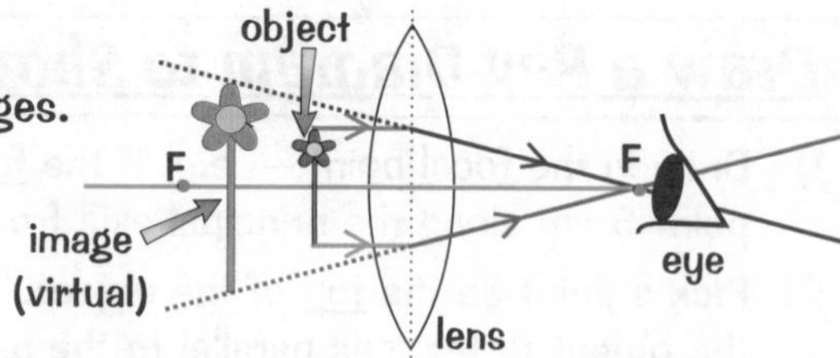

1) Magnifying glasses use convex lenses to create magnified images.
2) The object being magnified must be closer to the lens than the focal length.
3) The image produced is a virtual image.

Cameras Make the Image Smaller than the Object

When you take a photograph of a flower, light from the object (flower) travels to the camera and is refracted by the lens, forming an image on the light sensor (or film in old cameras).

1) The image on the sensor is a real image because light rays actually meet there.
2) The image is smaller than the object, because the object's a lot further away than the focal length of the lens.
3) The image is inverted — upside down.

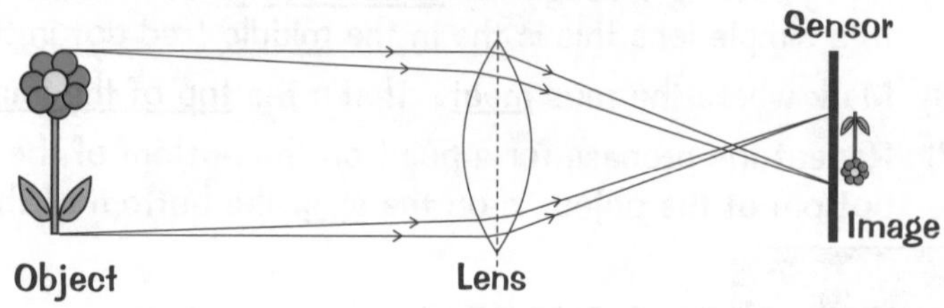

Projectors Make the Image Larger than the Object

Projectors work in a similar way to cameras, but the object is a lot closer than the focal length of the lens, so the image is larger.

1) When you project an image, the object needs to be placed upside down and very close to the lens.
2) The light from the object is refracted by the lens and produces a real, inverted and magnified image on a screen.

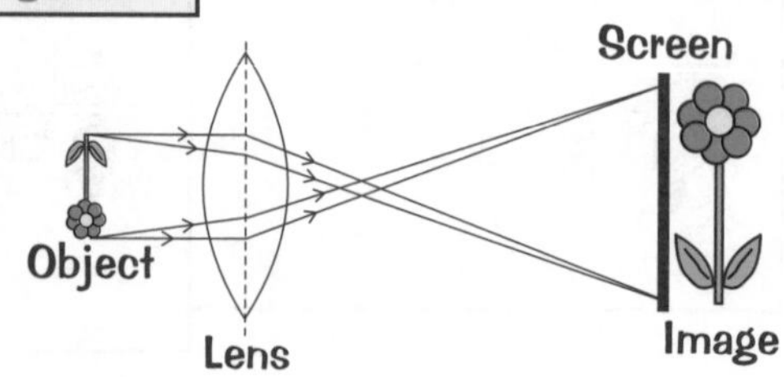

Images are Focused by Moving the Lens

1) An image will be in focus when the light that forms the image converges on the screen or the sensor.
2) In cameras and projectors the image is focused by moving the lens closer to, or further from, the object.
3) The closer to the object the lens is, the further from the lens the image will be formed (and vice versa).

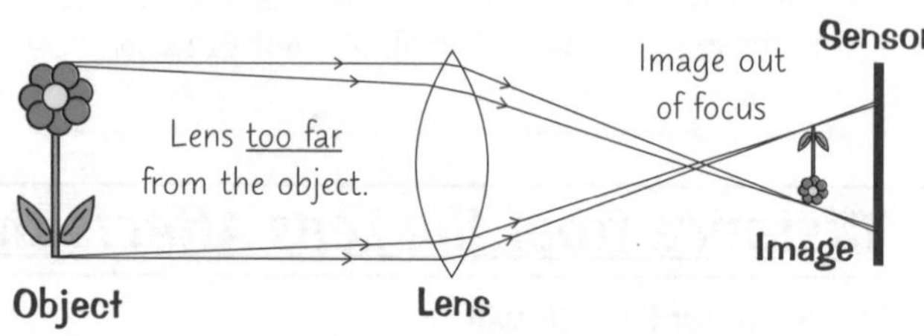

Learn the Magnification Formula

You can use the magnification formula to work out the magnification produced by a lens:

$$\text{Magnification} = \frac{\text{image size}}{\text{object size}}$$

Example: A coin with diameter 14 mm is placed a certain distance behind a magnifying lens. The virtual image produced has a diameter of 35 mm. What is the magnification of the lens at this distance?

magnification = 35 ÷ 14
= 2.5

In the exam you might have to draw a ray diagram to show where an image would be, then measure the image and work out the magnification of the lens. Another reason to draw those ray diagrams carefully...

Picture this — you've revised it, and it turns up on the exam...

Well done, you've almost made it to the end of this module. Celebrate by taking a picture of yourself.

Revision Summary for Module P5

Phew. Bit of a mixed bag, that section. If you reckon you know your stuff, then do these questions and prove it to yourself. If you can't do these questions now, you won't be able to do them in the exam.

1) What's the difference between speed and velocity? Give an example of each.

2)* A boat is sailing due south with a velocity of 0.5 m/s relative to the water. The river is flowing at 0.2 m/s due north. Draw a vector diagram to help find the boat's resultant velocity.

3)* A bird is facing due north and flying at 12 mph relative to the air. There is a 5 mph wind blowing due west. Draw a vector diagram to help find the resultant velocity of the bird.

4)* Find the distance travelled by a soggy pea as it is flicked from rest to a speed of 14 m/s in 0.4 s. (Assume constant acceleration.)

5)* A firework is launched upwards with an initial velocity of 13.4 m/s. Gravity causes it to accelerate downward at 10 m/s^2. It explodes when it's travelled 7 m. Find it's velocity at the moment before it explodes.

6) What shape is the trajectory (path) of a projectile?

7)* A sandwich is thrown horizontally off a skyscraper at 1.5 m/s. It hits the ground 10 s later.
a) How high is the skyscraper? Take $g = 10$ m/s^2 and ignore air resistance.
b) How far will the sandwich have travelled horizontally before it hits the ground?

8) Briefly describe Newton's third law and use it to explain recoil.

9)* If the total momentum of a system before a collision is zero, what is the total momentum of the system after the collision?

10) What happens to the pressure of a gas if:
a) the volume of the gas increases, b) the temperature of the gas increases?

11)* What happens to the size of the gravitational force if the distance between two masses decreases by a factor of three?

12) State three differences between a low polar orbit and a geostationary orbit.

13) Briefly explain why waves with a frequency higher than 30 GHz can't be used to carry satellite signals.

14) Briefly explain why satellite transmitting and receiving dishes need careful alignment.

15) Draw simple wave diagrams to show the difference between constructive and destructive interference.

16) Use a diagram to describe the diffraction of a beam of light through a single slit.

17) What effect does a polarising filter have on the light passing through it?

18) Draw a diagram to show the path of a ray of light as it passes from:
air → rectangular block of glass → air, meeting the block of glass at an angle.

19)* The refractive index of the mineral 'jet' is 1.66.
a) How fast will a ray of light travel through a piece of jet?
b) Will a ray of light be travelling towards or away from the normal when it exits a piece of jet into air?

20) For which colour light does glass have the highest refractive index — blue or red?

21) What will happen to a ray of light that enters a block of glass:
a) at the critical angle, b) at an angle greater than the critical angle?

22) What is a real image? How is it different from a virtual image?

23) Copy and complete this ray diagram to show the image formed:

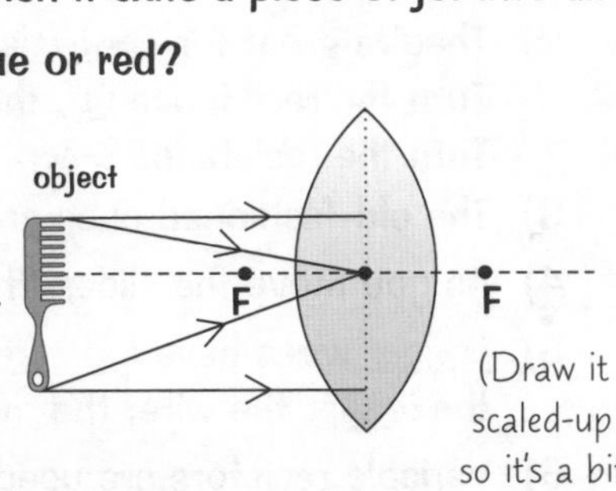

(Draw it scaled-up so it's a bit bigger.)

24)* Peter measures the length of a seed to be 1.5 cm. When he looks at the seed through a converging lens at a certain distance, the seed appears to have a length of 4.5 cm. What is the magnification of this lens at this distance?

* Answers on p. 124.

Circuits and Resistors

Isn't electricity great — hair straighteners, computers, life-support machines... Mind you, it's pretty bad news if the technical terms don't mean anything to you. So let's have a quick recap to start...

1) Current is the flow of charge (electrons) round the circuit. Current will only flow through a component if there is a voltage across that component. Current is measured in amps, A.
2) Voltage is the driving force that pushes the current round. Voltage is measured in volts, V.
3) Resistance is anything in the circuit that reduces the current. Resistance is measured in ohms, Ω.
4) There's a balance — the relative sizes of the voltage and resistance decide how big the current will be. If you increase the voltage then more current will flow. If you increase the resistance then less current will flow (or more voltage will be needed to keep the same current flowing).

You did a bit on circuits in P4.

Learn These Circuit Symbols

Circuit diagrams are a lot less scary if you know your symbols.

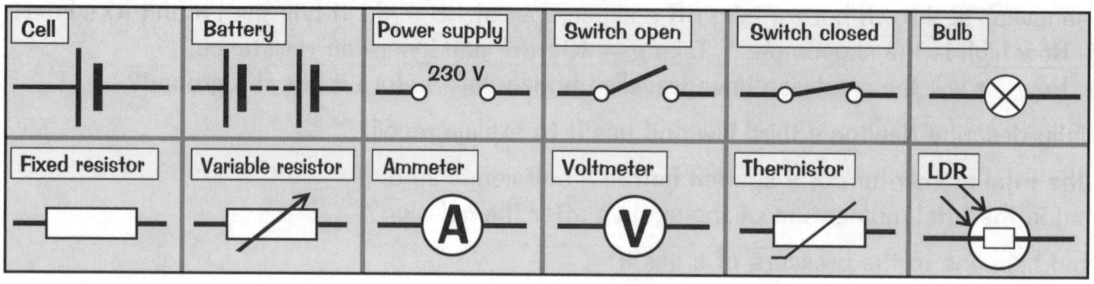

Resistance is Caused by Collisions in a Conductor

1) In a metal conductor, the electric charge is carried by electrons.
2) When electrons flow through a conductor they collide with atoms in the metal — this causes resistance.
3) Collisions between electrons and atoms cause the atoms to vibrate.
4) The more atoms vibrate, the more they get in the way of the electrons, so the more collisions there are.
5) So an increase in collisions causes an increase in the resistance of the conductor.
6) The increased vibration of the atoms also increases the temperature of the conductor.

Variable Resistors

1) A variable resistor (or rheostat) is a resistor whose resistance can be changed by twiddling a knob or something (you did a bit on these in P4).
2) They're great for controlling the current flowing through a circuit.
   Turn the resistance up, the current drops.
   Turn the resistance down, the current goes up.
3) The old-fashioned ones are huge coils of wire with a slider on them.

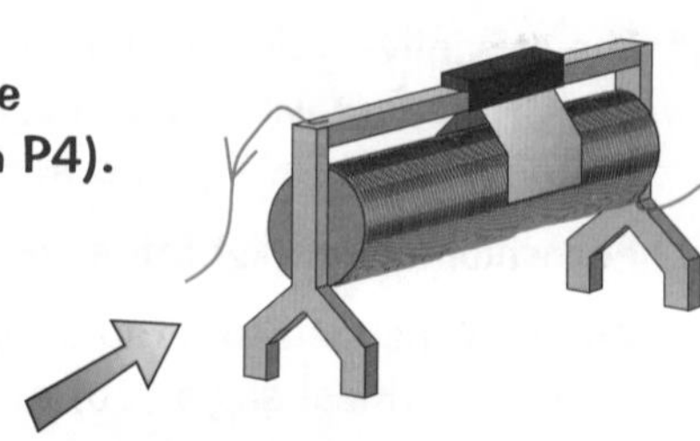

4) As you move the slider, the length of wire that has current flowing through it changes.
5) Longer wires have more resistance, so less current flowing through them. This is because the longer the wire, the more atoms the electrons will collide with, increasing the resistance.
6) Variable resistors are used for controlling the speed of motors and the brightness of bulbs. Turning the resistance down increases the speed of the motor or the brightness of a bulb.

Currently I'm trying to think of a joke about resistance...

The circuit symbols here are pretty simple ones that you should be familiar with. There's still a few more to come in this module, make sure you can recognise and draw them all before the exam. I like the one for a transistor.

Voltage-Current Graphs and Resistance

The resistance of a component can be measured using a standard test circuit. You saw one back in P4.

The Slope of a Voltage-Current Graph Shows Resistance

Voltage-current (V-I) graphs show how the current in a circuit varies as you change the voltage:

Different Resistors

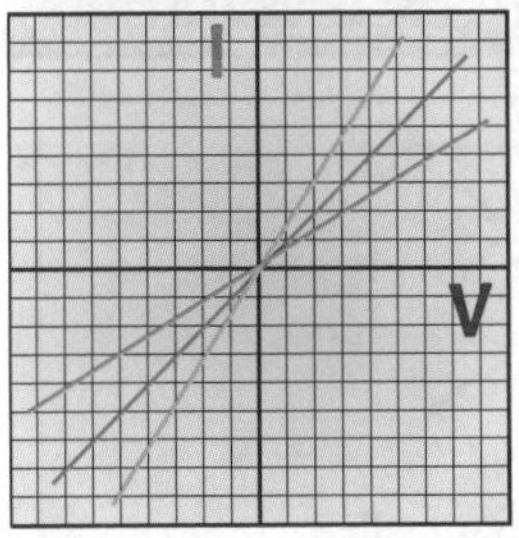

The current through a resistor (at constant temperature) is proportional to voltage. Different resistors have different resistances, hence the different slopes. Straight line graphs like this are for 'ohmic' resistors, which have a constant resistance.

A Filament Lamp

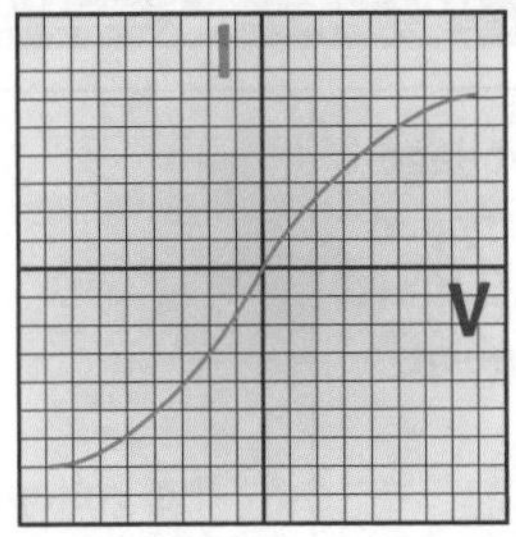

As the current increases, the temperature of the filament increases and so the resistance increases (hence the curve). Components whose resistance changes are known as 'non-ohmic' resistors.

Calculating Resistance: R = V/I (or R = "1/gradient")

For the straight-line graphs, the resistance of the component is steady and is equal to the inverse of the gradient of the line, or "1/gradient". In other words, the steeper the graph the lower the resistance.

If the graph curves, it means the resistance is changing. In that case R can be found for any point by taking the pair of values (V, I) from the graph and sticking them in the formula R = V/I.

$$\text{Resistance } (\Omega) = \frac{\text{Voltage (V)}}{\text{Current (A)}}$$

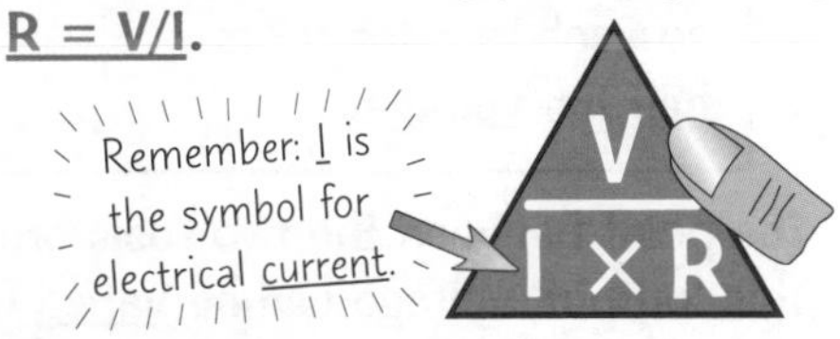

Remember: I is the symbol for electrical current.
V
I × R

Resistors in Parallel Reduce the Resistance in a Circuit

Sometimes a single resistor isn't enough — combining resistors changes the resistance of a circuit. Putting resistors together in series increases the resistance, connecting them in parallel decreases it.

1) In series circuits, the total resistance is just the sum of the individual resistances: $R_T = R_1 + R_2 + R_3$

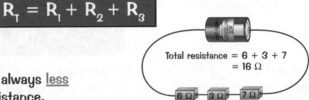

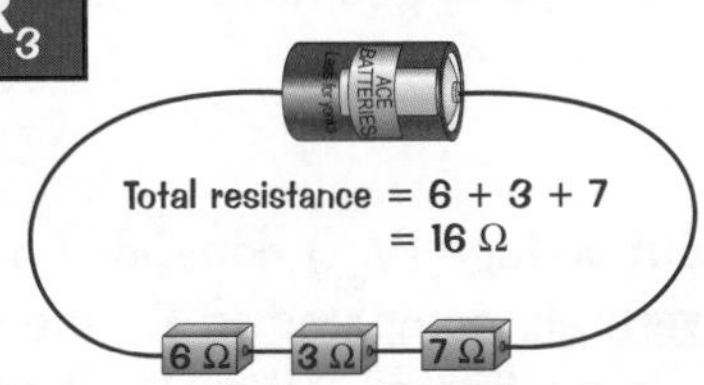

2) But resistors connected in parallel provide more paths for the current to travel down.
3) So the total resistance of a parallel circuit is always less than that of the branch with the smallest resistance.
4) A circuit with two resistors in parallel will have a lower resistance than a circuit with either of the resistors by themselves — which means the parallel circuit will have a higher current.
5) You can calculate the total resistance of resistors in parallel using this equation: $\frac{1}{R_T} = \frac{1}{R_1} + \frac{1}{R_2} + \frac{1}{R_3}$

$$\frac{1}{\text{Total R}} = \frac{1}{R_1} + \frac{1}{R_2}$$

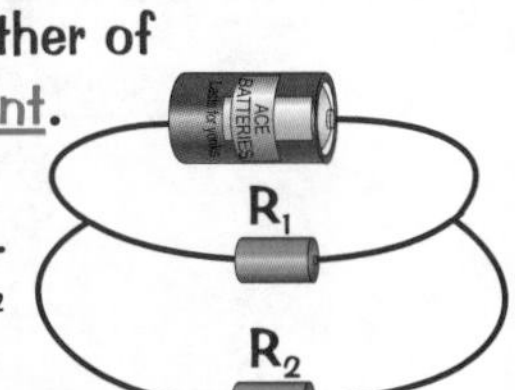

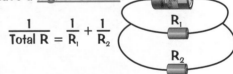

EXAMPLE:
Calculate the total resistance of the circuit shown in the diagram.

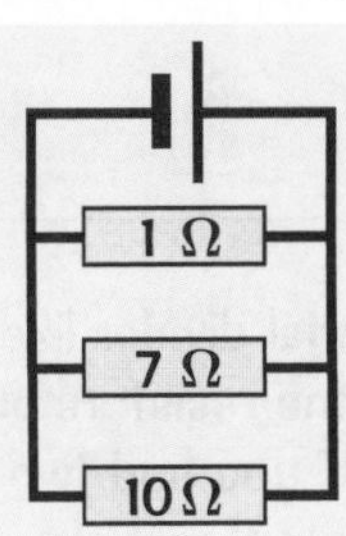

ANSWER:
Resistors connected in parallel, so use the equation $\frac{1}{R_T} = \frac{1}{R_1} + \frac{1}{R_2} + \frac{1}{R_3}$.

$\frac{1}{R_T} = \frac{1}{1} + \frac{1}{7} + \frac{1}{10} = 1 + 0.14 + 0.1 = 1.24$, so $R_T = 1 \div 1.24 = 0.8\ \Omega$.

Voltage-current graphs — also more fun than gravel*...

You have to be able to interpret voltage-current graphs for your exam. Remember — the steeper the slope, the lower the resistance. And you need to know the equations inside out, back to front, upside down and in Swahili.

*(see p. 54).

Potential Dividers

Potential dividers consist of a pair of resistors. They divide the potential in a circuit so you can get outputs of different voltages.

The Higher the Resistance, the Greater the Voltage Drop

A voltage across a pair of resistors is 'shared out' according to their relative resistances. The rule is:

The larger the share of the total resistance, the larger the share of the total voltage.

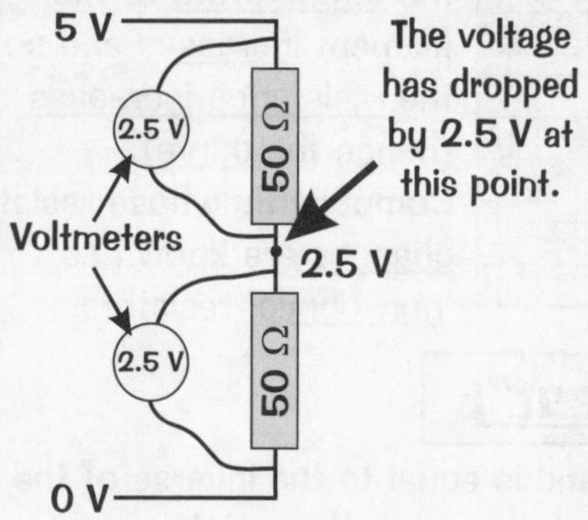

The resistances are equal, so each resistor takes half the voltage.

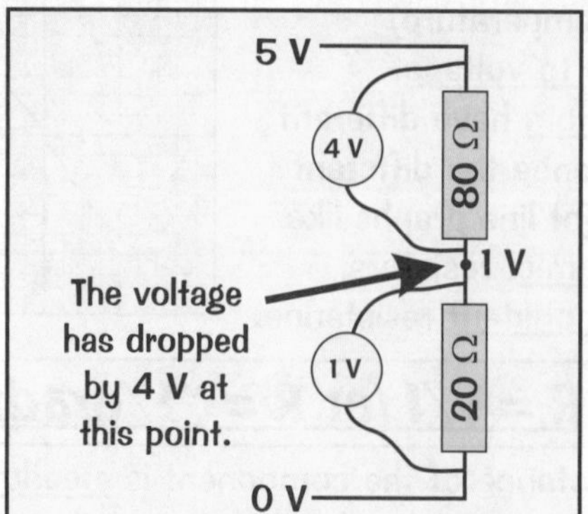

The top resistor has 80% of the total resistance, and so takes 80% of the total voltage.

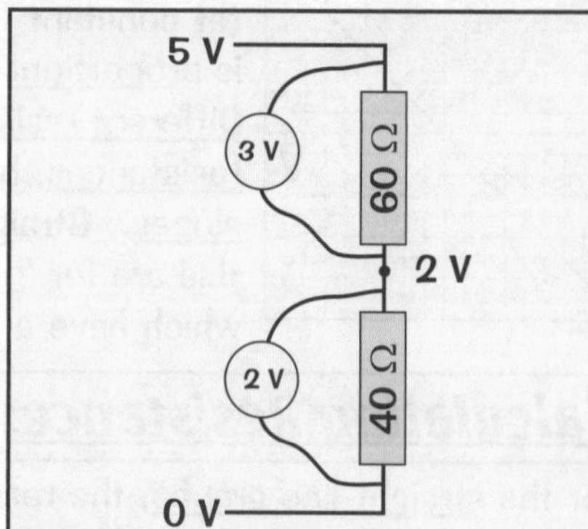

The top resistor has 60% of the total resistance, and so takes 60% of the total voltage.

The point between the two resistors is the 'output' of the potential divider.
This 'output' voltage can be varied by swapping one or both of the resistors for a variable resistor.

Potential Dividers are Quite Useful

Potential dividers are not only spectacularly interesting — they're useful as well.
They allow you to run a device that requires a certain voltage from a battery of a different voltage.
This is the formula you need to use:

$$V_{out} = V_{in} \times \left(\frac{R_2}{R_1 + R_2}\right)$$

The output voltage (V_{out}) depends on the relative values of R_1 and R_2. From the formula, you should see that if R_2 is very big compared to R_1, the bit in the brackets cancels down to about 1, so V_{out} is approximately V_{in}. But if R_2 is a lot smaller than R_1, the bit in brackets becomes so small that V_{out} is approximately 0.

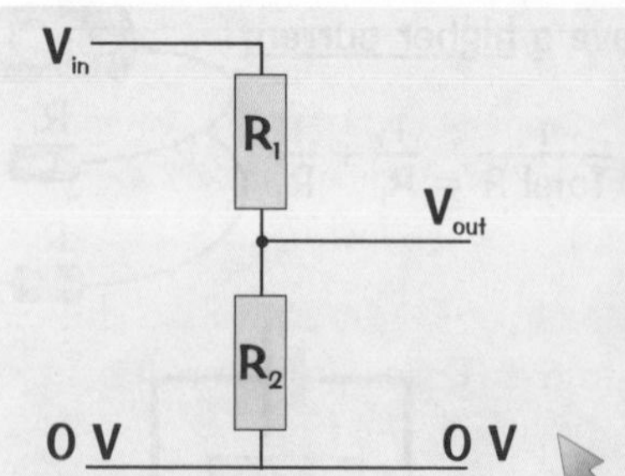

EXAMPLE:
In the diagram, the input voltage for the potential divider is 9 V. R_1 is 20 Ω and R_2 is 40 Ω. What is the output voltage across R_2?

ANSWER:

$$V_{out} = 9\text{ V} \times \left(\frac{40}{20 + 40}\right) = \frac{9\text{ V} \times 40}{60} = 6\text{ V}$$

A potential divider like this could be used to run a 6 V device from a 9 V battery. You could replace one of the resistors by a variable resistor, so that you could change V_{out} to any value between 0 and 9 volts. If you had two variable resistors you could have much finer control of an output voltage with an adjustable threshold — useful for controlling heat and light sensors (see next page).

My boyfriend's mother is a potential divider...

You won't believe this, but potential dividers get even more exciting on the next page. I know you're worried that you won't be able to cope with the adrenaline rush but it's just something you have to get used to with Physics...

LDRs and Thermistors

Some resistors change their resistance depending on the conditions.
You need to know about two of them — light-dependent resistors and thermistors.

Light-Dependent Resistor (or "LDR" to Thee and Me)

1) In bright light, the resistance falls.
2) In darkness, the resistance is highest.
3) This makes it a useful device for various electronic circuits, e.g. automatic night lights and burglar detectors.

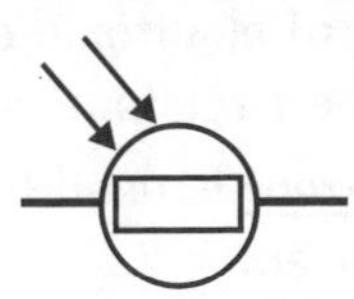
LDR circuit symbol.

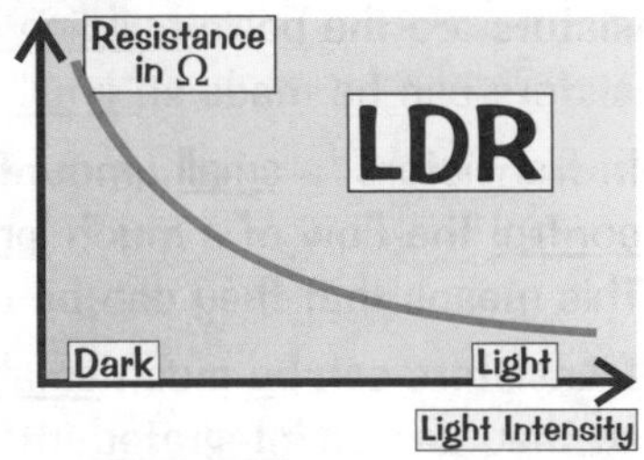

Thermistor (Temperature-Dependent Resistor)

1) In hot conditions, the resistance drops.
2) In cool conditions, the resistance goes up.
3) Thermistors make useful temperature sensors, e.g. car engine temperature gauges and electronic thermostats.

Thermistor circuit symbol.
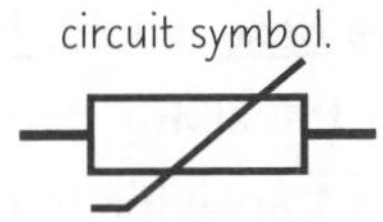

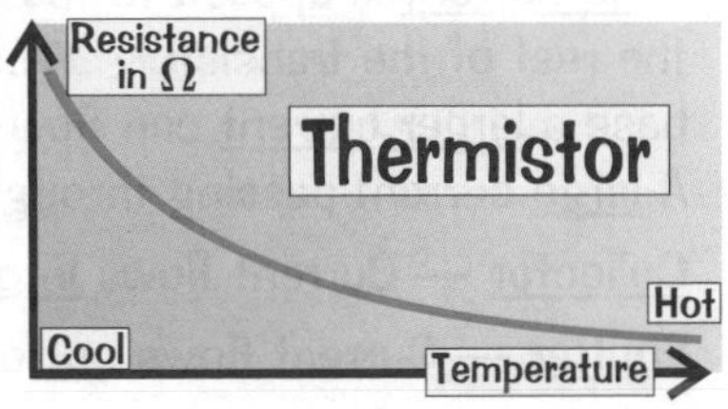

A Thermistor in a Potential Divider Makes a Temperature Sensor

1) Using a thermistor and a fixed resistor in a potential divider, you can make a temperature sensor.
2) You can make a temperature sensor that gives a high voltage output (a 'logical 1' — see page 109) when it's hot and a low voltage output (a 'logical 0') when it's cold. This is how it works...

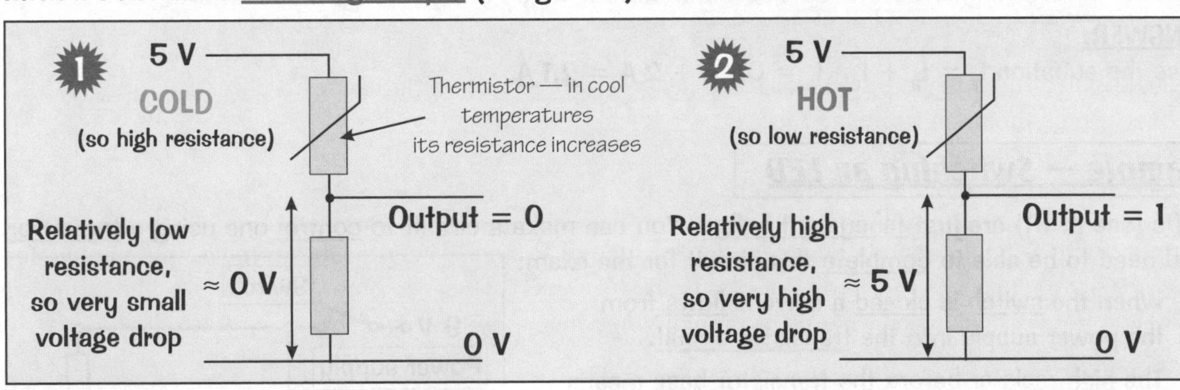

1 When the thermistor's cold its resistance is very high, so the voltage drop across it is almost 5 V, meaning the voltage of the output is nearly 0 V — a 'logical 0'.

2 As the temperature of the thermistor increases, its resistance falls dramatically. So the voltage across it is almost 0 V and the voltage of the output is nearly 5 V — a 'logical 1'.

3) In the circuit above, the thermistor is in the R_1 position (see previous page). If you switched the circuit around so the thermistor was in the R_2 position and the resistor was in the R_1 position then the output would switch round too. So, the output would be 1 when it's cold and 0 when it's hot.
4) If you replace the fixed resistor with a variable resistor, you can make a sensor that triggers an output device at a temperature you choose and can change whenever you like, e.g. in a heating system.
5) You can play around with that circuit to make different kinds of sensor. For example, you could use a similar circuit to make a light sensor — just replace the thermistor with an LDR.

How can this stuff be light-dependent if it's so dull...

Thermistors are used in computers as well. When you first turn the power on, the thermistor's cold, so its resistance is high. The high resistance prevents a surge in the current that could damage a silicon chip. Clever.

Transistors

Things you take for granted in the modern world couldn't exist without transistors — mobile phones, laptops, digital watches... so it's probably best that you learn a bit more about them.

Transistors are Electronic Switches

Transistors are the basic building blocks of electronic components.
Transistors can be made so small that the circuits of a modern computer may contain billions of them.

1) In transistors, a small amount of current is used to control the flow of a much larger current. This means that they can be used as electronic switches.
2) Transistors can be much smaller than mechanical switches, so they can be integrated into circuits, such as logic gates.
3) All transistors have three parts:
   a) Base — The 'switch' that controls the flow of current. If no current is applied to the base it stops current flowing through the rest of the transistor. When a small current is applied to the base a larger current can flow through the collector and emitter. A large current passing through the base would damage the transistor.
   b) Collector — Current flows into the transistor through the collector.
   c) Emitter — Current flows out of the transistor through the emitter.
4) The currents in each part of the transistor are related by this handy equation: $I_E = I_B + I_C$

Current in emitter = current in base + current in collector

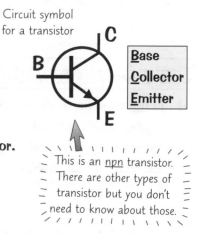

Circuit symbol for a transistor

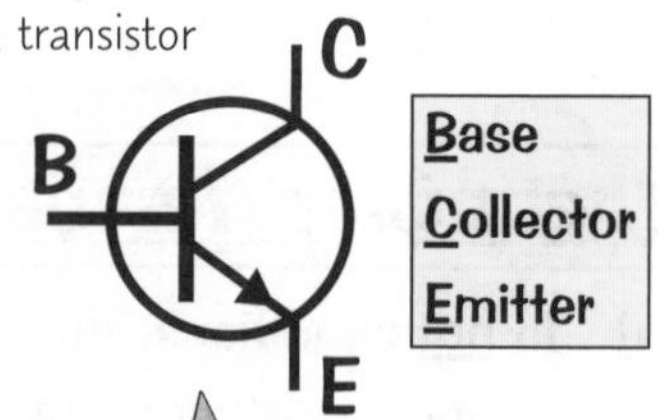

This is an npn transistor. There are other types of transistor but you don't need to know about those.

EXAMPLE:
A current of 0.1 A is applied to the base of a transistor. This allows a current of 2 A to flow through the collector. Calculate the current which flows through the emitter.

ANSWER:
Use the equation $I_E = I_B + I_C$. $I_E = 0.1\ \text{A} + 2\ \text{A} = 2.1\ \text{A}$.

Example — Switching an LED

LEDs (see p. 111) are just fancy light bulbs. You can make a circuit to control one using a transistor.
You need to be able to complete this circuit for the exam:

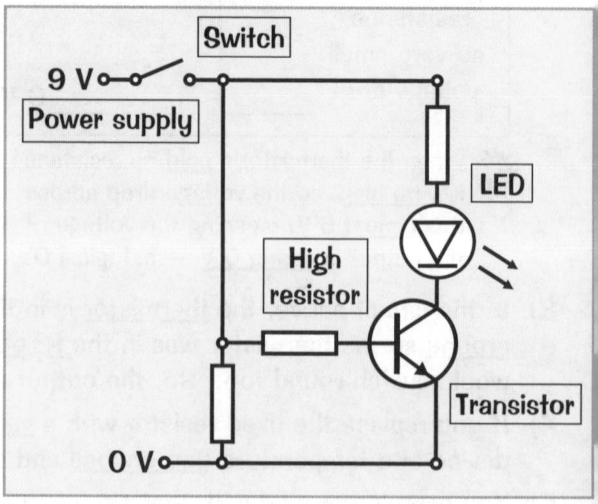

1) When the switch is closed a current flows from the power supply into the transistor circuit.
2) The high resistor before the transistor base means only a small current flows through the base.
3) The current through the base 'closes' the transistor and lets current flow through the LED, turning it on.
4) If the switch is opened, no current flows through the base, so it turns the LED off.

E.g. You could use this system to turn on an LED when the temperature in a room drops too cold. You'd just have a potential divider system with a thermistor in the circuit too. When temperature drops, V_{out} increases, the transistor is switched on, so the LED comes on too.

From a tenement window a transistor [radio] blasts...

Transistors can also be used to amplify a signal, so the first common devices to use transistors were radios. Before transistors, radios used bulky and fragile vacuum tubes. Transistors made radios portable and cheap.

Logic Gates

Transistors can also be combined to make logic gates, which process information and make computers work.

Digital Systems are Either On or Off

1) Every connection in a digital system is in one of only two states. It can be either ON or OFF, either HIGH or LOW, either YES or NO, either 1 or 0... you get the picture.
2) In reality a 1 is a high voltage (about 5 V) and a 0 is a low voltage (about 0 V). Every part of the system is in one of these two states — nothing in between.

A Logic Gate is a Type of Digital Processor

Logic gates are small, but they're made up of really small components like transistors and resistors.

They can be used to process information, giving different outputs depending on the input(s) they receive.

Each type of logic gate has its own set of rules for converting inputs to outputs, and these rules are best shown in truth tables. The important thing is to list all the possible combinations of input values.

NOT gate — sometimes called an Inverter

A NOT gate just has one input — and this input can be either 1 or 0, so the truth table has just two rows.

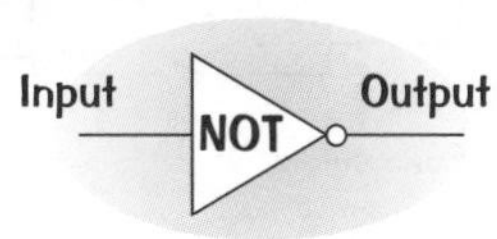

NOT GATE

Input	Output
0	1
1	0

Some AND and OR gates have more than two inputs, but you don't have to worry about those.

AND and OR gates usually have Two Inputs

Each input can be 0 or 1, so to allow for all combinations from two inputs, your truth table needs 4 rows. There's a certain logic to the names...

An AND gate only gives an output of 1 if both the first input AND the second input are 1.

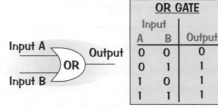

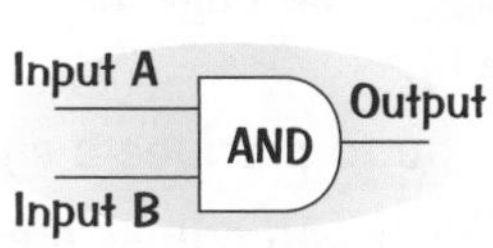

AND GATE

Input A	Input B	Output
0	0	0
0	1	0
1	0	0
1	1	1

An OR gate just needs either the first OR the second input to be 1.

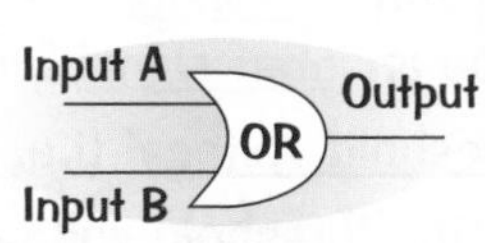

OR GATE

Input A	Input B	Output
0	0	0
0	1	1
1	0	1
1	1	1

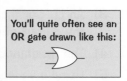

You'll quite often see an OR gate drawn like this:

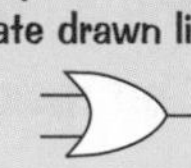

NAND and NOR gates have the Opposite Output of AND and OR gates

A NAND gate is like combining a NOT with an AND (hence the name):
If an AND gate would give an output of 0, a NAND gate would give 1, and vice versa.

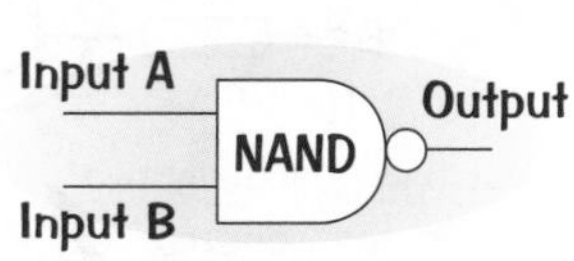

NAND GATE

Input A	Input B	Output
0	0	1
0	1	1
1	0	1
1	1	0

A NOR gate is like combining a NOT with an OR (hence the name):
If an OR gate would give an output of 0, a NOR gate would give 1, and vice versa.

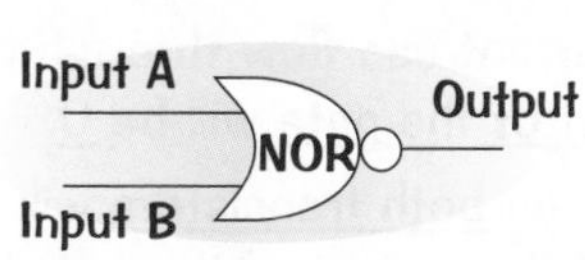

NOR GATE

Input A	Input B	Output
0	0	1
0	1	0
1	0	0
1	1	0

like physics, NAND chemistry, NAND biology...

Vell at least there aren't that many facts to learn on this page — it's more a question of understanding the inputs nd outputs for the five types of gate. It's a good idea to be familiar with the circuit symbols of the gates oo though. And practise writing out all the different tables — it's the quickest and bestest way to learn.

Using Logic Gates

You need to be able to construct a truth table for a combination of logic gates.
Approach this kind of thing in an organised way and stick to the rules, and you won't go far wrong.

'Interesting' Example — a Greenhouse

Once the gardener has switched the system on, he wants to be warned if the greenhouse gets too cold or if someone has opened the door. He only wants the warning system to work when the greenhouse gets dark.

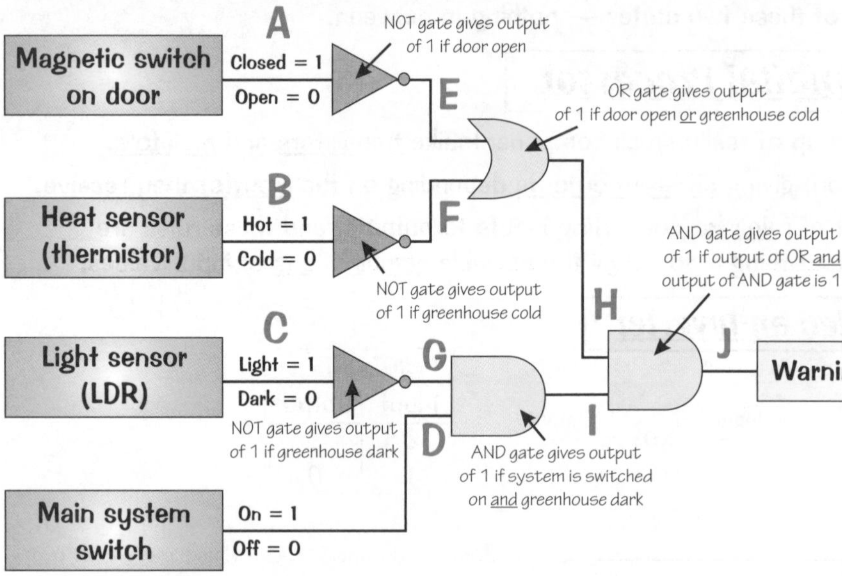

Inputs									Output
A	B	C	D	E	F	G	H	I	J
0	0	0	0	1	1	1	1	0	0
0	0	0	1	1	1	1	1	1	1
0	0	1	0	1	1	0	1	0	0
0	0	1	1	1	1	0	1	0	0
0	1	0	0	1	0	1	1	0	0
0	1	0	1	1	0	1	1	1	1
0	1	1	0	1	0	0	1	0	0
0	1	1	1	1	0	0	1	0	0
1	0	0	0	0	1	1	1	0	0
1	0	0	1	0	1	1	1	1	1
1	0	1	0	0	1	0	1	0	0
1	0	1	1	0	1	0	1	0	0
1	1	0	0	0	0	1	0	0	0
1	1	0	1	0	0	1	0	1	0
1	1	1	0	0	0	0	0	0	0
1	1	1	1	0	0	0	0	0	0

The warning light will come on if:

i) it is cold in the greenhouse OR if the door is opened,
ii) AND the system is switched on,
iii) AND the greenhouse is dark.

1) Each connection has a label, and all possible combinations of the inputs are included in the table.
2) What really matters are the inputs and the output — the rest of the truth table is just there to help.
3) An LDR or thermistor combined with a resistor makes a light or temperature sensor (see page 107), the output of which can produce an input signal for a logic circuit (as used above).
4) The resistance changes the 'threshold voltage' (i.e. how bright or hot it needs to be to produce a signal).
5) Using a variable resistor makes the threshold voltage adjustable — e.g. the gardener can adjust the temperature the warning light comes on at.

AND Logic Gates are Made From Two Transistors

1) AND logic gates give an output of 1 if both inputs are also 1.
2) AND gates are made using a series of two transistors.
3) Each input is connected to the base of a transistor.
4) If the signal of either input is 0, no current flows through the base of the transistor it's connected to. The transistor stays open, so no current can flow through the rest of the circuit and the output of the gate will be 0.
5) If both inputs are 1 then both transistors will be closed, current will flow through the gate and the output of the gate will be 1.
6) Other logic gates can be made from different combinations of two transistors.

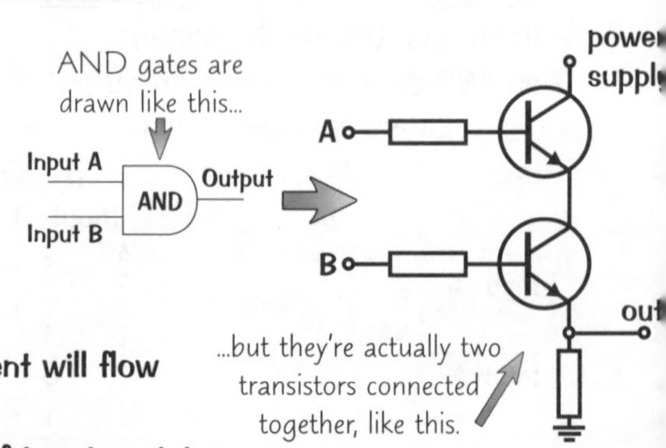

Now we can all sleep easy knowing the cucumbers are safe...

More hard stuff to get your head around here. Try copying out the diagrams of the greenhouse warning system and writing in the different inputs. Then follow them through to find the outputs. It's almost fun. Almost.

LEDs and Relays in Logic Circuits

Two main points on this page: 1) An LED can be used to display the output of a logic gate. 2) Logic gates don't usually supply much current, so they're often connected to a more powerful circuit using a relay switch.

LEDs — Light-Emitting Diodes

1) An LED is a diode (see page 119) which gives out light.
2) Like other diodes, it only lets current go through in one direction. When it does pass current, it gives out a pretty coloured light.
3) You can use a light-emitting diode (LED) to show the output of a logic gate. If the output is 1, enough current will flow through the LED to light it up.
4) An LED is a better choice to show output than an ordinary incandescent bulb because it uses less power and lasts longer.
5) The LED is often connected in series with a resistor to prevent it from being damaged by too large a current flowing through it.

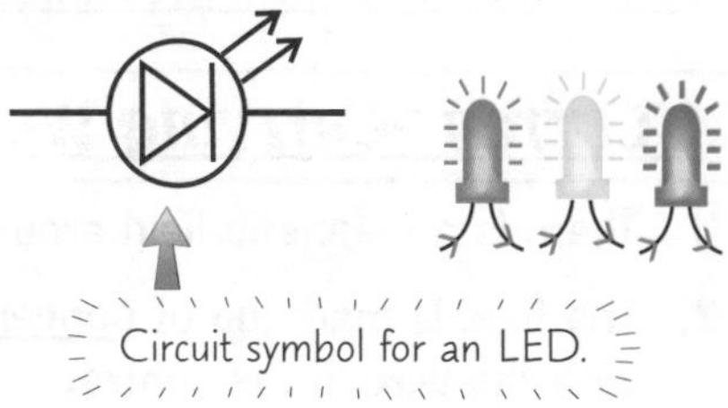

A Relay is a Switch Which Connects Two Circuits

1) A low-power logic gate would be damaged if you plugged it straight into a high current mains power supply.
2) But an output device like a motor requires a large current.
3) The solution is to have two circuits connected by a relay.
4) The relay isolates the low voltage electronic system from the high voltage mains often needed for the output device.
5) This also means that it can be made safer for the person using the device — you can make sure that any parts that could come into contact with a person are in the low-current sensing circuit. For example, a car's starter motor needs a very high current, but the part you control (when you're turning the key) is in the low-current circuit — safely isolated by the relay.

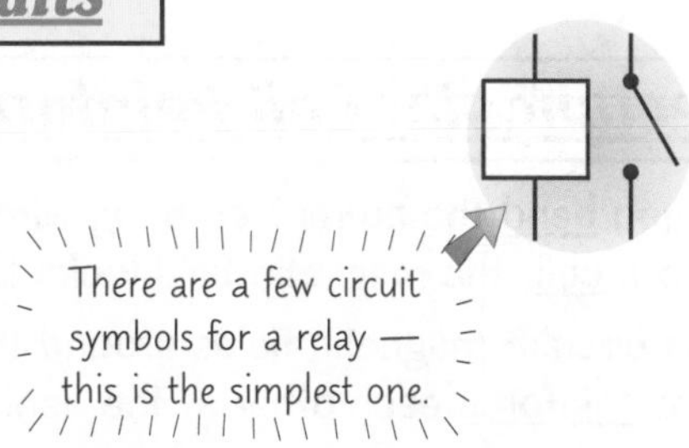

There are a few circuit symbols for a relay — this is the simplest one.

Here's How a Relay Works...

1) When the switch in the low-current circuit is closed, it turns on the electromagnet (see page 112), which attracts the iron contact on the rocker.
2) The rocker pivots and closes the contacts in the high current circuit — and the motor spins.
3) When the low-current switch is opened, the electromagnet stops pulling, the rocker returns, and the high current circuit is broken again.

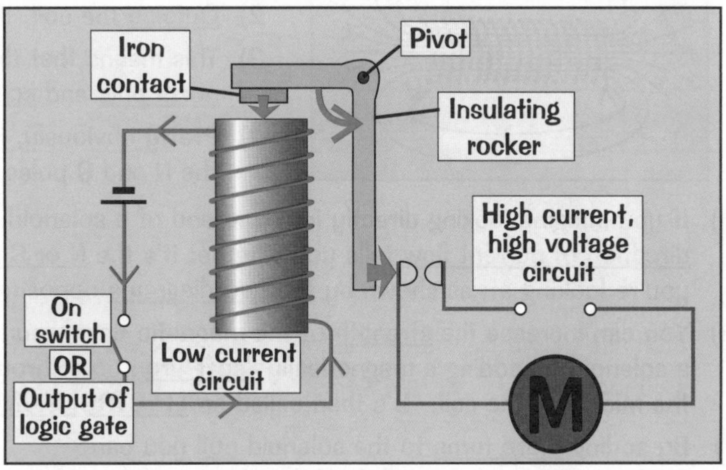

You should now be relay proud of yourself...

...'cos you've managed to get through all those pages on logic gates. I know it isn't always a barrel of laughs. There's a lot of tricky stuff here — a lot to learn, and a lot that's hard to understand. It's definitely a good idea to learn each page thoroughly before moving on, otherwise it'll all turn into a big tangled mess in your brain.

Magnetic Fields

Loads of electrical appliances use magnetic fields generated by electric currents.

> A MAGNETIC FIELD is a region where MAGNETIC MATERIALS (like iron and steel) and also WIRES CARRYING CURRENTS experience a FORCE acting on them.

Magnetic fields can be represented by field diagrams.

The arrows on the field lines always point FROM THE NORTH POLE of the magnet TO THE SOUTH POLE.

A Current-Carrying Wire Creates a Magnetic Field

1) There is a magnetic field around a straight, current-carrying wire.
2) The field is made up of concentric circles with the wire in the centre.
3) Changing the direction of the current changes the direction of the magnetic field — use the Right-Hand Thumb Rule to work out which way it goes.

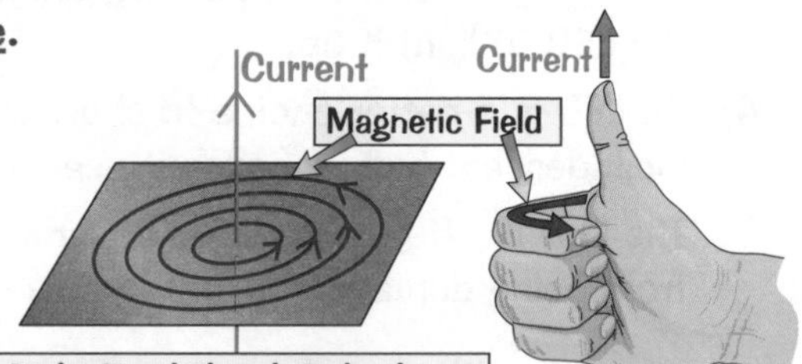

The Right-Hand Thumb Rule shows which way the magnetic field goes

A Rectangular Coil Reinforces the Magnetic Field

1) If you bend the current-carrying wire round into a coil, the magnetic field looks like this.
2) The circular magnetic fields around the sides of the loop reinforce each other at the centre.
3) If the coil has lots of turns, the magnetic fields from all the individual loops reinforce each other even more.

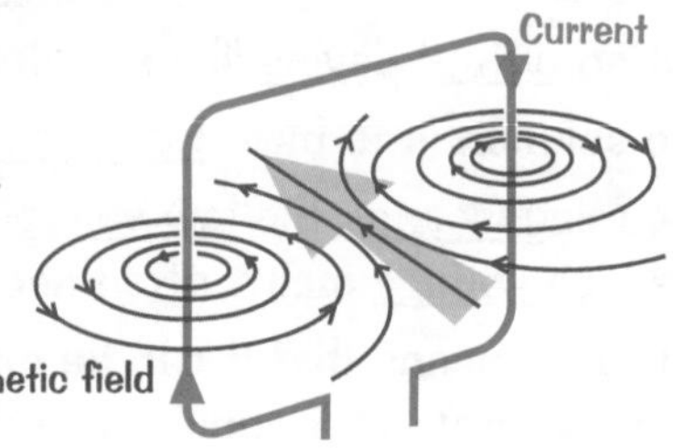

The Magnetic Field Round a Solenoid

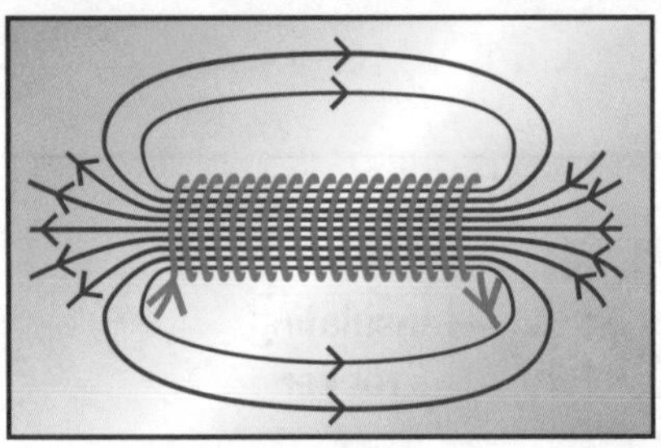

1) The magnetic field inside a current-carrying solenoid (a coil of wire) is strong and uniform.
2) Outside the coil, the field is just like the one round a bar magnet.
3) This means that the ends of a solenoid act like the north pole and south pole of a bar magnet.
4) Pretty obviously, if the direction of the current is reversed, the N and S poles will swap ends.
5) If you imagine looking directly into one end of a solenoid, the direction of current flow tells you whether it's the N or S pole you're looking at, as shown by the two diagrams opposite.
6) You can increase the strength of the magnetic field around a solenoid by adding a magnetically "soft" iron core through the middle of the coil. It's then called an ELECTROMAGNET.
7) By adding more turns to the solenoid coil you can further increase the strength of the electromagnet.

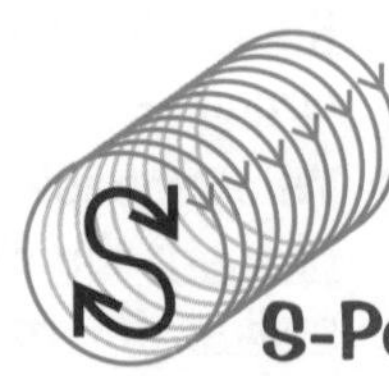

Current-carrying wires always get the thumbs up from me...

...and it's always my RIGHT thumb. Got that? Not my left, but my RIGHT thumb. Don't get them mixed up. You'll use your left hand on the next page, though, so it shouldn't feel too left out... (pun intended).

The Motor Effect

If you put a current-carrying wire into a magnetic field, you have two magnetic fields combining, which puts a force on the wire. The force can make the wire move — which can be quite handy, really.

A Current in a Magnetic Field Experiences a Force

When a current-carrying wire is put between magnetic poles, the two magnetic fields affect one another. The result is a force on the wire.

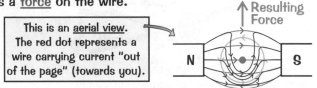

This is an aerial view. The red dot represents a wire carrying current "out of the page" (towards you).

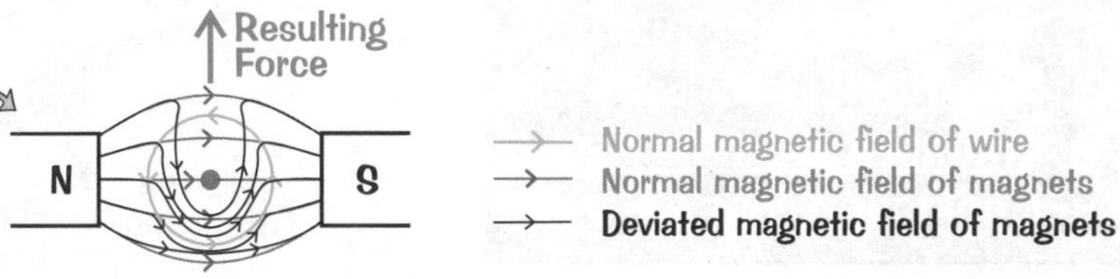

1) To experience the full force, the wire has to be at 90° (right angles) to the magnetic field. If the wire runs along the magnetic field, it won't experience any force at all. At angles in between, it'll feel some force.
2) The force gets stronger if either the current or the magnetic field is made stronger.
3) The force always acts in the same direction relative to the magnetic field of the magnets and the direction of the current in the wire. So changing the direction of either the magnetic field or the current will change the direction of the force.
4) A good way of showing the direction of the force is to apply a current to a set of rails inside a horseshoe magnet (as shown). A bar is placed on the rails, which completes the circuit. This generates a force that rolls the bar along the rails.

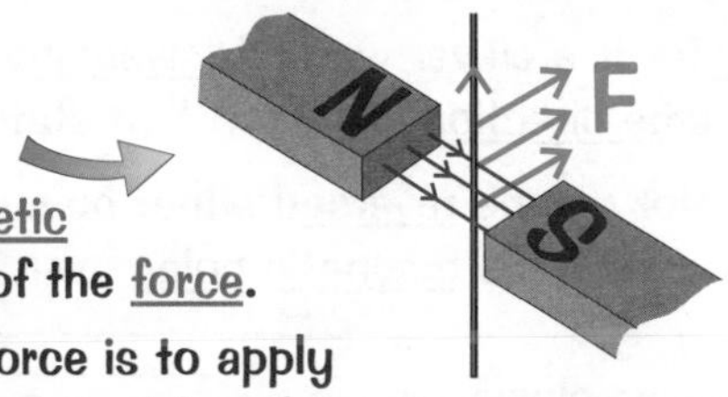

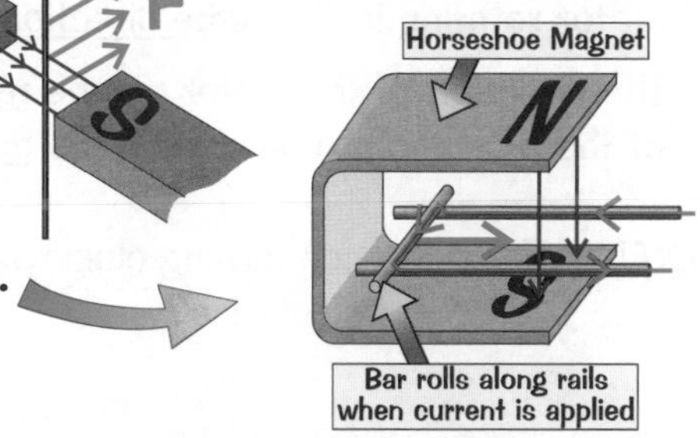

Fleming's Left-Hand Rule Tells You Which Way the Force Acts

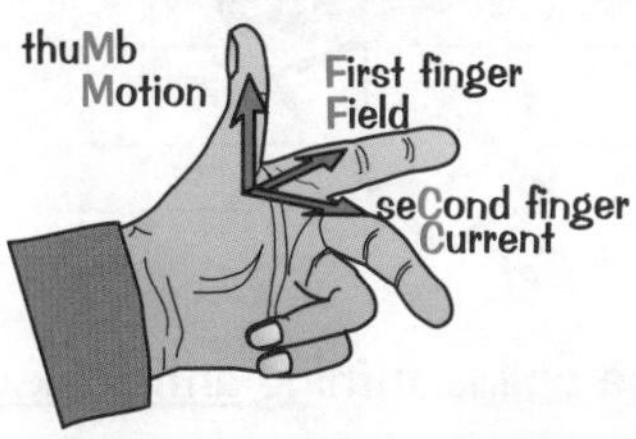

1) They could test if you can do this, so practise it.
2) Using your left hand, point your First finger in the direction of the Field and your seCond finger in the direction of the Current.
3) Your thuMb will then point in the direction of the force (Motion).

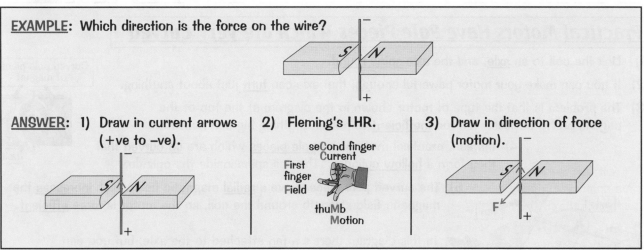

EXAMPLE: Which direction is the force on the wire?

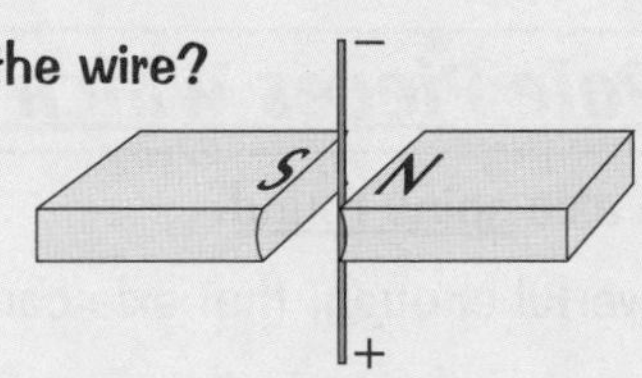

ANSWER: 1) Draw in current arrows (+ve to –ve). 2) Fleming's LHR. 3) Draw in direction of force (motion).

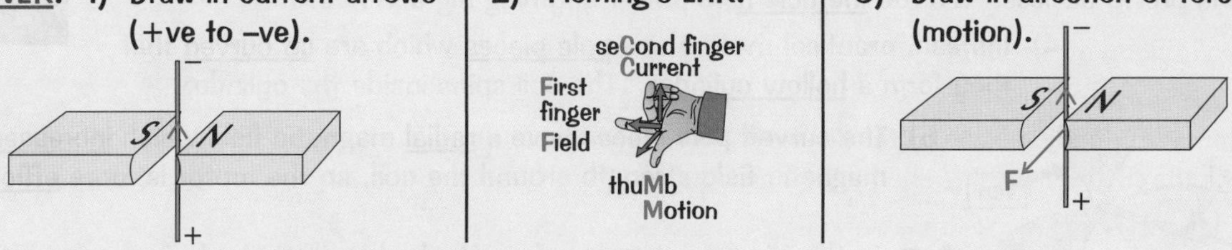

Remember the Left-Hand Rule for Motors — drive on the left...

See, I told you you'd need your left hand for this page. Learn the rule and use it — don't be scared of looking like a muppet in the exam. Learn all the details, diagrams and all, then cover the page and scribble it all down from memory. Then check back, see what you've missed, and try again (and again until you get it right).

The Simple Electric Motor

Aha — one of the favourite exam topics of all time. Read it. Understand it. Learn it.

The Simple Electric Motor

4 Factors which Speed it up

1) More CURRENT
2) More TURNS on the coil
3) STRONGER MAGNETIC FIELD
4) A SOFT IRON CORE in the coil

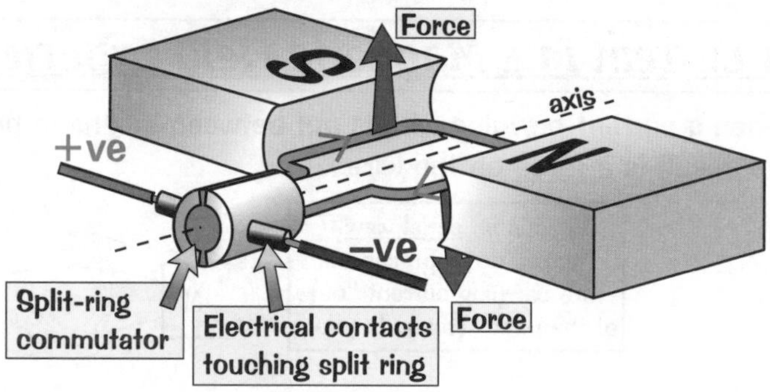

1) The diagram shows the forces acting on the two side arms of the coil.
2) These forces are just the usual forces which act on any current in a magnetic field (see previous page).
3) Because the coil is on a spindle and the forces act one up and one down, it rotates.
4) The split-ring commutator is a clever way of "swapping the contacts every half turn to keep the motor rotating in the same direction". (Learn that statement because they might ask you.)
5) The direction of the motor can be reversed either by swapping the polarity of the DC supply or swapping the magnetic poles over.

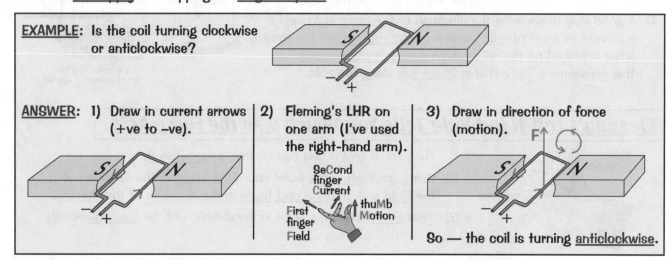

EXAMPLE: Is the coil turning clockwise or anticlockwise?

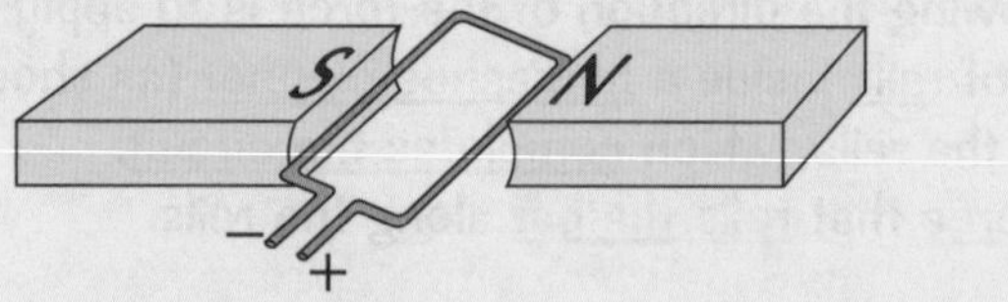

ANSWER: 1) Draw in current arrows (+ve to –ve).

2) Fleming's LHR on one arm (I've used the right-hand arm).

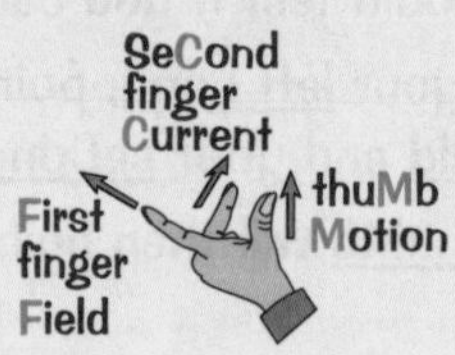

3) Draw in direction of force (motion).

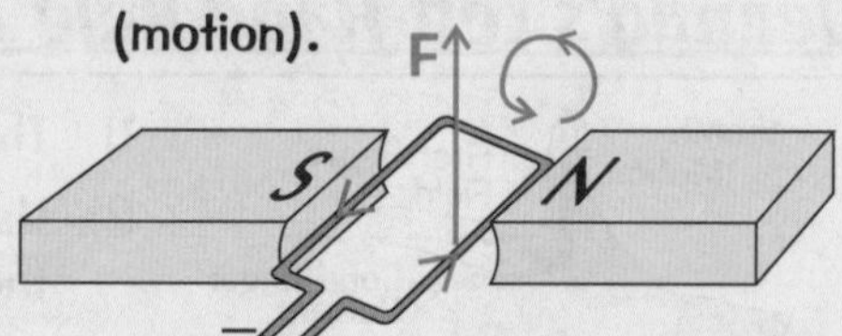

So — the coil is turning anticlockwise.

Practical Motors Have Pole Pieces Which are Very Curved

1) Link the coil to an axle, and the axle spins round.
2) If you can make your motor powerful enough, that axle can turn just about anything.
3) The problem is that the type of motor shown in the diagram at the top of the page is pretty useless. It's too inefficient to power anything big and heavy.
4) Instead, practical motors use pole pieces which are so curved that they form a hollow cylinder. The coil spins inside the cylinder.
5) The curved pole pieces have a radial magnetic field which increases the magnetic field strength around the coil, so the motor is more efficient.

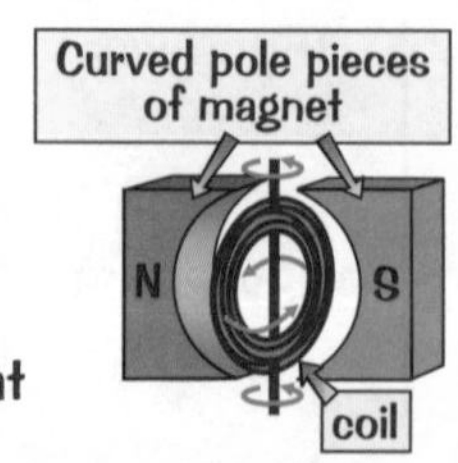

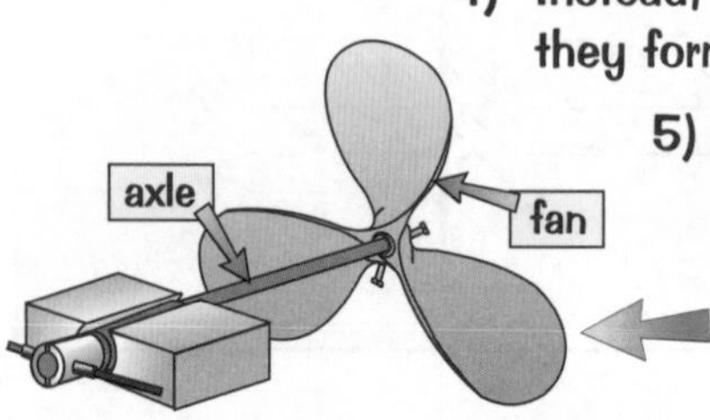

In this diagram there's a fan attached to the axle, but you can stick almost anything on a motor axle and make it spin round.

Hello Motor...

Loudspeakers demonstrate the motor effect. AC electrical signals from the amplifier are fed to the speaker coil (shown red). These make the coil move back and forth over the poles of the magnet. These movements make the cardboard cone vibrate and this creates sounds.

Electromagnetic Induction

Electricity is generated using electromagnetic induction. Sounds terrifying, but it isn't that complicated. Hopefully, some of the stuff on the next few pages will be familiar to you from P2.

ELECTROMAGNETIC INDUCTION:
The creation of a VOLTAGE (and maybe current) in a wire which is experiencing a CHANGE IN MAGNETIC FIELD.

(You'll sometimes hear it called the "dynamo effect".)

Moving a Magnet in a Coil of Wire Induces a Voltage

1) Electromagnetic induction means creating a voltage (and maybe a current) in a conductor. You can do this by moving a magnet in a coil of wire OR moving a conductor (wire) in a magnetic field ("cutting" magnetic field lines). Shifting the magnet from side to side creates a little "blip" of current.

A few examples of electromagnetic induction:

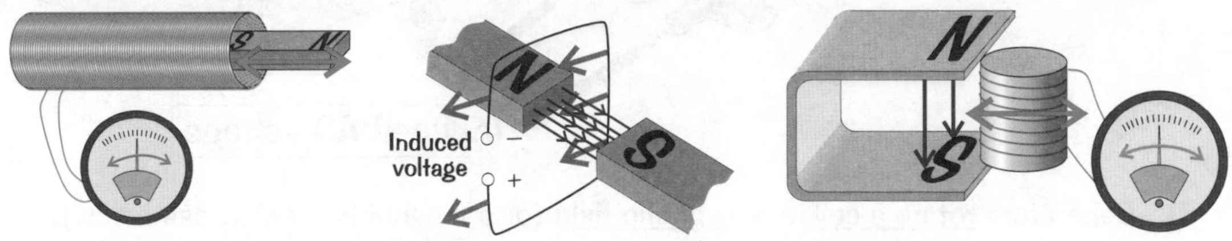

2) If you move the magnet (or conductor) in the opposite direction, then the voltage/current will be reversed. Likewise if the polarity of the magnet is reversed, then the voltage/current will be reversed too.
3) If you keep the magnet (or the coil) moving backwards and forwards, you produce a voltage that keeps swapping direction — and this is how you produce alternating current (AC).

You can create the same effect by turning a magnet end to end in a coil, to create a current that lasts as long as you spin the magnet. This is how generators work (see next page).

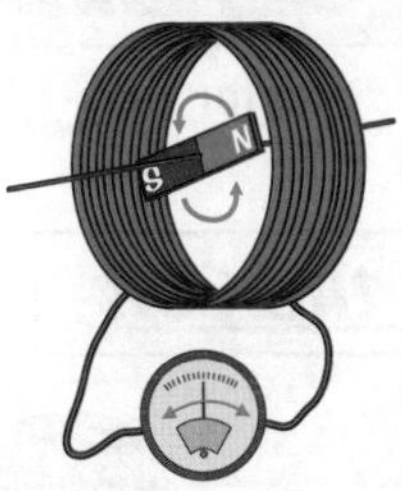

1) As you turn the magnet, the magnetic field through the coil changes — this change in the magnetic field induces a voltage, which can make a current flow in the wire.
2) When you've turned the magnet through half a turn, the direction of the magnetic field through the coil reverses. When this happens, the voltage reverses, so the current flows in the opposite direction around the coil of wire.
3) If you keep turning the magnet in the same direction — always clockwise, say — then the voltage will keep on reversing every half turn and you'll get an alternating current.

Four Factors Affect the Size of the Induced Voltage

1) If you want a different peak voltage (and current) you have to change the rate that the magnetic field is changing. For a bigger voltage you need to increase at least one of these four things:

1) The STRENGTH of the MAGNET	2) The AREA of the COIL
3) The number of TURNS on the COIL	4) The SPEED of movement

2) To reduce the voltage, you would reduce one of those factors, obviously.
3) If you turn the magnet faster, you'll get a higher peak voltage, but also a higher frequency — because the magnetic field is reversing more frequently.

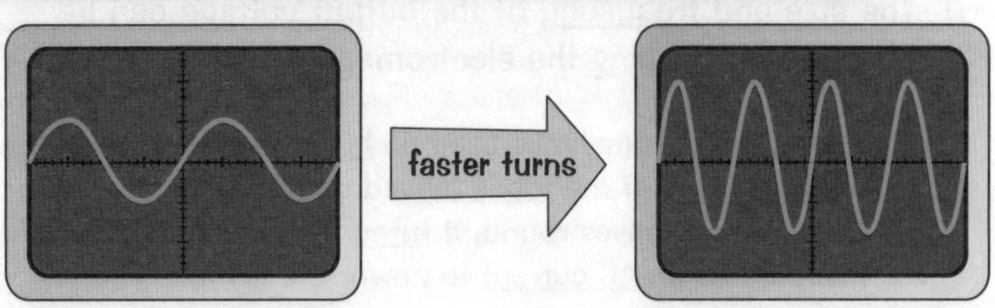

EM Induction — works whether the coil or the field is moving...

"Electromagnetic Induction" gets my vote for "Definitely Most Tricky Topic". If it wasn't so important maybe you wouldn't have to bother learning it. The trouble is, this is how all our electricity is generated, so it's important.

Generators

Think about the simple electric motor — you've got a current in the wire and a magnetic field, which causes movement. Well, a generator works the opposite way round — you've got a magnetic field and movement, which induces a current.

AC Generators — Just Turn the Coil and There's a Current

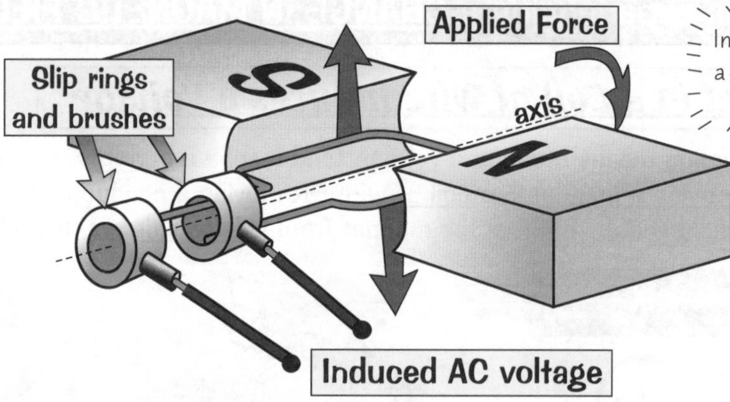

In an exam, they could give you a diagram like this and ask you to explain how it works.

1) Generators rotate a coil in a magnetic field (or a magnet in a coil... see below).
2) Their construction is pretty much like a motor.
3) As the coil (or magnet) spins, a current is induced in the coil. This current changes direction every half turn.
4) Instead of a split-ring commutator, AC generators have slip rings and brushes so the contacts don't swap every half turn.
5) This means they produce AC voltage, as shown by these CRO displays. Note that faster revolutions produce not only more peaks but higher overall voltage too.

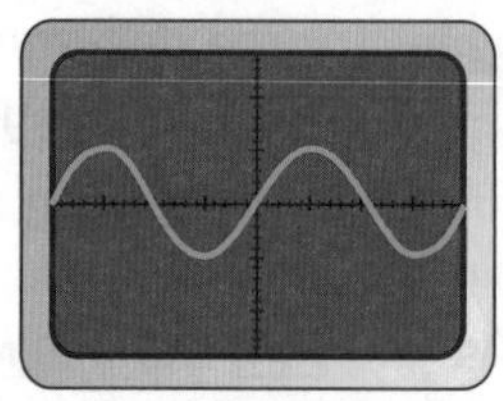

original

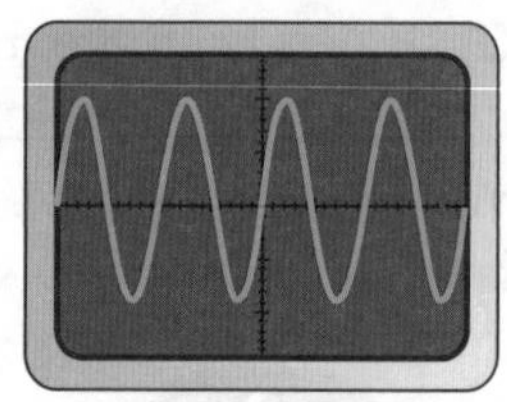

faster revs

Dynamos and Power Stations — Turn the Magnet Instead of the Coil

1) Dynamos are a slightly different type of generator. They rotate the magnet instead of the coil to produce alternating current.
2) This still causes the field through the coil to swap every half turn, so the output is just the same as for a generator.
3) This means you get the same CRO traces of course.
4) In a power station, electricity is generated by rotating an electromagnet in a coil of wire.
5) The size of the output voltage can be changed by adding more turns to the electromagnet coil.
6) The size and frequency of the output voltage can be changed by rotating the electromagnet coil faster.

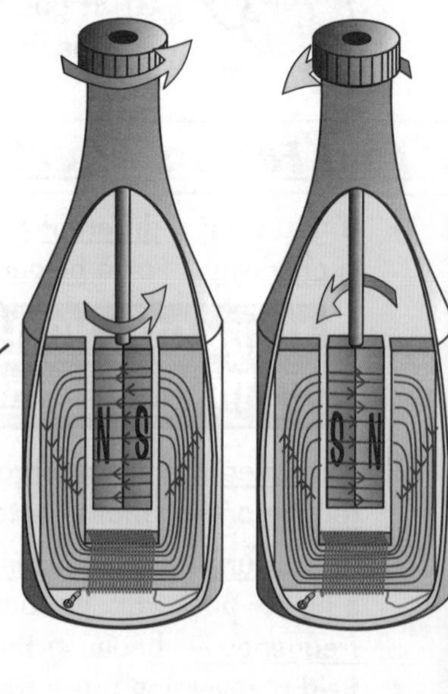

Dynamos are sometimes used on bikes to power the lights. The cog wheel at the top is moved so that it touches one of the bike wheels. As the wheel moves round, it turns the cog which is attached to the magnet. This creates an AC current to power the lights.

Dynamo Kiev — they like a bit of squad rotation...

The National Grid is fed by hundreds of generators. These are usually driven by steam turbines (and the steam usually comes from burning things). You can get small portable petrol generators too, to use where there's no mains electricity — on building sites, say.

Transformers

Transformers use electromagnetic induction to connect two circuits together.
Transformers mean that one circuit can power another circuit with a different voltage and current.

There are Three Types of Transformer

Transformers are basically two coils of wire wound round an iron core. They're used to change the size of an alternating voltage. There are three types — you need to know the differences between them.

STEP-UP TRANSFORMERS step the voltage up. They have more turns on the secondary coil than the primary coil.

STEP-DOWN TRANSFORMERS step the voltage down. They have more turns on the primary coil than the secondary.

ISOLATING TRANSFORMERS don't change the voltage at all. They have the same number of turns on the primary and secondary coils.

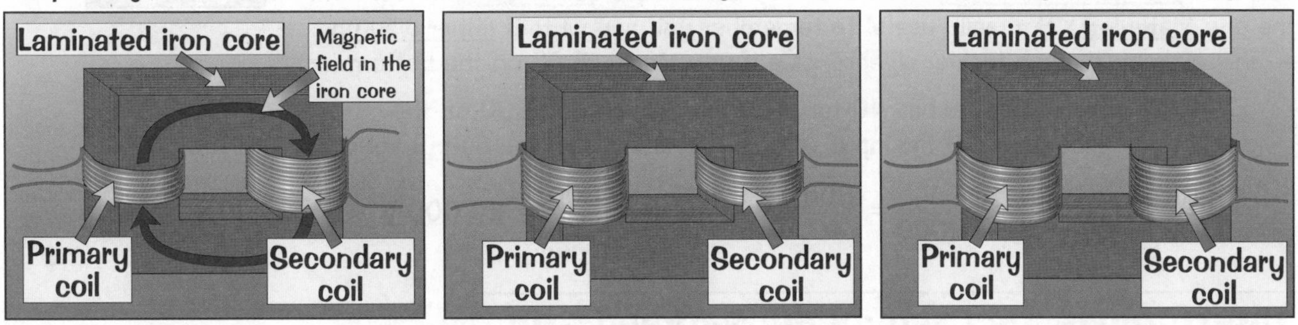

Transformers Work by Electromagnetic Induction

1) The primary coil produces a magnetic field which stays within the iron core. This means nearly all of it passes through the secondary coil and hardly any is lost.
2) Because there is alternating current (AC) in the primary coil, the field in the iron core is constantly changing direction (100 times a second if it's at 50 Hz) — i.e. it is a changing magnetic field.
3) This rapidly changing magnetic field is felt by the secondary coil.
4) The changing field induces an alternating voltage in the secondary coil (with the same frequency as the alternating current in the primary) — electromagnetic induction of a voltage in fact.
5) The relative number of turns on the two coils determines whether the voltage induced in the secondary coil is greater or less than the voltage in the primary.
6) If you supplied DC to the primary, you'd get nothing out of the secondary at all. Sure, there'd still be a magnetic field in the iron core, but it wouldn't be constantly changing, so there'd be no induction in the secondary because you need a changing field to induce a voltage. So don't forget it:

Transformers only work with AC. They won't work with DC at all.

Transformers are Nearly 100% Efficient So "Power In = Power Out"

The formula for power supplied is: Power = Voltage × Current or: $P = V \times I$.

So you can rewrite power in = power out as: $V_pI_p = V_sI_s$

V_p = primary voltage, V_s = secondary voltage
I_p = primary current, I_s = secondary current

You can use this equation to find the output current when the voltage has been changed. As both sides need to balance, for a fixed input power, the higher the voltage, the lower the current will be:

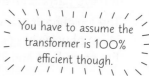

You have to assume the transformer is 100% efficient though.

EXAMPLE: The primary voltage and current into a transformer are 200 V and 5000 A. Find the secondary current, if the voltage is stepped up to 20 000 V.

ANSWER: $V_pI_p = V_sI_s$, so $200 \times 5000 = 20\,000 \times I_s$. $I_s = (200 \times 5000) \div 20\,000 = $ 50 A.

More on Transformers

The ratio between the primary and secondary voltages is the same as the ratio between the number of turns on the primary and secondary coils. You can either learn it that way, or learn the formula below.

The Transformer Equation — Use it Either Way Up

You can calculate the output voltage from a transformer if you know the input voltage and the number of turns on each coil.

$$\frac{\text{Primary Voltage}}{\text{Secondary Voltage}} = \frac{\text{Number of turns on Primary}}{\text{Number of turns on Secondary}}$$

$$\frac{V_P}{V_S} = \frac{N_P}{N_S} \quad \text{or} \quad \frac{V_S}{V_P} = \frac{N_S}{N_P}$$

Well, it's just another formula. You stick in the numbers you've got and work out the one that's left. It's really useful to remember you can write it either way up — this example's much trickier algebra-wise if you start with V_s on the bottom...

EXAMPLE: A transformer has 40 turns on the primary and 800 on the secondary. If the input voltage is 1000 V, find the output voltage.

ANSWER: $\frac{V_s}{V_p} = \frac{N_s}{N_p}$, so $\frac{V_s}{1000} = \frac{800}{40}$. $V_s = 1000 \times \frac{800}{40} = $ 20 000 V

Or you can say that 800 is 20 times 40, so the secondary voltage will also be 20 times the primary voltage.

Transformers Are Used on the National Grid

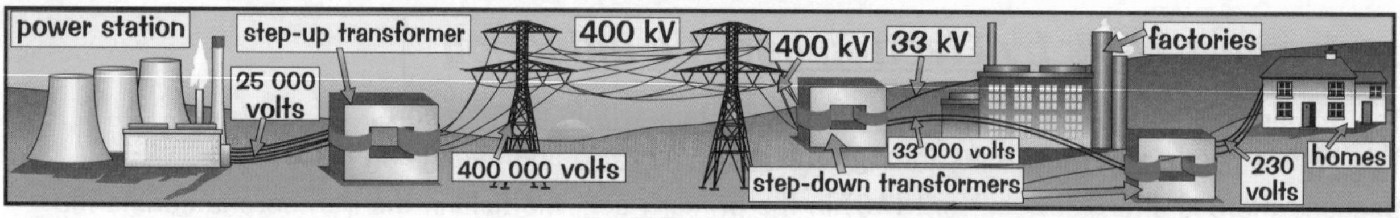

1) To transmit a lot of power, you either need high voltage or high current (P = VI).
2) The problem with high current is the loss (as heat) due to the resistance of the cables (and transformers).
3) The formula for power loss due to resistance in the cables is:

$$\text{Power Loss} = \text{Current}^2 \times \text{Resistance} \qquad P = I^2R$$

4) Because of the I^2 bit, if the current is 10 times bigger, the losses will be 100 times bigger.
5) So it's much cheaper to boost the voltage up to 400 000 V and keep the current very low. This requires transformers as well as big pylons with huge insulators, but it's still cheaper.
6) The transformers have to step the voltage up at one end, for efficient transmission, and then bring it back down to safe, usable levels at the other end.

Isolating Transformers are Used in Bathrooms

1) Isolating transformers have an equal number of turns in the primary and secondary coils, so also have equal primary and secondary voltages. They can be found in some mains circuits in the home, such as in a bathroom shaver socket.
2) Isolating transformers are there for safety. The mains circuit is connected to the earth, so if you touch the live parts and are also touching the ground, you will complete a circuit with you in it. NOT good.
3) The isolating transformer inside the shaver socket allows you to use the shaver without being physically connected to the mains. So it minimises the risk of the live parts touching the earth lead and likewise minimises your risk of getting electrocuted. Phew.

National Grid — heaven for noughts and crosses fans...

In most power stations, fuels are burned and the energy from this powers a massive generator. Not all the heat can be converted into mechanical power, though, so heat is often lost to the environment. What a waste.

Diodes and Rectification

Mains electricity supplies alternating current (AC), but many devices need direct current (DC). So we need a way of turning AC into DC. That's where diodes come in.

Diodes Only Let Current Flow in One Direction

1) Diodes only let current flow freely in one direction — there's a very high resistance in the other direction.
2) This turns out to be really useful in various electronic circuits.
3) You can tell which direction the current flows from the circuit symbol.

   The triangle points in the direction of the current.

Here the current flows from left to right.

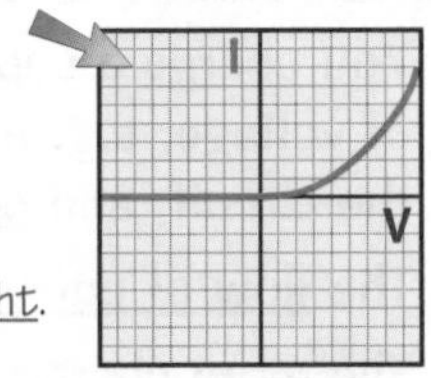

Diodes are Made from Semiconductors Such As Silicon

1) Diodes are often made of silicon, which is a semiconductor. This means silicon can conduct electricity, though not as well as a conductor.
2) Silicon diodes are made from two different types of silicon joined together at a 'p-n junction'. One half of the diode is made from silicon that has an impurity added to provide extra free electrons — called an n-type semiconductor ("n" stands for the "negative" charge of the electrons).
3) A different impurity is added to the other half of the diode so there are fewer free electrons than normal. There are lots of empty spaces left by these missing electrons which are called holes. This type of silicon is called a p-type semiconductor ("p" stands for the "positive" charge of the holes).
4) When there's no voltage across the diode, electrons and holes recombine where the two parts of the diode join. This creates a region where there are no holes or free electrons, which acts as an electrical insulator.
5) When there is a voltage across the diode the direction is all-important: Applying a voltage in the RIGHT direction means the free holes and electrons have enough energy to get across the insulating region to the other side. This means that a CURRENT FLOWS. Applying a voltage in the WRONG direction means the free holes and electrons are being pulled away from the insulating region, so they stay on the same side and NO CURRENT FLOWS.

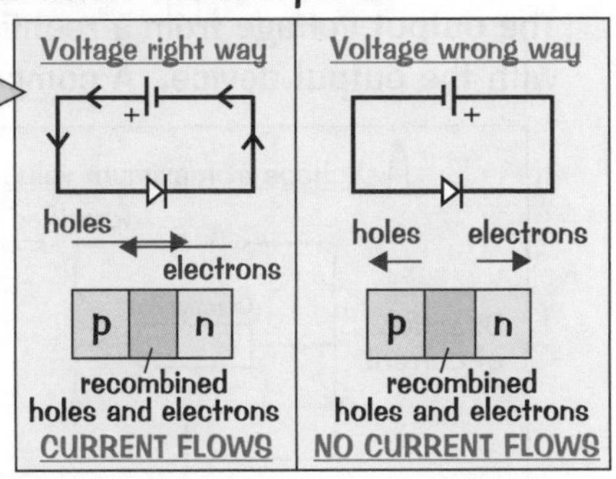

Diodes Can be Used to Rectify Alternating Current

1) A single diode only lets through current in half of the cycle. This is called half-wave rectification.

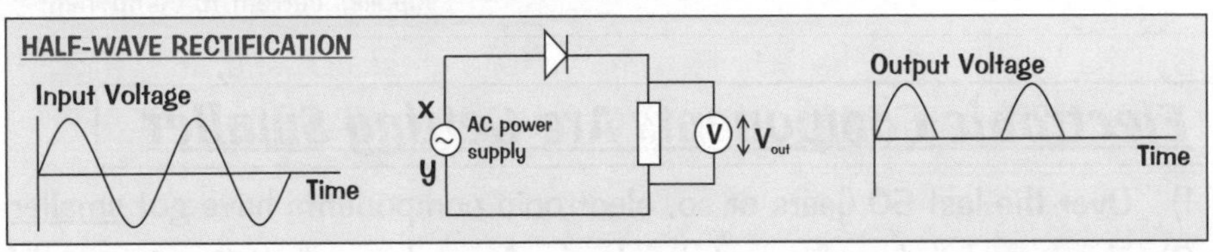

2) To get full-wave rectification, you need a bridge circuit with four diodes. In a bridge circuit, the current always flows through the component in the same direction, and the output voltage always has the same sign.

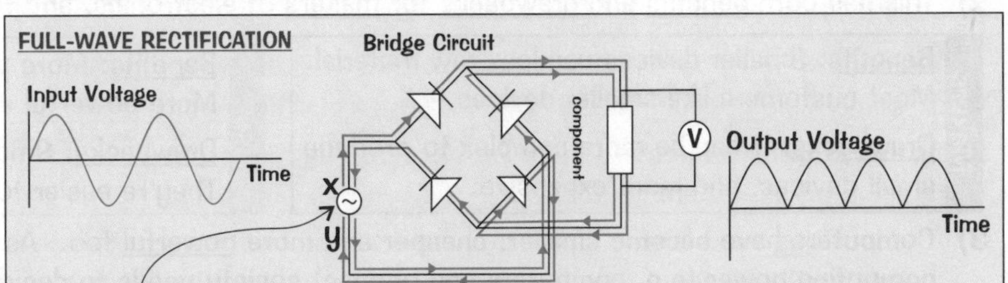

When X is positive and Y is negative, current flows along the red path (→).
When Y is positive and X is negative, current flows along the blue path (→).

Yep, it's all just common sense really...

Only joking — this stuff's flippin' hard. At least you've made it through to the other side though, well done.

Capacitors

AC voltage that has been rectified is not all that useful in its raw form. For example, computer chips are very sensitive to input voltage, and won't work with a voltage that looks like this: 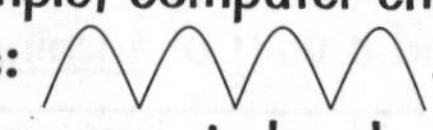.
They need a smoother voltage like this:  . This is where capacitors come in handy.

Capacitors Store Charge

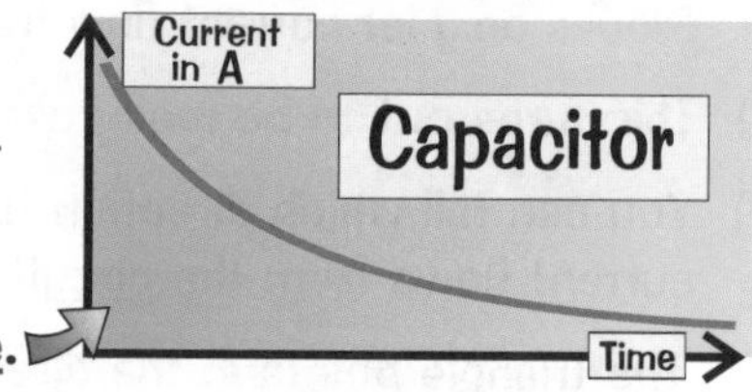

1) You charge a capacitor by connecting it to a source of voltage, e.g. a battery. A current flows around the circuit, and charge gets stored on the capacitor.
2) The flow of current decreases as you charge for longer periods of time.
3) The more charge that's stored on a capacitor, the larger the voltage across it.
4) When the voltage across the capacitor is equal to that of the battery, the current stops and the capacitor is fully charged. The voltage across the capacitor won't rise above the voltage of the battery.
5) If the battery is removed, the capacitor discharges — the flow of current is the same for discharging as for charging (see shape of graph above) but the current flows in the opposite direction round the circuit.

CHARGING:

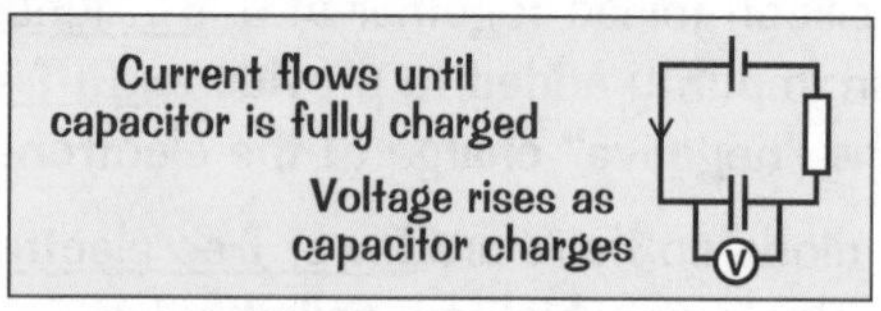

DISCHARGING:

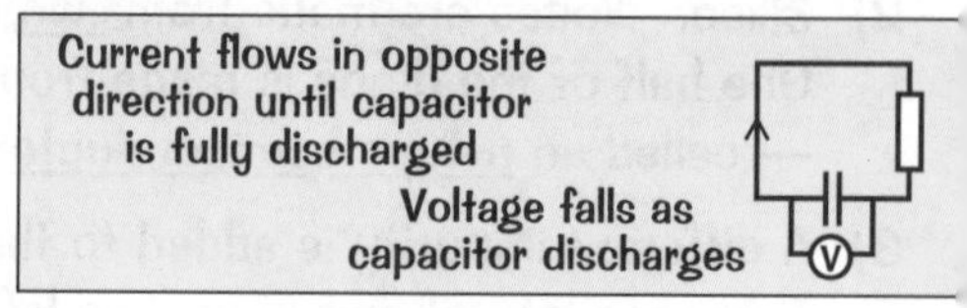

Capacitors are Used in 'Smoothing' Circuits

The output voltage from a rectified AC power supply can be 'smoothed' by adding a capacitor in parallel with the output device. A component gets current alternately from the power supply and the capacitor.

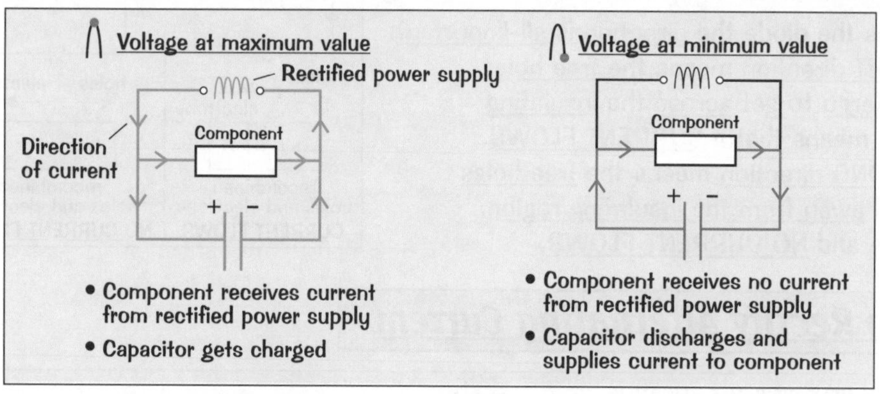

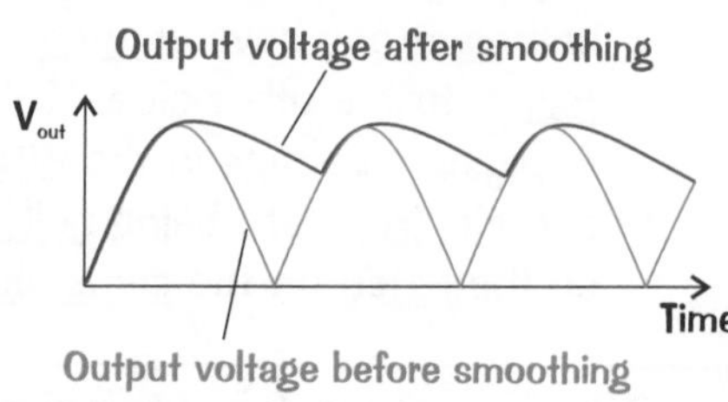

Electronic Components Are Getting Smaller

1) Over the last 50 years or so, electronic components have got smaller — it's known as miniaturisation.
2) This has both benefits and drawbacks for makers of electronics, and for the people using them:

Makers	Users
Benefits: Smaller devices use less raw material. Most customers like smaller devices. Drawbacks: It can be more complex to produce small devices, and more expensive.	Benefits: More portable electronic devices available. More powerful and feature-filled devices produced. Drawbacks: Smaller devices can be more expensive. They're easier to lose down the back of the sofa.

3) Computers have become smaller, cheaper and more powerful too. As more people have access to more computing power (e.g. computers and phones) society needs to decide how this should, or should not, be allowed to be used.
   For example, society needs to think about controlling hacking, piracy and access to personal data.

Current never flows through a capacitor...

Capacitors just store charge, and then send current back the other way when the voltage falls. Handy.

Revision Summary for Module P6

Electricity and magnetism. What fun. This is definitely physics at its most grisly. The big problem with physics in general is that usually there's nothing to "see". You're told that there's a current flowing or a magnetic field lurking, but there's nothing you can actually see with your eyes. That's what makes it so difficult. To get to grips with physics you have to get used to learning about things you can't see. Do these questions to see how you're getting on. Then you can relax, it's the end of the book. Ace.

1) Briefly explain what causes resistance in a metal conductor.
2) Sketch a voltage-current graph for: a) a resistor, b) a filament lamp.
3)* Find the current when a resistance of 96 Ω is connected to a battery of 12 V.
4)* Four resistors with resistances of 2 Ω, 4 Ω, 6 Ω and 3 Ω are connected in a circuit in parallel. Calculate the total resistance of the circuit.
5) Explain how potential dividers work.
6) State the formula for potential dividers. Do your own worked example, including a sketch.
7) Write down two facts each about: a) LDRs, b) thermistors.
8) Draw and label the circuit symbol for a transistor. Describe what happens in each part of the transistor.
9) Draw truth tables for AND, OR, NAND and NOR gates.
10) What are AND gates made from?
11) Explain how an LED can be used to show the output of a logic gate.
12) Make a sketch of a relay.
13) Give a definition of a magnetic field.
14) Sketch magnetic fields for: a) a current-carrying wire, b) a rectangular coil, c) a solenoid.
15) Make a sketch of the force on a current-carrying wire between two magnets. What is the name of this effect?
16) Explain how Fleming's Left-Hand Rule works.
17) Sketch a motor and list the four ways to speed it up.
18) What is electromagnetic induction? List four factors which affect the size of the induced voltage.
19) Sketch a generator, labelling all the parts. Describe how it works and what all the bits do.
20) Sketch the three types of transformer, and explain how they work.
21)* In a transformer, the primary voltage is 6 V, the primary current is 10 A and the secondary voltage is 3 V. What is the secondary current in the transformer?
22)* A transformer has an input voltage of 20 V and an output voltage of 16 V. If there are 64 turns on the secondary coil, how many turns are there on the primary coil?
23) Explain why power is transmitted at such a high voltage.
24) Write down three facts about isolating transformers.
25) Explain briefly how a diode works. What semiconducting material are diodes often made of?
26) Explain the two ways in which an AC current can be rectified. Include circuit diagrams and voltage/time graphs in your explanation.
27) What is a capacitor? How can it be used to smooth rectified voltage?
28) Electronic components are getting smaller. Explain why this could be a bad thing for:
    a) manufacturers of electronic devices, b) users of electronic devices.
29) Go and read up on quantum theory... no wait, I mean... go and put the kettle on.

* Answers on p. 124.

Index

Index and Answers

Answers

Revision Summary for Module P1 (page 31)

2) Energy = Mass × Specific Heat Capacity (SHC) × Temperature Change (Temp. Ch.), so SHC = Energy ÷ (Mass × Temp. Ch.) = 5000 ÷ (0.05 × 40) = 2500 J/kg/°C

4) Energy = Mass × Specific Latent Heat (SLH) = 0.5 × 2 260 000 = 1 130 000 J

8) Efficiency = Useful energy output ÷ Total energy input, so Useful = Efficiency × Total energy = 0.2 × 200 000 = 40 000. Wasted energy = Total energy input – Useful energy output = 200 000 – 40 000 = 160 000 J

Electrical Power (page 37)

1) Power = Voltage × Current = 230 × 12 = 2760 W = 2.76 kW

2) Energy = Power × Time, so Time = Energy ÷ Power = 0.5 kWh ÷ 2.76 kW = 0.18 hours = 10.8 or 10.9 mins

Revision Summary for Module P2 (page 52)

9) a) Energy = Power × Time = 2.5 kW × 0.05 h = 0.125 kWh
   b) Cost = Cost per unit × number of units = 12 × 0.125 = 1.5 p

Forces and Acceleration (page 58)

Resultant force = mass × acceleration
resultant force = 70 × 1.2 = 84 N
resultant force = driving force – drag
84 = driving force – 8
so, driving force = 84 + 8 = 92 N

Revision Summary for Module P3 (page 69)

1) u = 0 m/s, v = 0.08 m/s, t = 35 s
Distance = ((u + v) ÷ 2) × t
= ((0 + 0.08) ÷ 2) × 35 = 1.4 m

3) Acceleration = change in speed ÷ time = (14 – 0) ÷ 0.4 = 35 m/s^2

11) Force = mass × acceleration so, acceleration = force ÷ mass = 30 ÷ 4 = 7.5 m/s^2

16) Momentum = mass × velocity so, velocity = momentum ÷ mass = 45 ÷ 6 = 7.5 m/s

17) Force = change in momentum ÷ time so, change in momentum = force × time = 70 × 0.5 = 35 kg m/s

20) Work done = force × distance = 535 × 12 = 6420 J

21) G.P.E. = mass × g × height = 12 × 10 × 4.5 = 540 J

Answers

22) K.E. = ½ × mass × velocity^2
= ½ × 78 × 23^2 = 20 631 J

24) Increase in K.E. = Loss of G.P.E. = 150 kJ

25) Increase in K.E. = Loss of G.P.E., ½mv^2 = mgh
but mass stays the same, so can use h = v^2 ÷ 2g
v^2 = (h × 2g) = (20 × 2 × 10) = 400
v = √400 = 20 m/s

26) Work done must be in J = 540 × 1000 = 540 000 J.
Time needs to be in seconds, 4.5 × 60 = 270 s
Power = work done ÷ time = 540 000 J ÷ 270 s
= 2000 W or J/s (= 2 kW)

27) Power = force × speed = 500 × 20
= 10 000 W or J/s (= 10 kW)

<u>Plugs and Fuses (page 74)</u>

Power = Voltage × Current,
so Current = Power ÷ Voltage = 1200 ÷ 230
= 5.2 A. So the kettle will need a 7 A fuse.

<u>Resistance (page 75)</u>

1) Resistance = voltage ÷ current = 9 ÷ 3 = 3 Ω
2) Resistance = voltage ÷ current, so
voltage = resistance × current = 2.5 × 6.4 = 16 V

<u>Radioactive Dating (page 82)</u>

1) Original amount of carbon-14 is 1 part in 10 000 000.
So one half-life will be 1 part in 20 000 000. Two half-lives will be 1 part in 40 000 000... Four half-lives will be 1 part in 160 000 000.
4 × 5730 = 22 920 years old.

<u>Revision Summary for Module P4 (page 85)</u>

8) Power = voltage × current, so
current = power ÷ voltage = 400 ÷ 230 = 1.74 A
Need to use the fuse with the rating just above the current used — so need to use the 3 A fuse.

13) a) $^{234}_{92}U \longrightarrow {}^{230}_{90}Th + {}^{4}_{2}\alpha$
b) $^{230}_{90}Th \longrightarrow {}^{226}_{88}Ra + {}^{4}_{2}\alpha$
c) $^{241}_{95}Am \longrightarrow {}^{237}_{93}Np + {}^{4}_{2}\alpha$

14) a) $^{234}_{90}Th \longrightarrow {}^{234}_{91}Pa + {}^{0}_{-1}\beta$
b) $^{90}_{38}Sr \longrightarrow {}^{90}_{39}Y + {}^{0}_{-1}\beta$
c) $^{131}_{53}I \longrightarrow {}^{131}_{54}Xe + {}^{0}_{-1}\beta$
You won't have to remember the symbols for the elements in an exam, so you can stop memorising that periodic table for now.

21) Originally amount of carbon-14 was 1 part in 10 000 000. So one half-life will be 1 part in 20 000 000. Two half-lives will be 1 part in 40 000 000. Three half-lives will be 1 part in 80 000 000. 3 × 5730 = 17 190 years old.

<u>Refraction (page 98)</u>

Refractive index of sapphire
= speed of light in a vacuum ÷ speed of light in sapphire
= 3 × 10^8 ÷ 1.7 × 10^8 = 1.76
Light speeds up going from sapphire into air so the light would bend away from the normal.

<u>Revision Summary for Module P5 (page 103)</u>

2) 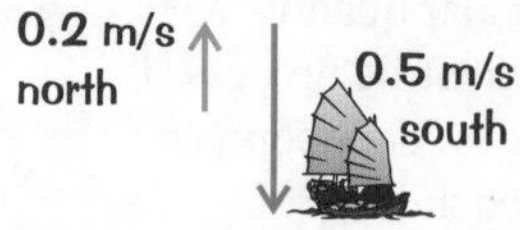

Vectors are directly opposite so overall velocity is (taking south as positive):
0.5 m/s – 0.2 m/s = 0.3 m/s south

3) 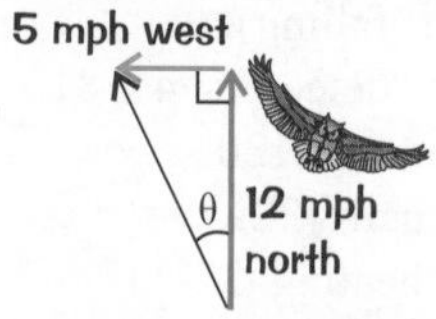

Use Pythagoras's theorem to find the speed:
speed^2 = 5^2 + 12^2 = 169
speed = √169 = 13 mph
Find direction using trigonometry:
tan θ = 5 ÷ 12 = 0.417
θ = 22.6°
So, the bird is flying 13 mph at 22.6° west of north

4) u = 0 m/s, v = 14 m/s, t = 0.4 m/s, s = ?
using s = ½(u + v) × t
s = ½(0 + 14) × 0.4 = 2.8 m

5) Make velocity upwards positive.
u = 13.4 m/s, a = –10 m/s^2, s = 7 m, v = ?
using v^2 = u^2 + 2as
v^2 = 13.4^2 + (2 × –10 × 7) = 179.56 – 140 = 39.56
v = √39.56 = 6.3 m/s

7) a) Taking the vertical motion: u = 0 m/s, t = 10 s, a = 10 m/s^2, s = ?
using s = ut + ½at^2
s = (0 × 10) + ½(10 × 10^2) = 500 m
b) speed = distance ÷ time
rearrange to find distance = speed × time
distance = 1.5 m/s × 10 s = 15 m

9) Momentum before = momentum after
so, momentum after the collision = 0.

11) The force will increase by a factor of nine.

19) a) Refractive index = speed of light in a vacuum ÷ speed of light in a medium. Rearrange to find speed of light in a medium = speed of light in a vacuum ÷ refractive index.
So, speed of light in jet = 3 × 10^8 m/s ÷ 1.66
= 1.81 × 10^8 m/s
b) The light would bend away from the normal.

24) Magnification = image height ÷ object height
= 4.5 cm ÷ 1.5 cm = 3

<u>Revision Summary for Module P6 (page 121)</u>

3) I = V ÷ R = 12 ÷ 96 = 0.125 A

4) Resistors in parallel, so use $\frac{1}{R_T}=\frac{1}{R_1}+\frac{1}{R_2}+\frac{1}{R_3}+\frac{1}{R_4}$.
$\frac{1}{R_T}=\frac{1}{2}+\frac{1}{4}+\frac{1}{6}+\frac{1}{3}$ = 1.25
so, R_T = 1 ÷ 1.25 = 0.8 Ω.

21) $V_pI_p = V_sI_s$, so 6 × 10 = 3 × I_s, so $I_s = \frac{60}{3}$ = 20 A.

22) $\frac{V_p}{V_s} = \frac{N_p}{N_s}$, so $\frac{20}{16} = \frac{N_p}{64}$. $N_p = 64 \times \frac{20}{16}$ = 80 turns

10:50
L2

MACMILLAN WORK OUT SERIES

Electronics

withdrawn

The titles in this series

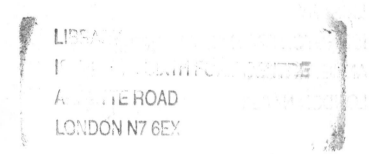

Dynamics
Electric Circuits
Electromagnetic Fields
Electronics
Elements of Banking
Engineering Materials
Engineering Thermodynamics
Fluid Mechanics
Heat and Thermodynamics
Mathematics for Economists
Molecular Genetics
Numerical Analysis
Operational Research
Organic Chemistry
Physical Chemistry
Structural Mechanics
Waves and Optics